PORTAL TO PARADISE

Portal to paradise.

(Photo: Brunner & Co.)

[*Frontispiece*

PORTAL
TO PARADISE

An Italian Excursion

Cecil Roberts

HODDER & STOUGHTON

First Published June 1955
Second Impression August 1955

MADE AND PRINTED IN GREAT BRITAIN FOR
HODDER AND STOUGHTON LTD., LONDON, BY
HAZELL WATSON AND VINEY LTD., AYLESBURY AND LONDON

CONTENTS

LIST OF ILLUSTRATIONS

What I love best in all the world
Is a castle, precipice-encurled,
In a gash of the wind-grieved Apennine.
Or look for me, old fellow of mine
(If I get my head from out the mouth
O' the grave, and loose my spirit's bands
And come again to the land of lands)—
In a seaside house to the farther South,
Where the baked cicala dies of drouth,
And one sharp tree—'tis a cypress—stands
My sentinel to guard the sands
To the water's edge. For what expands
Before the house, but the great opaque
Blue breadth of sea without a break?
Italy, my Italy.
Queen Mary's saying serves for me
(When Fortune's malice lost her Calais)—
Open my heart and you will see
Graved inside of it, 'Italy'.
    Such lovers old are I and she:
    So it always was, so shall ever be.

R. BROWNING, "De Gustibus—"

CHAPTER ONE

A TALE OF TWO CYPRESSES

I

THE bells rang in the romanesque church tower as I signed my name on a document, by which act I became the owner of a home in Italy. Outside in the bright noonday a February wind ruffled the palm trees in the piazza. At the bottom of the avenue a calm blue sea caressed the most perfect sandy bay situated midway between Nice and Genoa. As a dream, born some fifty years ago, became fulfilled, I reflected on the course of Fate as it moves through the days of our mortal lease.

Let me turn back from this pleasant Mediterranean scene to a Midland village, a thousand miles away in space and half a century in time. I evoke a boy who in the course of a Shakespeare lesson had been called upon to declaim a passage from *Hamlet*. "There's a divinity that shapes our ends rough, hew them how we will," he recited, and convulsed the class. Only too often does life follow that interpretation rather than the poet's. For myself a divinity had beneficently shaped my end, after some rough-hewing on my part, and the latest form, achieved in this Mediterranean sea-coast town, caused me to reflect. I had fulfilled my ambitious dream, a little late it is true; but is not hope the better part of fulfilment?

The story begins in this fashion. Fifty years ago I had walked some distance into the country to visit the house of a man who evoked something like hero-worship in my boy's heart, and whose kindness is among my first and clearest memories. At that time it had seemed a long journey for young legs, though it was scarcely six miles. My friend lived then in a small country house in a South Notts. village. It had been, I think, a farmhouse. It had double bay-windows facing a lawn and was hidden from the road by a high brick wall. It was painted white, and was most beautifully furnished as became the home of an English gentleman. That is a term which must be defined and defended today, because the gentleman has almost passed out of existence. The possession of privileges denied to others makes him now an anti-social figure. Our present age has taken its revenge on him. It has reduced him to near-poverty and turned him into an object of derision. By one of our less responsible politicians he has been stigmatized 'vermin'. Lord Henry, the owner of the house, was a handsome man, tall, with much distinction in voice and manner. It was easy for me to find in him my boyhood's hero. He seemed to me, in his country clothes, what Sir Galahad was in armour—the perfect knight of courage and compassion.

Tired at the end of my walk, I was ushered into a bright study by a dark young servant whose blue-tailed coat was decorated with brass buttons. He wore also a yellow-striped waistcoat and what seemed like a dress-shirt with a white bow-tie. He was a singular spectacle in this simple country house, the first of his doomed species I had seen. I surmised that he had been imported by my host from the ducal house where his brother lived in fabulous state, having succeeded, as 6th Duke of Portland, his kinsman the 5th duke, a famous eccentric who had burrowed underground at a prodigious expense. He built a tunnel, a mile and a half long and wide enough for two carriages to pass from his house to the village. He had constructed underground three library rooms 236 feet long, a ballroom 174 feet long, a corridor, and a conservatory with a glass roof 260 feet long. They were all heated by hot air and lit by 2,800 gas-jets. The duke forbade anyone to pass him in a corridor. He put his carriage, with blinds drawn, on a railway truck when he went to London. Nevertheless, he was on the friendliest terms with some four hundred workmen engaged on his crazy buildings; to each of these he gave a donkey and an umbrella to enable him to go to his work comfortably through the vast estate in Sherwood Forest.

Aware of this singular family background, I could not then understand why my host chose to leave such incredible, if curious, splendour for a simple farmhouse of ten rooms, even though it was embellished by a servant in blue livery. The furnishing was comfortable but not lavish. The chairs and divan in the study were upholstered in red leather. A fire blazed cheerily in the open grate. A large tiger-skin served as a hearthrug. There were china vases that held masses of flowers skilfully arranged. A large bay-window looked on to a green lawn with herbaceous borders. On bookshelves lining the walls there were leather-bound editions of Baily's *Hunting Almanac*, the novels of Thackeray, some French paper-backed novels, and many copies of Hansard's Parliamentary debates, for my host was a Member of Parliament. His contribution to this record of debates can have been only slight, for his political adversaries always asked what was the use of sending to the House of Commons a member who was mostly silent. I recall how deeply my boy's heart resented the epithet 'aristocratic nincompoop' thrown at him. Aristocratic, yes, but nincompoop, no. But he had critics in his own camp, who could not forgive him for voting for the reform of the House of Lords, old-age pensions, and an eight-hour day for miners. He was considered a traitor to his class, for he was always more liberal than the Liberals his party opposed.

The manservant, having shown me to a seat, threw a log on the fire and proceeded to light some candles in a *capodimonte* candelabra standing on a circular mahogany table.

"His lordship will be in soon, sir. He's gone to the stables, but he's expecting you. The air's quite nippy, sir, isn't it, but it's nice for walking?"

"Very nice," I agreed, my heart thumping. This unique person in the blue livery had addressed me as 'sir'. With a shock I heard him speak with a strong Cockney accent, but it made him more human. I discovered that he was indeed a Cockney and had come up from my host's Town house. "I like dogs and 'orses and even the mud you get walking," he said. He was a friendly, good-looking youth. He passed me a magazine to look at, with a smile. It was *L'Illustration*. I recall it fifty years later, for it contained a large picture of Sarah Bernhardt as L'Aiglon. It was the first time I had seen her name or learned of her. I could not know that some ten years later I should interview her in her dressing-room.

The observation about walking and mud made me conscious of my shoes. I wondered if I could wipe them with my pocket handkerchief and replace it in my pocket so that the mud wouldn't show. I was horribly aware that two of my finger-nails were dirty. I hesitated about taking the paper-knife on a writing-table in order to clean them. I took the risk and got back to my chair undiscovered. The open jaws of the tiger grimaced at me. I wiped my shoes on its chin.

The wintry-red sunset faded in the sky beyond the window, the logs blazed and threw out their heat. The room was very cosy in the candle-light. The great red-leather chair was comfortable. I began to feel drowsy.

On the wall by the fireplace there was a water-colour that fascinated me. The sunshine seemed to pour out of it. It was a painting of a villa with an overhanging red-tiled roof. It had long green shutters and windows that opened on to a sunny terrace. On it stood great terra-cotta jars filled with scarlet geraniums. Below the terrace, at the foot of a wide flight of balustraded steps, a fountain cast a jet of silvery water. It sparkled between two slim dark trees that pierced the bright blue sky like giant spears. The dramatic beauty of the scene fascinated me. I wondered where it could be. Somehow I found myself walking along the terrace, down the marble steps towards the fountain whose water tinkled in the basin between the great sentinel trees.

A hand touched my knee and a voice said gently, "It's a pity to wake you, young man, but I'm sure you want some tea!"

I started. It was my host, greatly amused. The fountain I had heard must have been the rattle of tea-cups, for the servant had just wheeled up a tea-table in front of my hostess, who sat by the fireplace with a white Borzoi hound stretched in front of her. Lord Henry laughed to find me sleeping after my walk. He did not know on what a far journey I had been, to a scene of great loveliness where a silvery jet of water

Alassio and Capo Mele from the villa.

The island of Gallinaria, like a snail.

played on the lower terrace of a green-shuttered villa. My first question was to ask where it was.

"That? Oh, that's a villa in Italy, near Florence, where we spent our honeymoon. It was my mother's," said my host.

"And those trees—what are they?" I asked.

"Cypresses; you see them all over Italy. They're like a stage-set for the garden of *Twelfth Night*—Malvolio strutted around them, I'm sure."

"I love them," said Lady Olivia; "but they're too funereal for England. They want a blazing blue sky as a background."

"Is Florence very far away?" I asked, fascinated by the water-colour.

"Oh no—not very far; you can get there in thirty hours."

In thirty hours! That seemed to me a very long way off, and getting there must cost a lot of money. Yet nothing should prevent me. I there and then determined to go to Italy, to live in a villa under a vivid blue sky, to have a terrace on which stood two black cypress trees.

Thirty hours? Signing the deed that made me the possessor of a home in Italy with a terrace and two black cypresses against an azure sky, I reflected that the journey to fulfilment had taken me fifty years. In that time, two great wars had changed the face of the world. My host and his lovely wife had long since vanished from the scene. Perhaps the youth in the blue livery was now a grandfather—the world of those who rang bells and those who answered them was no more.

But one thing had not changed—the ambitious hope of a boy in a Midland village who had come upon that painting of a villa in Italy. The desire born then had found fulfilment on this late day. The portal to Paradise had opened.

II

It has been said that Englishmen are born with two ineradicable loves—one for the England that breeds them, the other for the Italy that lures them. It is understandable. It arises from more than a craving for sunshine by those who live in a land whose green loveliness owes much to its rains and mists.

Our cultural inheritance has deep roots in the Italian soil whence came many of the things that grace our civilization. English poetry, an incomparably rich inheritance, could not have reached its greatness without Italian forebears. Chaucer took from Italy his stories and metre. Shakespeare, the very heart of England, felt the pulse of Italy, drawing from its strong beat the tales he transformed, the scenes and histories he made immortal. The young Milton, who could write a sonnet in Italian with the same facility as one in English, found there the storehouse of his muse. The better part of Shelley's genius flowered on the shore that received his body; and Keats, although he saw it only when the film of death dimmed his eyes, owed to it imagery that glows with the colours of the Renaissance. Italy nourished the best years of Byron, who repaid his debt lavishly. As for Browning, he was wholly its child from that youthful moment when Pippa passed, to the closing scene in the great Venetian palace when the last leap of the flame of genius gave us the lovely lines to Goldoni. Expressing a lifelong debt, the last book, published as he lay dying in Venice, took its title, *Asolando*, from a village in the Venetian foothills so dear to him.

Our architecture carries across its noblest façades the signature of Palladio. Our art had in Italy its roots. Much of the music that gives us delight, from Palestrina to Verdi, is of Italian birth, as also the very language and instruments dedicated to its expression—the oboe, viola, violin, violoncello and pianoforte. Italy lives in the very script one writes, derived from past generations of monastic pedagogues, forerunners of that immigration of Italian dancing, fencing and music masters from whom the Elizabethan youth took the modes of gallantry. Need we wonder that we are drawn so strongly to the Italian scene, so many things in us calling back to their ancestral sources?

I knew nothing of all this on the day I looked upon my host's water-colour of an Italian villa. I knew not the name of those dark trees that hypnotized me with their dramatic beauty. A little ahead of me lay the intoxication of English poetry—Shelley's 'Ode to the West Wind', born of the Italian day; Byron's apostrophe:

> *Thou art the garden of the world, the home*
> *Of all Art yields, and Nature can decree;*
> *Even in thy desert, what is like to thee?*
> *Thy very weeds are beautiful, thy waste*
> *More rich than other climes' fertility;*

Browning's repeated magnificence, whether in the 'Toccata', 'The Ring and the Book', or 'Love Among the Ruins', and in his tribute

> *Open my heart and you will see*
> *Graved inside of it, 'Italy'.*

Lastly and overwhelmingly there is Shakespeare's immortal gallery of characters, Brutus, Coriolanus, Othello, Shylock, Portia, Malvolio, Romeo and Juliet.

> *The Englishman Italianate*
> *Is the Devil incarnate,*

runs the couplet.[1] But what a loss to literature, art, music, architecture and life itself would be entailed were the Englishman not Italianate.

Dr Johnson long cherished the hope of visiting Italy. Boswell has told us of the Doctor's desire, in 1766:

"I was glad to understand from him that it was still resolved that his tour to Italy with Mr and Mrs Thrale should take place, of which he had entertained some doubt. . . . A journey to Italy was still in his thoughts. He said, 'A man who has not been to Italy is always conscious of an inferiority, from his not having seen what it is expected a man should see. The grand object of travelling is to see the shores

[1] The Puritans of the Elizabethan era firmly believed this. Italy was a seat of vice in their eyes, as Paris became later. When Sir Philip Sidney departed for Italy in 1573 his diplomatic friend, Languet, extracted from the nineteen-year-old youth a promise not to visit Rome, seat of the Catholic sorceress. Sidney promised, to his lifelong regret. The Italianate Englishman had been given a wide notoriety. "Suffer not thy sons to pass the Alps, for they shall learn nothing there but pride, blasphemy and atheism," wrote Lord Burghley. But two centuries later Italy was in high favour, and the Grand Tour was considered essential for the completion of the education of all cultivated Englishmen.

of the Mediterranean. On these shores were the four great Empires of the world—the Assyrian, the Persian, the Grecian and the Roman. All our religion, almost all our law, almost all our arts, almost all that sets us above savages, has come to us from the shores of the Mediterranean.'. . . . I dined with him at Mr Thrale's. Before dinner, Dr Johnson and I passed some time by ourselves. I was sorry to find it was now resolved that the proposed journey to Italy should not take place. . . . He said, 'I am disappointed, to be sure.' "

III

After many wanderings I settled for a quarter of a century in an Elizabethan cottage at the foot of the Chiltern Hills. It was a halcyon spot, and inspired much of my best work in those highly productive years. There I wrote some eighteen books. One of them, *Gone Rustic*, and its sequel, concerned my life in the cottage and brought to its clematis-covered porch readers from all parts of the world. I fretted at the ceaseless knocking at my door, but I had brought it upon myself and it would be hypocritical of me to deny that this attention was flattering, for surely we write to be read? From time to time I made refreshing excursions abroad. I travelled in France, Germany, Austria, Hungary, Spain, Italy, Greece, North Africa, the United States and Canada. Sometimes I stayed for long periods. I took houses, villas, apartments or lodgings in Vienna, Budapest, Venice, Paris, New York and Miami, all of which had unique charm; but always I returned to my cottage in the Chilterns, with its four poplars, its apple trees, and its hawthorn hedge. It was a green paradise, vocal with birdsong, encompassed by an emerald lawn. On the north side the old tiled roof had nestled down in its green bed for three hundred years. These tiles were new when young Shakespeare went by the gate on his way to London.

I thought I should be there for the rest of my days—that poplars, not cypresses, would mark my last abode. By all my friends and readers I was deeply embedded in Pilgrim Cottage. They were naturally shocked when I sold it and moved away. How could I be so faithless to something I had written about so lovingly? But time can manacle us with memories. There were too many ghosts in the garden and on the stairs. Many of those whom I had loved and who had lived happily there had died—one in his youth after a long and gallant fight; another struck down swiftly in all her loveliness; another with his boy's laughter still echoing, sacrificed to Moloch on the African sands. Often, sitting in the quiet of the garden, they came upon me. Once I counted them, nine all told, who had loved this scene. Suddenly I realized that I had begun a fatal thing—I was living in the past, evoking the irretrievable. Moreover, the books I had written here began to get in my way. Visitors would recall characters in them, and it was with an effort that I remembered them. Sometimes I failed, and my visitors would wonder why I was so absent-minded. The creative artist must look forward not backward, and here I was always being made to evoke the past. Age accumulates a burden of memories, and there falls on one the weight, unknown to youth, of invidious comparisons. "Do you remember how we ..."; "The russet tree has never had blossom as in '38 ..."; "What wonderful weather we had for Henley Regatta eight years ago when ..."

A heavier shadow lay over the old house. There had been a long, devastating war. One September day in 1939, some days after it had broken out, a friend motored down to say good-bye, for we were all being scattered to our various tasks. He paused at the gate on leaving and looked down the garden path. "What wonderful times we've had here, it will never be the same again," he said. "Oh, don't be pessimistic; of course it will, unless we're all blown up," I retorted. He was right. The place looked just the same when I opened the garden gate one May day six years later. The russet apple tree was in full bloom, the lawn was a brilliant green, the daffodils were golden flames. But I soon found out that it was not the same. There were restrictions on food and transport, the housekeeper could not ring up the tradesmen for supplies, there was a matter of coupons, also they would not deliver to the door. It made guests impossible. My morning *Times* had to be posted to me by the newsagent not two miles distant so that I received it in the evening. The fares from Town had gone up and the service had been cut down. Petrol restrictions limited travel. People thought twice before coming down to lunch or tea. Many of my former visitors had vanished, casualties of war or of finance. I had been a convenient halfway-house, a place of union between parents and their boys at Oxford. Many of those boys were dead; a generation we knew not took their places. Old neighbours had moved away. "All, all are gone, the old familiar faces," I echoed with Charles Lamb. That lovable handsome pair, Tony and Ann, no more rushed down the garden path, having borrowed mother's two-seater. Tony at twenty-six had inexplicably faded away with a mysterious disease. His young sister, in Army service in Malaya, had been murdered in an ambush.

Faces still familiar had somehow changed. There was Henry whom I encountered one day in London and invited down to the cottage for old times' sake. In the pre-war years he had been a bright young man about town. Tall, extremely handsome, witty, a good dancer and bridge player, he was popular with mammas who had disposable daughters. He dressed impeccably. He never owned a car, but always seemed able to borrow or to be transported in an expensive one. He flitted along the French Riviera; he visited some of the best houses in England. During the war, a good linguist, he had found employment with the B.B.C. and lived in his elegant little flat, which escaped bombing.

When Henry came down to me, I saw he was a bundle of nerves under a superficial gaiety, a visible war casualty. He was worried because his job had ended and his servant had walked out after ten years; but what really distressed him was that a butterfly life had come to an end. He was still handsome, but no longer young, being thirty-eight. He had not married, for the latest girl had always gone off, largely because she was not prepared to offer the incense Henry craved. The era of house-parties was at an end, food shortage, servant worries, finance, closed the lovely houses he had frequented. The week-ends he now must spend in London depressed him.

I noticed the alacrity with which he accepted my invitation. There were the same quips at the table, but the gaiety was forced. I caught him glancing a little anxiously in the mirror, although he was still faultlessly dressed. It was the week-end before Henley Regatta, and I was shocked to hear him canvassing my guests for an invitation, which happily he secured. "It's been an absolute paradise; I needed the change so badly," he said on departing. I inquired delicately whether he had any money worries. If he had he was too proud to tell me. "Oh no, old boy, thank you—I just manage somehow," he said with his famous smile. He seemed elated because he departed in a shining Jaguar, a calling friend having offered him transport to Town. He turned up half of the collar of his camel-hair overcoat, his hat at a jaunty angle, in the old debonair manner as he waved good-bye. A few weeks later, while visiting a friend in Devon, he took a gun from the cloakroom, went into the woods and shot himself. The deeper tragedy was that he left behind a devoted mother of eighty.

There was another ghost, a lovely one, that of Nadja Malacrida. She was Lord Cowdray's niece and had married the Marchese Peter Malacrida, a handsome young Italian who worked in London. They were a popular young couple, and one seemed to meet everybody at their London house. Young, beautiful, Nadja appeared to have the world at her feet. I recall a fancy-dress ball to which she came as La Camargo, and captured the floor with her vivacious beauty. The poet Humbert Wolfe was always at her feet with delicate tributes of verse, not only to herself but to the things she collected and loved—her fan, her Buddha, her pet dog. She was a good athlete and she was among the first women to take an air-pilot's certificate.

One day, after lunching at Pilgrim Cottage, she said, "I could live here for ever, it is so beautiful and peaceful!" I laughed. "You couldn't live here for a week, you would pine for the fleshpots of Town," I replied. She strongly dissented. I was about to leave on a Greek cruise. I offered her the cottage for a month. Peter was absent on the Continent on a business trip. She accepted my offer. Every day she exchanged letters with her husband. When he returned he joined her in the cottage, and they were so enchanted with the surrounding country that they began to negotiate for a large Elizabethan house on the hill above, not knowing that from a boat in the Ægean I, too, was negotiating for the house on behalf of a friend on our cruise! We got the house with a higher bid. Nadja and Peter were heart-broken, all of us unconscious that I was the villain of the piece.

The evening before Nadja left Pilgrim Cottage, she wrote me a letter saying the halcyon month was at an end and she would never forget it. The next morning she left in her Hispano-Suiza racing-car. Five minutes later she was dead. Her car left the road just over Henley Bridge, and she lay beneath it with a broken back. No one knows how it happened. A friend met me in Paris with my letters and a copy of *The Times*. One letter was from Nadja, written a few hours before her death, thanking me for my hospitality. In it she wrote: "May the ghost of my happiness haunt your garden for ever." *The Times* carried the story of the accident. So another ghost walked my garden.

After twenty-five years, happy, industrious years, but heavy with memories both beautiful and sad, I felt it was time to leave Pilgrim Cottage. I had written my books there, but perhaps the place will hold a memory of me more lasting because of another achievement. I had saved this enchanting little corner of England from destruction. It was an American woman who had found two almost derelict Elizabethan cottages, had bought them and converted them into one. Here, having made a garden, she lived happily for ten years and died. Being the returned descendant of a Pilgrim Father, she named it Pilgrim Cottage. When I bought it and went there, there were three derelict condemned cottages of the same construction, all inhabited. I bought them, the borough council having given me an undertaking that the demolition order would be rescinded if I restored the cottages to its satisfaction. There were sitting tenants, and I could do nothing until their deaths. They were all old.

The story now takes a Hans Andersen flavour. In one

cottage lived two brothers, woodcutters. They never spoke to each other, having quarrelled many years earlier over a girl. The cottage was indescribably filthy, the garden a weed-grown rubbish heap. Thirty years earlier their mother had won a prize in a competition for the prettiest cottage garden in England. During long absence on a war mission in the United States, I received news of the death of the brothers. People clamoured for the derelict cottage. I reconstructed it by cable from America, and let it to an acquaintance who made a lovely garden. It stands next to Pilgrim Cottage, and is such a gem that artists sometimes sit down to paint it, thinking they are painting the cottage of my books.

My other property, also condemned, was two semi-detached cottages near 'The Golden Ball'. These had two tenants. More different types of the human race one could not imagine. In one cottage lived a little old man, a retired hedger of eighty-four, with his wife of eighty-two. His pride was his hedge. He went out every morning with a sickle and shaved it. Green and smooth as a billiard table, the haw-thorn hedge embraced a garden full of flowers. His wife came right out of a fairy-tale. She was a little woman with rosy cheeks, beautiful manners, and bright blue eyes in which a smile always lurked. She glistened with cleanliness, and was always seen in a snowy white apron. They contrived to live on their old-age pension. Their little two-roomed cottage was spotless, a scene of comfort, with a big tom-cat purring by the steel fender.

Alas, next door a frightful creature dwelt in a state of utter filth. The village called her a witch and things that were worse. In her youth she had been seduced by someone with whom she had been in service. She had an illegitimate child. But the real offence was her filthiness and her whining obsequiousness. She was a female Uriah Heap. No one could cross her threshold, the stench was so frightful. She had torn out cupboards and doors for firewood. I once attempted to enter the cottage to see what temporary repairs could be effected, but fled, as others had fled, revolted by the appalling smells. She lived on public assistance.

In the course of time the rosy-cheeked old lady died, the

23

husband went to the infirmary. A little later the local authorities removed the filthy old witch to a place where she could be superintended. I was in Rome when, one morning, I received a letter from my solicitor saying that the cottages were empty, that the local authorities had given me fourteen days in which to demolish them, and that they had already pulled out the doors and windows to render them uninhabitable. This high-handed procedure was in complete repudiation of the pledge they had given me that the demolition order would be rescinded if I restored the cottages.

Hot with indignation, I flew home and went into action. They were adamant, and declared that the new housing regulations, following the war, cancelled their pledge. I protested against this outrageous breach of faith. I pointed out that these cottages with their beautiful roofs were part of the legacy of ancient England. Nothing like them could ever be built. They were as beautiful as Pilgrim Cottage and its neighbour. They settled into the landscape at the end of the old lane, companions of 'The Golden Ball' with its bow-window. "No, they must be demolished," they said. The regulations could not permit them to remain however much I spent on them.

I interviewed the Clerk of the Council, I had an architect draw up plans, I argued with the Borough Surveyor, with the County Surveyor, with the County Council. I canvassed the Housing Committee, which seemed to have an active hatred of old cottages, possibly enamoured of modern mould-built council houses. Finally I appealed, wholly on artistic grounds, to the Ministry of Housing. I pointed out that my books had drawn thousands from all parts of the world to visit Pilgrim Cottage, that these old cottages were part of the renowned beauty of Britain, a beauty used as a bait by the 'Come to Beautiful Britain' campaign of the official Travel Association, subsidized by the Government at the cost of many thousands of pounds a year. I produced an advertisement in an American paper. It showed an old cottage exactly similar to my condemned cottages, with the caption 'England's Incomparable Heritage'. This advertisement, in colour, had cost twelve hundred pounds in dollars. The Ministry of Housing sent down its official. He looked the place over, reported that it had no historic merit and should be demolished. In vain I pointed out that it was not a question of history but of beauty. I was defeated at every step. The regulations could not be changed.

But I knew from long experience that official Bills, Orders and Regulations always carry somewhere within their wordy labyrinths an escape clause by which the Government can do just what it wishes. I carried on the battle and won. I converted the two cottages into one. Out of a queue of prospective buyers I sold it to a charming young couple who created about it a beautiful garden. So today, within the space of a few hundred square yards, there are four of the loveliest old cottages in England, set in a beautiful landscape amid the Chiltern beechwoods.

I had saved my corner of England from destruction. I could now leave it without misgivings as to what might happen. It seemed that my work was done. As for my own cottage, with its ghosts of vanished happiness and crowded with memories that pulled me into the past, all things considered I sadly decided that it was time to go. I turned southwards towards Italy and the shores of the Mediterranean Sea that had witnessed the birth of our civilization, towards the cypresses of my early dream.

CHAPTER TWO

A VILLA IN ITALY

ONE day, seeing an advertisement in *The Times* of a furnished villa to let on the Italian Riviera, I wrote and took it for the following winter. I was at that time staying with friends in Palm Beach, Florida. On the same day that I completed the transaction with the English owner, I went to dinner at a neighbour's house. We dined in a beautiful patio on a warm starlit February evening. At the end of the garden the palms bordering Lake Worth were silhouetted in moonlight. Somehow the talk turned to winter resorts, and I remarked that, perhaps rashly, I had taken, unseen, a villa on the Italian Riviera for the following winter.

"Where on the Riviera?" asked one of the guests, a young Dutchman with a pretty American wife.

"At Alassio. I've never been there, I hope it is nice," I said.

"Alassio is lovely," he commented. "What's the name of your villa?"

"The Villa Perdita."

"I know it very well! We lived in it for two years. It's charming! You've not seen it? Well, if you will dine with us tomorrow night I'll show you a colour film I took of it."

Thus in Palm Beach, Florida, I had my first view of the villa. It bore out his eulogy. It looked enchanting, perched on the mountain-side.

"Has it any cypresses?" I asked.

"Cypresses, palms, lemon, tangerine and mimosa trees. There's purple bougainvillæa on the terrace and a brier-rose pergola down the path to the gate," said my host. "You'll love it—and such views over the town and bay!"

I had one brief glimpse of the villa before going to it in the following September. In July, motoring with friends from Venice to Monte Carlo, we passed through Alassio. After some time we found the villa, on a terrace above the town, but it was surrounded by a high wall, dusk had fallen, and the gate was locked. All we could see from the road above the villa were the red tiles of the roof and two balconies and green-shuttered windows. The view of the town, sea and mountains was superb. Two other things I saw: a pair of giant cypresses black against the darkening sky. My friends were in a hurry to reach Monte Carlo for a dinner party that evening, so we had no time to find the gardener and to inspect the villa. When we resumed our journey through the town, full of lights and with a carnival gaiety, I felt well satisfied with my adventure.

We moved into the villa early in October. We had taken on with the place a resident maid. She was an old retainer of the owner's, a sturdy little woman in her sixties with a brown wrinkled face like a walnut. She was a cheerful, willing soul, but, alas, stone deaf. All communications were by sign or had to be written down. Since we were surrounded by a wall, gated on the north and the south, and Anna could hear no bell, no knocking, callers found it almost impossible to get in to us.

For some reason, despite my affability, I inspired terror in this good soul. Possibly it was my strange form of earning a living, by writing cabbalistic signs on a sheet of paper, for in any reference to me she would fold her hands on her breast and roll her eyes as if seeking protection from the Virgin Mary. Although our relationship became in time quite affectionate, I know she thought I was 'strange'. "*Il Signore ha qualche cosa!*" she would murmur, tapping her brow significantly—"The Signor has 'something'!" Within a month she fell down and broke her wrist so that she was almost useless; but we kept her on, and fed her in a manner she will never forget. She was a good, devoted soul.

The villa was all that I had hoped it would be, and more. It was only five minutes' walk from the centre of the little town and had been built about eighty years earlier on a terrace of an olive grove. These olive orchards are rapidly disappearing, alas. Those near the town are absorbed by building extensions. The more remote ones up in the foot-

hills often give the steep slopes the appearance of a vast
Greek or Roman theatre. They are now deserted and falling
into ruin. Their creation was a result of back-breaking
labour. They are remote from social centres and reached by
tortuous *salitas*, or mule tracks, made by the patient labour
of dead generations. Every terrace is built up on a dry-stone
wall. Neglect of these walls, after rainstorms have broken
them down, entails patient reconstruction by hand.

Viewing these miles of dry-stone terraces on which the
olive trees are planted, I have often wondered how many
centuries have gone to their creation. Since we know that the
Romans owned olive groves, some of them must date back
nearly two thousand years. Now they are disappearing. The
stone walls collapse, the earth slides, and the terraces are
obliterated. With them disappear the village communities
that cultivated them. On walks along the mountain tracks
one comes upon deserted villages and old farm dwellings
without roofs and windows. The last war hastened this
devastation. The great Ansaldo shipbuilding and engineering
works at Genoa drained off the peasants from their home-
steads. The demand for labour in war-time by vast industrial
enterprises offering high wages started a migration from the
mountains that has never ceased. It is not to be wondered at
when one contemplates the lonely, hard lives led through
the centuries by peasants always on the verge of poverty.
Their only diversion was unrestricted copulation, which in
turn increased the problems of sustenance and habitation.
The visitor to Italy, observing from train and car the villages
so picturesquely perched on the ledges of the mountains,
amid the olive groves and vineyards, has no conception of
the utter squalor and frightful insanitation of these romantically grouped dwellings. If he should venture up the
arduous paths, he will suffer a great disillusionment. He will
find amid the loveliness of vines, wistaria, orange and lemon
trees, in steep alleys that have lovely vistas of the Italian
landscape, noisome hovels, waterless, airless, with primitive
sanitation or none at all. Here are bred those dark-eyed
children whose beauty ravishes the tourist. He will find sitting at the doors old crones, sun-withered, prematurely aged

by early and long labour in the fields, who have carried up and down cobblestone tracks heavy burdens on their heads in mule-like patience.

It is true that these mountain villages are being transformed. Smooth roads have made them accessible, and the motor-bus and motor-cycle, particularly the ubiquitous Vespa now ridden by the lads of the village, have banished isolation. The radio is heard through dark doorways. Lipstick and nylon stockings are not unknown to Maria and Lucrezia. Less and less are the sturdy mountain women seen carrying on their heads pitchers of water from the communal tap. There are striking incongruities. The electric iron will be found in hovels whose 'convenience' is a hole in the ground beyond the hen-pen. An electric press extracts the oil from the olives. But the bullock still pulls the ploughshare on the steep mountain-side, and the donkey wearily revolves on its track around the well. At night a heavy black silence falls upon the lonely village, lit by only one bare electric bulb, not turned off in daylight as though forgotten by man. Need one wonder that youth migrates from the meagre wages, hard labour, and isolation of these crumbling villages? The bus, the cinema, the bevies of girls in their town finery, the lights, the better-paid work and social amenities, are irresistible lures.

So the terrace walls crumble, the olive groves go unattended, and a slow ruin covers a landscape cultivated in patience and sweat through a thousand years. A man once reckoned his wealth by the number of olive trees. His taxes are still based on them. The law has heavy penalties for their destruction, but it has no power to keep the men on the land. All around Alassio the beautiful terraces of olive trees are crumbling into ruin.

There are other causes for these changes in the landscape. A terrace with a view, accessible to the town, has value as a building plot. The villas creep higher and higher up the mountain-side; then come roads, then electric light, then more villas. There has also been a change in seasonal habits. Of old, wealthy winter tourists flocked to this enchanted coast, escaping the rigour of a northern winter, but taxation and currency restrictions, and a change in the channels of wealth, have eliminated them. There is no winter season as of old. Many of the hotels are shut, the tea-rooms empty. A new clientele now descends upon this coast in what was considered the intolerable heat of summer. The cult of nudism and the fried skin brings proletarian multitudes to the Mediterranean shore. The sands and rocks are covered almost to invisibility by the human body exposed in all its unloveliness, for not two per cent. of mortals are enhanced by shedding their clothes.

Since the French and Italian Riviera coasts are predominantly rocky, any resort with a sandy beach reaps a fortune. In this respect Alassio is supreme, from Marseilles to Genoa. It has a wide stretch of fine golden sand in a perfect bay. Nor does it suffer, as so many of these resorts, from a railway dividing the beach from the town. The line runs, discreetly masked, behind the town. Alassio tilts its nose in superiority over its fashionable neighbour, much advertised San Remo, which has no sand but only a shore of craggy rocks bordered by the railway separating it from the town. On a coast-line two hundred miles long, very few places are blessed with a beach like Alassio's. For this reason, in the months of July and August the Italians descend upon it like an obliterating cloud of locusts. For the rest of the year it is almost deserted. Let me be accurate. It happens that the Italian Riviera is the quickest approach to the sun for the Swiss and the Germans. They come as early as March, and splash in water that is regarded as arctic by the Italians, for nothing will induce the latter to enter the sea before the first of June and after the thirty-first of August, be it a hundred degrees in the shade. The Germans, and their near neighbours the Swiss, are impervious to cold. As early as March and as late as November, they offer us a copious display of those breasts and buttocks, especially the female species, with which the Germans are so liberally endowed. They wallow like pink hippopotami along the shore.

It happened that from the Villa Perdita one could see the railway station but not the line. This was no defect; on the contrary, it was an attraction. We delighted in the nocturnal

30

aspect of the station whose roof alone was visible. It had a carnival air on the approach of a train, for it sprang into light, its name picked out in luminous, bright blue letters. Since our route into town ran parallel for some distance with the railway's low viaduct, we came to be familiar with and to love our part of the line and the station. The latter was a floral affair, the platforms gay with palms, scarlet canna, wistaria, clematis and purple bougainvillæa, while the lamp standards were hung with baskets of flowers. It was also a place of romance, exciting the imagination whenever trains came in. The route boards on the coaches were visible from the road. They had quite an intoxicating effect on me, in whom the wanderlust has never died.

The Riviera line is mostly a single track, operated on the block system, owing to the fact that it has been cut along terraces of rock overhanging the sea. Frequently it runs in and out of tunnels that plunge into mountainous promontories. Journeying along this line from the Italian frontier at Ventimiglia as far as Spezia beyond Genoa, some two hundred miles, one is constantly shuttering in and out of blazing sunshine and black darkness. There are sometimes gaps in the tunnels where one has a blinding glimpse of dazzling blue sea. Someone wittily likened this coast journey to 'running down a flute'. When I first made it in 1922 the line had not been electrified, and one was blackened and suffocated by the acrid sulphurous fumes from the vile coal these trains burned. They penetrated the closed windows of the dark carriages in which one sweated at a temperature of ninety degrees. All this has changed with electrification. One can now travel with open windows.

This line is a highway to Rome and southern Italy. It is one of the oldest routes in Europe, for along this coast the Romans built their famous Via Aurelia that carried them from Rome to their province of Gaul, and subsequently to the British Isles. It threaded its way through Liguria via Genoa, La Turbie above Monte Carlo, Fréjus, Marseilles (the Greek colony Massilia), Arles, and eventually to Paris and the English Channel. I once lodged in a villa on the Via Aurelia in Rome. The main road threading Alassio is also called by this name. It pleased my fancy to think that in my cottage in the Oxfordshire Chilterns I was living on an extension of this highway, for it stood on the old Roman road along which the XXth Legion marched on its way to the camp at Dorchester, near Oxford.

The Riviera highway has been traversed by Cæsar, Scipio, Marc Antony, Augustus, and a hundred famous Roman generals. The motorist coming down through Provence and along the French coast still follows, for the main part, the Via Aurelia on its way to Rome. Italy is entered at the frontier town of Ventimiglia or Vintimille. This name has nothing to do with Twenty Miles, so it is useless to speculate on twenty miles from where; the name is derived from the Roman town, Intemelium. Ventimiglia is the venue of all trains taking the Mediterranean coastal route, with the result that little Alassio is given something of an international air by the names displayed on the carriages going east and west. When the trains halt in the station and we are walking down the slanting road by the viaduct, we are on eye-level with names on through-carriages to Marseilles, Paris, Bordeaux, St. Jean-de-Luz, Cerbère (for Spain), Rome, Venice, Trieste, Innsbruck, Klagenfurt, Vienna, etc. I soon realized that nothing would dispel the restlessness they provoked save to pack a small bag and take any one of these coaches halting at Alassio and go through to its final destination. When the lights of the station suddenly went up as I sat at supper in the Villa Perdita, I thought how that, tomorrow morning, I could have coffee at Florian's in the piazza at Venice, or in that azalea-bowered café on the Pincio terrace overlooking Rome, or in the Englischer Garten at Munich, or by the lakeside at Lausanne, or in a Tirolean chalet above Merano, or on the Champs-Élysées. All very unsettling for an author who had vowed he would begin the next chapter, now delayed a month.

But I anticipate future joys and dilemmas. We have just arrived at the villa. The housekeeper has been installed a week, the trunks are unpacked, and as a reminder of work she has placed my manuscript on a writing bureau in a large bow-windowed room with glorious views. It overlooks the town. The ancient romanesque campanile of the parish church of Sant' Ambrogio rises above the red roofs. Its name is that of an old friend. Thirty years earlier I had made my first visit to this enchanted coast, staying first at Rapallo, later at Levanto. I carried with me a letter of introduction to Max Beerbohm from my publisher-to-be, for my first novel was in the press. I sent the letter in advance to the Villino Chiaro, and received from the Incomparable Max an invitation to lunch. It was, for me in the first flush of authorship, like calling on Parnassus, and the summons there, a minutely pencilled missive, was addressed in a manner that overwhelmed me. It was addressed *all' Illustrissimo Signor* Cecil Roberts, inviting me to lunch on the morrow. I felt like the Doge of Venice on receiving this charming exaggeration calculated to overcome my shyness. "To the most Illustrious. . . ."

That evening, to make sure that I should correctly time my appearance at the villa, about two miles along the Via Aurelia, I made a rehearsal trip, but somehow, out of Rapallo, took the wrong path and ended, lost, on an olive-tree shadowed piazza high in the mountains. It was a warm July night with the fireflies jewelling the velvet darkness. The white façade and tall campanile of a baroque church glimmered in the starlight, while far below, in a great curve of the bay out to the promontory of Portofino, shone the thousand lights of Rapallo and Santa Margherita. I stood breathless with the beauty of the scene before me. It was made more theatrical by the dark cypresses standing in the wings of this celestial set. I was hot, tired and lost. The Villino Chiaro had eluded me, but what enchantment I had fallen into! While standing there I became aware of voices and silhouetted figures sitting on a parapet overlooking the distant bay. I approached and asked for direction. A little priest in a black soutane detached himself. This was Sant' Ambrogio. The Villino Chiaro was far off, down on the coastal road. I thanked him and disappeared into the night.

The next noonday I found the villa and lunched memorably with Max. I could not foresee that when I lunched there again he would be an immortal of eighty and I a man of sixty with much of my writing career accomplished. The evening prior to that long-spaced reunion, on the day of my sixtieth birthday, I climbed once more to the church of Sant' Ambrogio. It was foolish to awaken ghosts of the past after thirty years, but I felt impelled there in the desire to see how much of reality there was in something that had become a dream evoked in starlight. That long-lost occasion had been commemorated by me in some lines I had then written, lines subsequently widely quoted.

> *The priest of Sant' Ambrogio will grow old*
> *And some day I*
> *Shall no more climb mountain mule-tracks*
> *Where the cypress stands on guard against the sky;*
> *He will tend his flock and hear their last confessions,*
> *Doze and totter—but will always be for me*
> *A shadow 'mid the olives in the moonlight*
> *On a small piazza high above the sea.*

As I gained the piazza through the verdurous dusk of a warm May evening, there was a jangle of bells in the campanile, and I found a small congregation coming out of the church, a scene that reminded me of *Cavalleria Rusticana.* I asked a lovely Santuzza the reason of this occasion, and she informed me that it was the festival of a boy saint. I went inside, and at the beautiful marble altar-rail found a young priest engaged in extinguishing the candles. It was from him that I learned the name of my little priest of Sant' Ambrogio, encountered thirty years earlier. Much beloved, he had died a few years previous, and lay buried in the cathedral church of Savona.

The name Sant' Ambrogio is a common one along this Ligurian coast, with reason. Ambrogio, or Ambrose, was born in Treves in A.D. 340. Educated in Rome, he entered the civil service and was made Prefect of Emilia and Liguria. In this capacity he went to Milan to settle a dispute between the Catholics and the Arians, about the election of a bishop. While addressing the multitude a child's voice was heard proclaiming "Ambrose shall be Bishop!" Taking it for a sign from heaven the people forthwith elected him, although

he was not even a baptized Christian. Handing over his
secular affairs to his brother, he began to study the sacred
books and prepare himself for his office. Statesman, theo-
logian, philosopher, poet, he soon achieved the reputation of
a saint. He raised the services of the Church to great dignity
and beauty, and the hymns he composed are still sung. The
Eastern mode of chanting, adopted by him, became known
as the Ambrosian Chant. With St Augustine he composed the
Te Deum Laudamus for the occasion on which he received St
Augustine into the Church. During his tenure of office in
Milan, he became the intimate friend of Theodosius, the last
of the great Roman Emperors, but his friendship did not
prevent him from rebuking and demanding penance from
the Emperor for a crime he had committed. The Governor
of Thessalonika had thrown into gaol a professional charioteer who had made advances to a favourite youth at his court.
The mob rose in anger at this treatment of their popular
charioteer, debarred from appearing in the circus. They
broke into the gaol, released the charioteer and lynched the
governor. Theodosius, angered by this murder of his
representative, planned an atrocious retribution. He invited the inhabitants of Thessalonika to special games in the
Circus. Then, closing the gates, his soldiers massacred seven
thousand of them. There was not a family left intact in the
city. Ambrose, horrified at this massacre, denounced the
Emperor and fearlessly refused him admittance to the church
at Milan. Only after eight months' retirement, submission
and public penance before the whole congregation would he
readmit Theodosius to the church and the sacrament. It was
a show of righteous strength that filled the country with awe
and respect for the rule of the Church over the civil and
regal power. The scene of Theodosius's submission was long
a favourite theme with artists. St Ambrose is also familiar in
art as one of the four great doctors of the Latin Church—
St Ambrose, St Augustine, St Jerome and St Gregory.
Whenever the bells jingle in the campanile of St Ambrogio
at Alassio, I recall my first acquaintance with his name on
that far-off night on the mountain-side above Max Beerbohm's villa.

At the Villa Perdita we found ourselves steeped in an ecclesiastical atmosphere. It had belonged for many years to a spinster lady of a very tough constitution, as will appear later. She loved bishops and canons of the English Church, and was strategically placed to entertain them when they visited Alassio. On the other side of the cobbled track that passed by her north gate was the English church. The British colony grew too large for its little church in the town and being a well-to-do community built, across the railway-line, a new church. Alongside it they also built a large octagonal room, to house the twenty thousand volumes of the English library and a tea-room annexe. A garden and a long pergola walk connected the church and the library. The community was inspired in its selection of an architect. Without question, this is the most beautiful and sensibly de-signed English church in Italy. The sad thing today is that with the dwindling of the English colony from five hundred residents to fifty, a number formerly swollen to two thousand in the winter season, the church rarely has a congregation above fifteen, comprising the honorary chaplain, a blithe and rubicund eighty, in the pulpit, and his wife at the organ. This beautiful church, in happy juxtaposition to the Villa Perdita, gave the occupant a privileged start in the honour of entertaining the itinerant Bishop of Gibraltar, a bishop with a see and no seat, and other pillars of the Church. She im-proved the occasion by adding to the villa a north room with a wide bay window from which there is a magnificent pano-rama of Alassio between the two promontories, Santa Croce and Capo Mele, of the curving bay. A reminder of the 'Church Militant' was included in this view, for seawards stood the snail-like island of Gallinaria, once associated with the soldier-bishop, St Martin, and later a monastery of Benedictine monks.

To facilitate the passage of the visiting potentates of the Church, the hostess had cut a gateway in her north wall which corresponded, across the *salita*, with a back entrance into the church. The bishop could robe in the ample north room and then pass undetected in all his vestments into the church.

Beyond the south wall of the villa the Roman Church was also in evidence in the guise of the nunnery of Santa Chiara. Whenever a large hotel or villa gets into financial difficulty, it seems to fall for little or nothing into the hands of one of the Orders of nuns or monks. They can fill these derelict buildings and maintain them, being exempt from taxes. They have various means of income, apart from endowments and legacies, such as teaching, nursing or sewing, and selling Masses.

The one at the bottom of our garden nursed, received female paying guests in the holiday season, and took in sewing. We overlooked this nunnery. It appeared dead. The windows on the garden and road sides were always close-shuttered and showed no signs of life. Between this institution of the Catholic Church and that of the Anglican Church, as represented by the Villa Perdita, there was at least one occasion of contact. A canon of St Paul's staying at the villa had played so vigorously at the English Tennis Club that he had split his white duck trousers. Mending these was a simple problem. They were sent over to the industrious sisters in the convent. Towards evening a novitiate, a most gentle soul, appeared at the villa with the canon's trousers, saying that she would call for them the next morning as their repair had not been completed. "Then why not keep them and bring them when they're finished?" she was asked. To this she responded gently: "The rules do not permit us to keep male garments in the convent overnight."

It was in the ecclesiastical wing of our villa, in the large downstairs north sitting-room under the guest bedroom, that I started to work, but I found the glorious views, morning, afternoon and evening, with their permutations of beauty transforming sea, mountains and town, somewhat distracting. Later something more distracting drove me out of this delightful room—the intense cold when winter came.

The first survey of the villa made me fall in love with it. It was small, picturesque and stood in a garden that ran in two terraces on either side of the house. On these grew wistaria, lemon, orange, tangerine and grapefruit trees that kept us in fruit throughout the winter. There were beds of violets,

freesias, jonquils and jasmin. There were also palm, olive
and mimosa trees. A great locust tree had spread itself over
the wall into the nuns' domain. There was a large vine and
a brier-rose pergola that ran from the house to the back gate.
Dominating all, towered half a dozen palms and four giant
cypresses. The south side of the villa had a projecting terrace
that was smothered in bougainvillæa. On the first floor of
this south front two bedrooms had French windows that
opened on to small wooden balconies painted a bright blue.
The pantiles above these were red. The balconies and terraces had exquisite views over sea and mountains. The villa
had been 'occupied' during the war, and then had suffered
from a succession of temporary tenants who had neglected
the house and the garden. I put in two months of hard work
cutting out the overgrowth, pruning the trees, and opening
vistas through the dense palm branches. The villa, high on
its terraces, had nothing to obstruct the view, but immediately
behind it, level with our roof, ran a road. This side of the
house and garden had been built into a cliff-cutting.

Inside, the feature that delighted me most was a white
Carrara marble staircase. It was quite large enough to be
seigniorial and ran up from the hall to the first and only
floor. It was something to be able to boast that we had a
marble staircase, and I made a great entertainment of this
by marching up and down it singing "I dreamt that I dwelt
in marble halls". Anna, emerging from the kitchen, observed this exuberant performance. Stone deaf, she could not
hear the song, and had she heard it the words would have
been unintelligible to her, but she had no doubts about the
maestro's performance. With a look of sadness she pointed a
finger to her brow and muttered '*C'è qualche cosa!*'—'There's
something (wrong) there!'

There was a small dining-room and, opening off it,
through folding doors, a salon with a French window leading
on to the terrace. Windows looked east and south. It was
simply and pleasantly furnished. I chose the large north
room, the Bishop's Room, as I called it, for a workroom.
Upstairs there were five bedrooms, including the maid's.
Two of these had balconies. It was all very compact and

pleasing. But the establishment broke down badly in the two most important sections. The bathroom had no hot water. The bath was supplied by a wood-stoked geyser, efficient when the fire had been kindled. Hot water for the hand bowl had to be transported upstairs by kettle or jug. The kitchen was lamentable. It was small, possessed only a cold-water tap, and cooking was by a wood-burning range, a sooty abomination supplemented by a single gas-ring. With no hot water, a small wood stove and a gas-ring, it required the agility of a circus-master to keep a three-saucepan performance going. Nor was my housekeeper's temper improved by the willing assistance of the smiling but stone-deaf, one-handed Anna. When it was demanded of her how the late owner had contrived to live she replied, "She ate cakes!" The amazing preponderance of cake shops and shoe shops in Italian towns has made me wonder if they are not due to these obsolete culinary arrangements, causing their owners to be everlastingly running out to buy cakes to eat.

Nevertheless, we settled in happily. With flowers and fruit in the garden, glowing sunrises and sunsets, the noondays so warm and sunny that we ate on the terrace until the end of November, it seemed a halcyon existence. With copious notes, supplemented by the excellent English library at my doorstep, I began to work on the long-contemplated *And So To Rome*. There were the attractions of the town and the beach when I wearied of labour.

The chief avenue of commerce in Alassio is a narrow main street, over a mile long. The high houses on either side are buttressed with flying arches. On the sea side one looks down narrow alleys that end in blinding vistas of the blue sunlit sea and shore. Through centuries of irregular building the street and houses have achieved an enchanting diversity of shapes. The roofs, windows, chimneys and balconies stand at all angles and levels, with an infinite gradation of colour washes. We are losing all this in our age of hideous concrete. Houses like packing-cases are tied together with telephone wires. Only that summer in Venice I had seen the concrete machine-gun casement which the lovely old Danieli Palace

Hotel had built as an annexe, and the neon-lit glassy horror erected as a façade for the Hôtel Bauer Grünwald. They are as appropriate to Venice as a gold tooth in the smile of a beautiful woman. Alassio today is also consumed by a cancer of concrete five-storied apartment houses eating into the beauty of its hills. The old sea front, once picturesque with clusters of fishermen's houses, is being ecstatically demolished.

The English at some time dubbed the long narrow main street 'The Drain', with a sense of humour that will ever be incomprehensible to the natives. The name infers nothing disparaging, for it no longer smells and the only odours it emits are the somewhat alluring ones from shops stocked with every known delicacy and "such sweet jams meticulously jarred as God's own Prophet eats in Paradise" to quote James Elroy Flecker. It was along this narrow highway that one April day in 1796 Napoleon Bonaparte, newly gazetted to command the French Army in Italy, marched on his spectacular conquest of that country. He found the narrow street of the town so lengthy that he called the place Longueville. The name of the street was then the Corriera. It was called later, at the end coming in from France, the Via Roma, and since it leads to Rome its earliest name was the Via Aurelia. But Italian street names are unpredictable. They are apt to change with the blue, red, green, grey, purple or black shirts of the popular political creed of the day. As any old *Baedeker* will prove, the Piazza Italia in any city may have been Piazza Garibaldi, Piazza Umberto, Piazza Emmanuele, Piazza Vittorio Veneto, Piazza Republica or Piazza Matteotti. At present The Drain changes name in its length from the Via Roma to the Via Brennero, then again to the Via Vittorio Veneto, formerly Via Vittorio Emmanuele, and finally to the Via Venti Settembre, formerly Via Umberto. In its picturesque course, with overhanging eaves and arches and divergent alleys, it swells into open piazzas in three places.

The plan of the town is gridiron fashion. Lengthways there is the sea front, then, parallel, The Drain, then the Corso Dante Alighieri, and then the Via Aurelia, now the main traffic route. Behind all these lies the railway line, where the

foot-hills with their villas and olive trees rise into the amphitheatre of mountains that enfolds the town. The wide Via
Aurelia that passes the gardens of the public piazza changes
its name to Via Mazzini, and later to that of an Englishman,
the Viale Hanbury. This last name is still potent on the
Italian Riviera, recalling the famous gardens at La Mortola,
where Sir Thomas Hanbury, with a fortune made in the
China trade, bought an Italian promontory near Ventimiglia, and with fifty gardeners created a botanical and ar-
boreal paradise. He bought land in order to preserve the
beauty of Alassio, built villas for himself and friends, created
the splendidly housed English Club, and generally played
the Mæcenas at a time when wealthy Englishmen abroad
could enact that rôle. The name Viale Hanbury, originally
planted with plane trees, is a gracious Italian tribute to his
munificence and memory. The Hanbury tradition was maintained by his younger son, Daniel, who built the excellent
Lawn Tennis Clubhouse and spent many happy years in the
place he loved.

Alassio's gold-mine is its beach running the whole length
of a three-mile bay. It is closed at each extremity by mountains that descend steeply towards the sea. Their precipitous
faces have been nicked by a new highway that traverses the
plain between. There is one astonishing fact about this
noble bay. Every person coming from the north to the
Riviera imagines it faces south. Actually the bay turns in on
Italy and faces east. If you flew directly from it you would
pass, in turn, over Viareggio, Lucca, Florence and Ancona
in Italy, Split in Yugoslavia, Sofia in Bulgaria, and Istanbul
on the Bosphorus. Standing on the beach, I could never get
used to the fact that England was on my left and the French
Riviera and Ventimiglia, through which one comes in, at
my back. At the southern extremity of the bay, under the
shadow of the great Capo Mele, lies the little fishing village
of Laigueglia, an antique place not yet quite absorbed by
Alassio, whose promenade has extended almost into it.
Out of this village comes the fishing fleet whose boats, using
acetylene flares, extend in a great arc that lies like a diamond
necklace on the dark throat of the night. The fishermen here,

and in Alassio, are rapidly disappearing along with their fantastic tumbledown houses, hung with coloured washing, fishing-nets and lobster-pots. These houses have outside staircases and balconies of all shapes and hues that seem to have been plastered on by giant house-martins.

About a mile off the promontory of Santa Croce lies the small island of Gallinaria. It is crowned with a castle and a tower, some ruins of an ancient monastery and a church. In early Roman days it witnessed the coming of Mago, the Carthaginian, to aid his brother, Hannibal. It is mentioned as early as Varro (116 B.C.), who declared that it took its name from the flocks of sea-birds that lodge there. After Mago and Varro, we hear little more of Gallinaria until the era of St Martin of Tours. He became a familiar figure in art by virtue of the famous painting of the young soldier on horseback who stoops to give half of his cloak to a naked beggar. It is one of the most arresting works of El Greco, a wistful portrayal of a famous incident in the life of the saint—*"Jeune homme qui fait la grâce de son manteau à un compagnon moins favorisé"*, in Barrès' words.

St Martin was born in A.D. 316 in Hungary, in the reign of Constantine the Great. His father, a military tribune, was stationed with his Legion at Pavia, and here Martin was educated. The parents were *gentiles*, that is, pagans. While Constantine was making Christianity fashionable, the boy Martin ran away to a monastery. Like normal fathers, Martin's refused to permit him to take a contemplative life in a new creed for which he felt little sympathy. He put his son in the Imperial cavalry. As a young officer Martin was sent to Tours, where the nobility of his character and his kindness soon made him popular among his fellow soldiers. To their astonishment, he demonstrated that the Christian virtues were not incompatible with the profession of arms. The winter of 362 at Amiens, where he was stationed with his Legion, was a very bitter one. One day by the city gate he saw a half-naked beggar shivering with the intense cold. Taking his sword he cut his mantle in two and gave one half to him. That night in a dream he had a vision of Christ wearing on his shoulders the half-cloak he had bestowed on the beggar.[1] His vocation seemed clear at last. He was baptized and, nearing forty, asked for release from service in order to devote himself to religion. He was taunted by the Emperor Julian, who insinuated that it was only a device to escape from an imminent battle; whereupon Martin proclaimed that he would march naked, armed only with the Cross, in front of the army. The Emperor took him at his word, but before the test came the enemy sought peace. The Emperor saw in this divine intervention and released his officer from service.

But Martin's troubles were only beginning. It was at a period when the Church was split by the Arian schism, a wordy and venomous quarrel among the Fathers of the Church based on one of those hair-splitting theological controversies that have so often brought Christian communities into bloody conflict. Arius, a bishop in Upper Egypt, came into collision with the ecclesiastical authorities on a point of doctrine. He denied the Bishop of Alexandria's assertion that the Trinity contained one single essence or indivisibility of substance. Like a flame, the dispute spread across the Christian world, and excommunications and persecutions almost wrecked the Church. In despair of these fanatical bishops, the Emperor Constantine called the famous Council of Nicæa. Three hundred and eighteen bishops attended from all parts of the Christian world. The proceedings became like a modern session of the United Nations. Arius defended his opinions, asserting that the Son of God was created out of nothing, had not always existed, was not immutable or impeccable, remained holy through free will, could have sinned if he wished, was not of the same substance as the Father, and, though the Son of God, was not the Word. He split the conference and was most bitterly assailed by an eloquent young deacon called Athanasius, who persuaded the Council to define the doctrine of the absolute unity of the divine essence and the absolute equality of the

[1] This cloak was for long one of the most valued of French relics, and was carried as a banner in war. It is said that the word chapel, in French *chapelle*, is derived from cape, French *chape*, meaning the tent in which St Martin's cloak was preserved, and that chaplain or *chapelain* was the person entrusted with the care of the cloak.

Three Persons. All the bishops save Arius and two colleagues submitted. The three Arians were banished.

This was not the end of the trouble, as Constantine had hoped, but only the beginning. The controversy flared, with varying fortune for the opposing factions, and although the Church endorsed the Athanasian creed, it burned for another fifteen hundred years. John Milton was an Arian, and even the Wesleyan Methodist Society toyed with the Arian denial of the eternal sonship as late as 1832, when its Conference suppressed the doctrine as heretical. Then Arianism was superseded by Unitarianism. "If they had won, Christianity would have dwindled away to a legend", wrote Carlyle.

In this fierce controversy St Martin was caught up. An adherent of Athanasius, he was persecuted by the temporarily dominant Arians. He took refuge with some companions in a cave on the island of Gallinaria, and here he remained in hiding for a year, until the winds of the controversy favoured the Athanasians. It was with dismay that he heard he had been elected Bishop of Tours, for he had enjoyed his life as a hermit on the pleasant Italian island. When the deputation came from Tours he hid from it, but was betrayed by the quacking of a goose at his side. That is why he is so often portrayed in church paintings and statuary as a bishop with a beggar and a goose at his side. He went to Tours, living the same simple life as a bishop, where, greatly loved, he reigned many years until he returned to the great Benedictine abbey of Marmoutier, which he had founded and where he died in 397. The patron saint of Tours and Lucca, and of Knights, Tailors and Repentant Drunkards, his legend became a favourite one of Italian painters.

There are two grottoes on Gallinaria, and one of these is named after the saint, where his altar was shown as late as 1880. We next hear of the island in the tenth century, when the Benedictines founded there an abbey which they named in honour of the two saints, St Martin and St Hilary. They seem to have become powerful on the mainland at Alassio, where they built the priory of Santa Croce on the promontory. The monks and their abbey are mentioned in a charter of 1028. Their power became so great that Alassio placed herself under the jurisdiction of the abbot. His rule extended as far as Andora in the near-by valley, where its men were recorded as 'serfs of the monastery', while the men of Alassio remained free subjects. To the island, driven there by a storm, came Pope Alexander III. He said Mass in the monks' chapel, and in grateful remembrance placed the monastery under the special protection of the Apostolic See. The same Papal Bull mentions the church of Sant' Ambrogio and the church at Andora, with the serfs and the land.

An historian, Navone, records that the monks with great labour made a subterranean passage from the monastery to the cave where St Martin had lived, as a refuge from the piratical invasions of the Saracens, who ravaged the coast until William, Count of Provence, temporarily wiped out this terror in 975. I have not been able to find the corridor, and doubt whether it ever existed; an impossible task for a handful of men in the pre-dynamite era. The jealousy of the bishops of Albenga on the mainland opposite, together with ecclesiastical quarrels, finally destroyed the abbey. The abbot sold the disputed fief to the Commune of Albenga in 1303. The Alassians have always asserted that the deed was a forgery. Bishop Giustiniani informs us, around 1513, that two centuries earlier the Podestà of Genoa, one Lazario di Giraldone, occupied the island, and that the tower still standing was part of his fortifications. The modern house on the top of the crest, incorporating these ruins, was built in the nineteenth century by a banker from Porto Maurizio. The island is still privately owned.

In summer a visit to Gallinaria, with its exquisite little harbour and its path winding up through scented pine-woods to the summit, is a favourite boat excursion from Alassio. Some hardy souls swim to it. It provides the most lovely views, from Capo Mele as far as the promontory of Portofino, with shining glimpses of the white mountains of Carrara.

From the windows of our villa, Gallinaria was clearly visible like a blue-grey snail stationary on the sea. It stood, a black silhouette against the sunrise, and at evening, when the sun set over the land, its buildings on the summit shone rosily in the last light against the darkening sea and sky.

Let us return to the beach at Alassio. The promenade in the old part of the town is called Passeggiata Italia. It is a pleasing jumble of houses, cafés and restaurants. It blossoms with pergolas, pillars, balconies, arched alcoves, terraces, seventeenth-, eighteenth- and nineteenth-century façades, with a few twentieth-century horrors composed of concrete, glass and gas-pipe verandahs. The promenade is gay with palms, awnings, sun umbrellas and chairs in fancy colours that make a Picasso pattern on the sand. It is best seen in spring and autumn before the bathing-huts have created an obscuring wall between the houses and the sea. Midway along the Passeggiata is the pier, a very chaste and uncluttered affair that ends in no oriental-coloured glass-house such as forms a rusty excrescence on most English piers. A few boats can come to it on the translucent jade-green water, but large boats must stand off. When a passing merchantman has an Alassian on board, its siren gives forth echoing blasts so that relatives in the town may know he is looking at them. This is the beach Edward Lear loved, then more primitive, when he stayed here in 1864, on a sketching tour. A few years ago, when the contents of some English villas were sold, fifty of his paintings went for three or four pounds each. Some of the English residents were lucky enough to purchase examples of his delicate art, for the famous *Book of Nonsense* was only a sideline to the work of a serious artist.

Before one reaches the pier there is a tall house with pseudo-Venetian Gothic windows on the second floor. Between two of these windows a marble plaque commemorates the fact that in this house, in 1885, lived Amilcare Ponchielli. And who is he, you may ask? There are some composers who, like poets, are fated to be known by one composition long remembered after their names are forgotten. *The Dance of the Hours* has been played by every esplanade and tea-room orchestra *ad nauseam*. Few know it is by Ponchielli, still fewer that in the middle of the nineteenth century one of his

operas, *La Gioconda*, had a considerable vogue.[1] The plaque
has some charming Italian verses to his memory:

> *On the willow hangs the harp,*
> *But its chords sing as of yore,*
> *Touched by fingers that our eyes*
> *Can see no more.*

Alassio has known other composers. I always wonder in
which hotel or villa Elgar wrote his *Symphony of the South*, in
part dedicated to Alassio.[2]

There is one feature of many of these old houses that is not
really as romantic as it appears. This is the built-on balcony
that leads into a little tower, usually glassed-in and accessible
through French windows. The little verandahs and towers
are the modern sanitary amenities more easily added on to
the exterior than the interior. The ground floors offer some
fine examples of groined and arcaded ceilings, their arches
springing from massive walls. Another feature is the colours
in which the houses are painted: pink, chrome, russet. The
hideous new concrete apartments are all a glaring white.

Alassio has known earthquakes in its time. One half of the
tiles in the town are grey, the other half red, the latter being
the roofs restored after the earthquake of 1887. We speculate
today on which buildings would stand best another earthquake—the old houses with massive walls or the new five-
storied apartment houses, shells of three-inch concrete
poured over quarter-inch iron rods. Dwellers in the latter
nourish a belief that, being flimsy, they would gracefully bend!
The occupants of the fortress-like houses scoff at this idea.

Since the bay faces east, the sun rises like a ball of fire from
the cool grey horizon of the sea. Beautiful as these sunrises
are, they are surpassed by the sunsets. When the sun goes
down behind the mountains to the west, the sea receives a

---

[1] Ponchielli's opera was first performed with great success at La Scala in
1876. The libretto was by Boito, who afterwards wrote his own opera, *Mefis-
tofele*, and supplied Verdi with the librettos of *Otello* and *Falstaff*. *La Gioconda* was
based upon a play of Victor Hugo's, and *The Dance of the Hours* is the music of
the ballet in the opera. Ponchielli taught Puccini and helped to strengthen the
rôle of the orchestra in opera.

[2] "Do you like music?" said Elgar to young Hanbury. "No!" was the
response. "Good!" said Elgar. "Now we can talk about yachting."

beautiful rosy light that does not blind the eyes. It touches with gold not only the island of Gallinaria but also the ships that happen to be in the bay. As we are on the route of liners going to or coming from America, those departing from and returning to Genoa often call at Cannes, wherefore we have a frieze of ships moving along the horizon. In the evening their white decks and stacks stand out in the rosy light. At night, illuminated, they shine like diamonds on black velvet.

To the beach with its three-mile arc of beautiful sand, shut in at either end by the mountain promontories, Alassio owes its livelihood. There are two months when tourists cover the beach in such density, together with huts, umbrellas and chairs, that the sand is almost obliterated. Then, the eight weeks gone, the beach becomes spacious and visible again. This brief summer vogue of the Rivieras is a growth of the last fifty years. For centuries Alassio's chief source of livelihood was boat-building and fishing. Its sailors went as far south as Sicily, not only as fishermen for tunny but also for coral. Large fortunes were made out of this. Some of Alassio's churches were founded on the coral-fisher's prosperity. But, above all, through the centuries Alassio was a recruiting ground for the navies of Genoa and Pisa. When Admiral Andrea Doria set about driving the French out of Genoa in 1528, Alassio contributed no less than eighteen galleys. At the battle of Lepanto in 1571, when the combined navies under Don John of Austria defeated the Turkish armada, four ships from Alassio were in that great sea fight. The town was also a prosperous shipbuilding centre. Nothing of this remains in an iron age. The pines and larches that covered the mountainside and supplied the keels and hulks have all disappeared. The slopes, alas, are denuded of trees, two recent wars completing the deforestation.

How Alassio contrives to live on so short a bathing season has remained for me a complete mystery. Hotels, pensions, restaurants and shops stretch mile on mile in increasing numbers. For eight months of the year they hardly see a customer. The English no longer flock here in the winter months. Nevertheless, one look reveals the fact that Alassio is a thriving and enterprising place.

CHAPTER THREE

A FEW CHARACTERS

I

AT the Villa Perdita, October and November passed. They were halcyon days. We walked along the sand, sunned ourselves at cafés on the Passeggiata, and lunched on our balcony, often with the awning down. But we became aware of a menace in paradise. The evenings began to be cold. Moreover, the balcony went out of use. We discovered that owing to its position under the hill it lost the sun by two o'clock. The temperature in the house fell quickly.

It is an illusion of visitors from the north that the winter on the Riviera coast is warm and sunny. When the sun shines it can be very warm, but Phœbus Apollo knocks off early in the daytime in winter, and his span is often shortened by the mountains behind which he drops. An intense cold falls with the sunset. Riviera villas and apartments are seldom constructed to withstand cold. The price of coal being prohibitive, wood is burned in the grates. No fire is more charming or more unsatisfactory. It will burn for a few minutes with a cheerful flame, and then it will smoulder for hours. If the logs happen to burn brightly, then their swift consumption is at a ruinous cost. The grates in these houses are inefficient and suitable for wood only. Little heat is forthcoming from them. Our hall had a wood-burning stove, but the marble staircase in which we had exulted became a malignant enemy. It defeated the stove and made the hall an ice-box that set the temperature of the house. It became an act of courage to walk upstairs to bed. I made vain attempts to heat the large north-east room, the Bishop's Room, that I had chosen for a study. I bought a large round stove, one of those ancient contraptions that used to heat parish rooms and station waiting-rooms, with a great stove pipe up to the ceiling. Apparently this was no innovation, for there was a hole made for a former pipe. My stove had been Italianized or, more correctly, Hellenized. Its white-stone exterior carried an embossed design of Pan, satyrs, nymphs, youths and maidens in procession around it, reminding me of Keats' 'Ode on a Grecian Urn'. It had a cavernous interior that swallowed half a tree. Hopefully I had this stove installed. It had no effect whatever and consumed prodigious quantities of wood. After a week we closed the room. As for the bedroom above it, I wondered how any visiting bishop, whether from Gibraltar or Alaska, had survived in it. Inquiries produced the information that the Bishop of Gibraltar only toured his diocese in the spring. Wise man.

Desperate with the cold, I cabled to New York for a fur overcoat that I had left there, believing that I should never encounter elsewhere the arctic winters that visit that city. Wrapped in this, plus a blanket, and ensconced on a couch pulled up to the grate in the small salon, with a hot-water bottle at my feet, I endeavoured to write in the evenings. When I inquired how the clergyman-loving lady who had lived here had survived the cold, I learned that after November, until the coming of the spring, she had made the salon a bed-sitting-room. This gave me an idea. I stayed in bed each day until noon, writing, but while my body was warm my hands were icy. I overcame this by purchasing a small electric stove which I ran off the light, turning its reflector towards my hands. Thus I laboured with *And So To Rome*. Ironically *The Times* often carried a travel advertisement, "Visit the Italian Riviera where winter never comes." This had an illustration of a blazing sun shining on palm trees by a sparkling sea. There was a list of these halcyon haunts of summer warmth, including Alassio.

Now, the strange thing about this experience was that one never lost hope or the illusion that one was living in a summery paradise while in England they were shivering under dark rainclouds. The reason was that every day, or almost every day, by ten or eleven o'clock, one was in a world of warmth and radiance; the sea sparkled, the air was balmy, the whole landscape was so entrancing that it made the rigours of the night seem a chimera. The cold spell had gone, one felt assured, casting off the overcoat and gloves, and forgetting the defeated stove and the feeble grates in the 'Villa Frigidaire', as I now called it. In the growing gaiety of the radiant day one forgot that at sundown the Riviera swung into the sub-arctic zone.

I was not alone in my misery. Elderly ladies and gentlemen living in the hotels and pensions complained that the heating was inadequate except in a few hotels all booked up. They thought wistfully of tea and toast and bright coal fires at home in England—until the morning mail brought them envious letters describing the rigours of a land wrapped in a thick fog or saturated with rain, where it was dark at three o'clock, where the electric power was cut off when most needed, and coal was so strictly rationed that only one fire could be lit in the evening. Reading these letters at a café in front of a sparkling sea, where the light was so great that sunglasses had to be worn or the awning lowered, we realized our good fortune and believed it could not be as cold tonight as it was last. This discomfort is unknown in properly equipped villas; but how few are properly equipped! Since the thermometer never falls to freezing, it requires only a little heat in a well-insulated house to be comfortably warm. The owner of the Villa Perdita, I discovered later, had never spent a winter in her villa, which she had inherited. She was indignant when I complained of the absence of amenities. Later she spent a winter there, suffered a revelation, and confessed that she wondered how I had ever been able to hold a pen in my hand. She then dealt with the heating and cooking deficiencies.

There was another spectre haunting our paradise. It was something on which Alassio maintained a conspiracy of silence. Wind. I thought I knew something about wind: I had crossed the Atlantic in winter gales; I had battled for survival on what I regarded as the coldest, bitterest spot in the world, the corner of 59th Street and Fifth Avenue in New York. There, on a January day, one is blasted by a wind that starts from Alaska, twenty below zero, blows straight across the prairies of the Middle West and, screaming over

New York's open Central Park, lashes its victims caught on
the corner of 59th Street. I had known strong men, fortified
by ten cocktails, blanch at the thought of emerging from
adjacent hot-house hotels into that arctic whirlpool. But 59th
Street is no worse than Alassio when the wind is in its most
vicious mood. I used to wonder where it came from and how
it could reach us. We were deeply enfolded in an amphitheatre of hills soaring up to fifteen hundred feet. That seemed
ample protection. It was not until I had mounted up to one
of these heights, looked down on a wide valley and had seen,
farther inland, the great snow-covered expanse of the
Ligurian Alps, that I began to understand where the icy
blasts came from.

One January day, motoring to the opera at Milan, I
had another revelation. After surmounting the barrier of
these Alps, on a perilous ice-bound road, we descended to the
Piedmont plain and the valley of the Po in which Milan is
situated. It was like entering the arctic zone. A hoar frost
whitened the landscape, a thick chilling mist lay over the
plain, a bitter wind lashed the trees. Here was the ice-house
that generated the blasts that descended upon us. It began
to explain something that had always puzzled me. Most
English visitors go to Italy in the spring, summer and
autumn—they are summer birds. It is for them a land of
sunshine, blue seas and lakes, sun-browned natives, grapes
hanging in luscious clusters, flowers in profusion, warm,
scented nights—in short, an enchanted scene. Knowing only
the Mediterranean shore with its palms, oranges and sub-
tropical vegetation, they think it is a land perpetually
bathed in sunshine and balmy breezes. With such a limited
knowledge of the Italian scene, I used to speculate about the
Roman soldier. Had the physique of the Italians degenerated,
for how otherwise could the Legions have withstood the
rigours of foreign service? How had they sustained the
freezing cold and damp of the sunless lands they had conquered and settled in? How, for instance, was it possible for
a Roman, clad in classical kilt, to live by Hadrian's Wall or
in such settlements as Carlisle? Now I no longer wonder. The
Italian who can survive the winter climate of Italy's northern

plains, or of the Apennine and Abruzzi hill-towns, can survive anywhere. No wonder that our soldiers who knew only
the winter campaign in Italy regarded it as a mountainous
Siberia.

The icy winds swept down on Alassio with sudden fury.
Out of a calm clear sky the *Tramontana*, as it is called, would
smite us. I knew that the *Bora*, which curses Trieste, can lift
a man and blow him into the sea, but here in Alassio I was
almost knocked down one morning by a hooligan wind that
leapt on me from the back of the post office—this under a
blue, smiling January sky. There are other winds also, not so
violent but unpleasant in their manifestations. There is one
that blows across the sea from the south-east, the *Libeccio*. It
picks up the sand on the beach and blows it into your eyes,
ears and mouth. It covers the café tables with sand, and
gradually piles it up in banks on the Passeggiata so that the
municipality is put to considerable expense in transferring it
back to its precious beach. We used to wonder why the
natives walked along with their heads swathed in woollen
scarves like Arabs coming out of a sandstorm. We soon
learned. If it was not the *Tramontana* or the *Libeccio* that
leapt on us, then it was the *Greco* from the north-east, the cold
Levante from the east, the hot, humid *Scirocco* from the
south-east, the rain-bearing *Ponente* from the west, or the
Maestrale (the wearisome *mistral* of Provence) from the north-
west. As a result, the great bay of Genoa is subject to the most
sudden furies that make it a treacherous zone; as Nelson well
knew, having had his fleet blown away during his vigil on
Napoleon's transports.

I had a warning of these bitter winds very early in my
sojourn at the villa. One day I discovered in a drawer a
small pocket-diary for the year 1888. It had daily entries
written in a very small, neat hand; feminine, I assumed. It
proved a very poignant document. There was no name in it,
and the entries suddenly ended in May. The writer appeared
to be in the last stages of consumption. There were notes of
temperatures, of night-sweats, of violent attacks of coughing,
of recurrent weakness, followed by optimistic comments
that had a special poignancy—"Much better, feel I am

improving"; "A good night, not so weak"; "The sunshine lovely today, sat out for an hour—happier in spirit". There was a list of books read. For some reason I surmised that the diarist was a young woman, a guest or resident in the villa. Among these entries, in the months of January, February and March, there were references to the wind. "Awake all night, frightful wind storm"; "The wind drove in the rain and my bedroom floor was flooded"; "Bitter wind, could not go out"; "Icy winds from the mountains"; "Blowing hard all day"; "Have not been in the garden for three days, icy wind".

I noticed these entries with surprise, for I read them one December morning basking in the warmth of the sun. A week later I had reason to know how true these were. A friend arrived in Alassio for Christmas. I went to escort her from her hotel up to our villa for the Christmas dinner. We had to fight every inch of our way up the hill, and on arrival in the porch felt we had emerged from a boxing-ring after a violent buffeting. One day my guest was accosted in the street by a lady who expressed alarm for her. She had her own head swathed in a woollen scarf—"*Signora*, it is perilous for you to go about like that," she said, alluding to my friend's hat. "This wind can make you stone-deaf."

For a time I believed that wind was the Achilles Heel of Alassio, that for some reason the mountains under which it is nestled offered no protection, and that its position made it subject to the prevailing easterly winds. Later, I found that Alassio was no worse than most of the Riviera resorts. One day in the late autumn I went to Monte Carlo to lunch with a friend. There was a dog show held on the beautiful promenade that faces the Casino, with its vista of the French and Italian coasts; but it was impossible to visit the show, for at any moment it seemed as if the violent wind would blow the whole thing into the sea below. I never saw anything more miserable than the great Danes, English bulldogs and giant wolfhounds cowering in their cages along the deserted avenues. Here and there the apprehensive owners of Skye terriers, pekes and pugs tried to give their precious pets shelter under umbrellas and mackintoshes. It was the final day, but the prize-giving on the promenade was abandoned. Monte Carlo boasts of the great Tête-de-Chien whose massive cliff is reputed to protect the town, but on this day the great dog wholly failed to protect the little dogs.

On another occasion I was the luncheon guest in Monte Carlo of Lord Sackville, a debonair lad of eighty-five. In his unfailing courtesy he had come down to the station to meet me. Leaving Alassio, I had been almost knocked down by an icy January gale. I remonstrated with my host for coming out to meet me on such a windy day. "Wind? What wind?" he demanded. There was not a movement in the air, it was like a fine summer morning. The wind bloweth where it listeth. On the Riviera one may be in halcyon calm while thirty miles away the gale is up.

Having said my worst about the climate in which we live, let me give the whole picture. It would be safe to say that out of the three hundred and sixty-five days three hundred of them are as perfect as any that God has designed for this world of tribulation. Sleet, snow, fog and damp are unknown to us. When it rains, it rains in a fierce downpour that performs its refreshing business quickly and thoroughly. The next day the sky is blue again, the pavements dry. Those dark, sodden grey days that for week after week are so depressing in England are unknown here. The daylight lasts until almost 5 p.m. in mid-winter. The mornings are bright and mostly sunny at 9 a.m. The winter climate of Florida and South California is justly famous, but a sticky sirocco can make both day and night miserable. After April the heat and insects render life there a trial. In the dry air of Alassio, with the cooling sea adjacent, the heat is rarely oppressive. The swift, short spells of winter cold are bracing and dry.

The real testimonial to the climate is in the prodigious number of octogenarians. It is a place where old people do not know how to die. To be eighty in Alassio is to achieve an age at which one is listened to by one's elders. We have in our midst the Perfect English Gentleman. He emigrated from England at eighty-five. The father of a famous general, at eighty-six he is the Beau Brummell of the beach. Tall, slender, erect, rosy-cheeked, with a clear eye and the brightest of minds, he is the cause of despair in the hearts of those who are living on capital in their closing years. Having planned to vanish from the scene at eighty-five, coincident with the last instalment of their money, they are perturbed by someone who is still in need of it for the vivid enjoyment of protracted youth. He upsets their confident calculations. We have also in a beautiful villa just above the town a nonagenarian who is an awful warning. I met him in town one bright February morning, more buoyant than ever after a little stimulant in a local bar. He informed me jauntily that he had just been to order two suits. "And I've been measured for some shirts. There!" he said, pointing to the shop. "They make them very well—and not expensive."

I have said he is an awful warning, and I would not infer insobriety or unbecoming gaiety. The story is quite different. In late middle-age, a lively bachelor, he fell in love with a pink-cheeked English nun of the Order of the Blue Sisters, who had nursed him during an illness in its convent hospital at Fiesole. Recovered and reluctant to part with the Blue Sister, he set all the town gossips by the ears by marrying her. They settled in Alassio in a perfect villa embowered in flowers. Since he was twenty years her senior, he thought it prudent to make over to his delightful young wife the villa in which they lived, to ensure that she should not be evicted from paradise when he died. It seemed a wise thing, but, alas, she died first. The lonely widower then discovered that his wife had left the villa to the Blue Sisters! A Mother Superior descended upon the wolf who had raided the nunnery, and informed him that after his death they would take possession.[1]

One March morning, walking along the Viale Hanbury,

---

[1] All my life I have experienced coincidences such as no novelist would dare to use. Travelling one day from the Edinburgh Music Festival to London, I utilized the train journey in correcting the proofs of this book. Two Blue Sisters sat opposite and one, overcome by curiosity, asked me if I was an author and what I was writing. I informed her that I was checking at that moment the story of a villa at Alassio inherited by the Blue Sisters. "I know the villa. I am the Mother Superior of the Order and live at Fiesole," she said, and invited me to visit them. She was a genial Australian and travelled all over the world visiting their convents.

by the orange trees where the café tables, bright with coloured covers and flower-pots under striped awnings, are well patronized, two young ladies drinking coffee unmistakably gave me the 'glad eye'. I felt such conduct should be reproved and, stopping, admonished them. But they were quite unrepentant at eighty-four and eighty-two respectively. The younger one had given me earlier proof of her abundant vitality. One day I was invited on a mountain excursion by car. My hostess was a sturdy seventy-nine, her companion was my 'glad eye' friend. I did not then know her age, utterly misled by a dainty pair of legs, a neat waist and the slender figure of a débutante. There was a twinkle in her eye and not a grey hair in her neat brown head. At a great altitude, amid the snowfields, we stopped to pick flowers: gentians, the early crocus, wild daffodils, hepatica and the beautiful spider orchid—*Ophrys granifera*. Presently, high up the slope I espied a small valley. With my passion for exploring, I saw that it ran round the back of the headland and that I could thus reach the main road and walk back to the car. I was correct in my surmise, but the walk proved longer than I anticipated, with the result that my companions, alarmed and fearing I might have fallen down a precipice, began to search for me. Returning, I was astonished to find that, like mountain deer, seventy-nine and eighty-two were careering over the lofty crags and loudly making the herd call. On descending, they sternly reproved me for rashly wandering. I was contrite. I would have been more contrite had I discovered that they were out of breath. They were not.

The climate on this coast naturally attracted retired civil servants, many of whom had passed their lives in India and other warm countries, and had felt unable to face the rigours of the English winter. A further inducement was the low cost of living. In their lovely villas they settled down in the evening of their lives. It has been the fashion to deride these Blimps, Pooh Bahs and elderly Kims, who seem to have come out of Kipling's India. In a recent copy of *The New Yorker*, a journal that epitomises the sophistication of the dollarocracy of America, a clever, slick journalist derided Kipling and his generation. Kipling was "a minor writer but a major disaster for the British Empire. . . . The heroes of the *Jungle Book* and *Kim* are pre-adolescent males, and so are all Kipling's other protagonists, even when they are six-feet-four and big in proportion. His style has descended to us through the speeches of Winston Churchill, who was saturated with Kipling when he was a young journalist and contracted an incurable grandiloquence. . . . Viewed in retrospect, Soldiers Three (Ortheris, Mulvaney and Learoyd) are merely dialect comedians in red suits. . . . Kipling seldom wrote a good story, but he often wrote parts of bad ones well."

Several British novelists have descended upon Alassio and found the general air of propriety offensive. It would be difficult for the English colony here to achieve that Bohemian camaraderie which marks the gayer sectors of the French Riviera, with its aggregation of drug addicts, drunkards, divorcees, debased royalties, pseudo-princes, ex-gaol-birds, crooks, pimps, 'pansies' and gigolos. Alassio has a less intoxicating air; to our livelier scribes it offers only a depressing respectability. Alassio in its English colony has no local drunk, sponger, dope fiend, sexual maniac, social charlatan, shady peer or run-to-seed baronet.

The old Anglo-Indians are rapidly vanishing. The ex-governors of provinces and Indian Civil Servants lie in the cypress grove on the hill. A few of the breed are still to be found. I attended the eightieth birthday party of one of them. A cruel malady has imprisoned him in a chair and shuts off all sound, but under his polished cranium glows the best scholar's brain, Balliol-trained, in Alassio. In the same age-bracket an ex-judge sallies forth with a dog and a shopping basket to exercise, in grocers' shops, a judgment that once measured the litigious passions of India's millions. Slim, of incomparable courtesy, I would trust his incorruptible honesty in any matter vitally affecting me. Perhaps here, in these ancient few, most of them with sadly diminished incomes, is a microcosm of that greatness which made us a nation whose history, possibly now written, is the most incredible in the long saga of human achievement.

The frozen and devalued pound played havoc with the

British colony. Incomes reduced by a war were further reduced by Stafford Cripps. The latter's astonishing somersaults in Washington, with five firm denials of devaluation, repudiated overnight, shook badly the elderly British in Alassio. Too old to return to a country whose climate would kill them, without adequate incomes to meet the rise in the cost of living, they sold their villas, gave up their servants and gardeners, and astonished the Alassio shopkeepers, brought up in a tradition that every Englishman is a Mæcenas, by buying margarine instead of butter and counting the paper lire as if they were banknotes. For some the annual visit to England became too expensive. A phenomenal rise in fares cut them off. They grew older and lonelier. From time to time a local Italian banker who transacted their affairs put his hand in his pocket and buried them. Gone were the pre-war days of carriage drives, theatrical parties, dinner parties at the English Club, the side excursions to Venice, Florence, Rome, Montecatini and Como. The Blue Train and the Compagnie Internationale des Wagons-Lits knew them no more. In the back rooms of cheap pensions they put out their sad souvenirs of happier days, photos of the villa's garden in spring-time, the husband dead for twenty years, the sons and daughters and friends who had preceded them to the exit they craved and could not reach.

"But surely England won the war!" exclaimed the astonished shopkeeper when old Miss Smith counted her lire and bought a very small cake in a shop that was mountainous with them, and which the returning Germans, with new automobiles and a revalued mark that sneered at the pound, bought by the dozen. "Did they mint their gold in the incinerating ovens of Dachau and Belsen?" asked one old lady bitterly, as a bursting Frau walked out with an enormous confection. The last straw for Miss Smith, governess-trained, was the sudden horde of English tourists, loud, garish, the new travelling public, speaking a language she could hardly understand and astonishing the natives with a noisy exuberance that brought Hampstead Heath to the Mediterranean shore. One could forgive them their brash ignorance, but it was difficult to endure their aggressiveness. Happily there are other kinds of English in Italy. I travelled in an autobus from Rome to Florence one summer's day. A quiet middle-aged Englishwoman sat next to me. In the course of conversation I learned that this was her first journey abroad. Somewhat courageously she had chosen to travel independently during her fourteen days' trip. "I wanted to have time to absorb things and not be rushed around," she said. She was a cashier in a Leeds drapery shop, and had saved up for this Italian tour. It was dark when we arrived in Florence. She knew no Italian nor the geography of the place. She had only four more days before she returned to England. I escorted her to a small pension, and as we parted I expressed the hope that she was not disappointed in Italy. She looked at me earnestly and said with quiet conviction, "It's beautiful, it's all so beautiful— it's like evensong in a cathedral! I shall live on these memories for ever!"

II

By Christmas we had met all the members of the English colony. It would be more accurate to say that we had met them a dozen times over. At cocktail parties, on the promenade, in The Drain, at the Agency Galleani, so ubiquitous in service to the English that many of them contrived never to have learned fifty words of Italian in twenty years of residence, you encountered the same faces and were familiar with all their foibles. All considered, I never encountered a nicer community, polite, considerate, well-mannered and hospitable. This agreeable colony never felt itself to be alien in a foreign land. The long and warm tradition of Anglo-Italian friendship was confirmed by the local Italians on their part, whose kindliness and natural hospitality were never failing towards those who were never allowed to feel strangers in their midst.

Among the English residents there were, of course, some 'characters'. One met the colony most frequently at the English library, situated in the octagonal-towered room adjacent to the church. The days of its glory had also departed with diminished subscribers and the ravages of war, but it survived somehow. The early founders had been enterprising and intelligent. It owed much to a Miss Lamport, a well-to-do resident. It contained an excellent collection of works of history and biography, and a large section of fiction, well-catalogued. Since the library dated from 1878 the volumes belonged to the generous years when book production had not been demeaned by paper and binding economies, and when works of scholarship were not truncated or products of shifty journalism. In the late-Victorian and Edwardian eras authors had the means and leisure to devote themselves to research and were able to produce works of erudition whose quality was assessed by critics capable of sound judgment. Book production was then part of the spaciousness of the age. The author was not told that more than ten illustrations would price the book out of the market, that maps were an unthinkable luxury, and that three hundred pages were the 'commercial' limit. Just as economic pressure has driven us from the mansions to the mews, so have we been driven from the well-bound volume to the flimsy pocket-book. The latter has virtues of compression and portability, but it caters for a meaner world.

The library, voluntarily run, opened two mornings a week. By its very nature it was the chief gossip exchange. If Mr Snaith had not been seen at his favourite café table on the sea front, we learned why—he had slipped in the bath and sprained his back. Mr Blake, rubicund and noisy owing to deafness, for he could not hear himself bellow, was unusually subdued. It was not his kidneys, he was in the doghouse, having made two disastrous trips to the casino at San Remo. The local bore, of such amiability and generosity that he was irrepressible, would turn up, looking for a victim to take off to coffee on the piazza. Mrs Netherby, all of a twitter like a starling at sundown, would drop her glasses, her bag, her books, and be uncertain whether she had read the book she was taking out. "They're all so much alike, don't you think? But original books are rather trying, aren't they? I mean, you never know what they mean, do you, even if they mean something, which I suppose they do?"

Then came Sir Job Scattergood, with a large canvas hand-bag. He had to be watched or he would sneak off with half a dozen books that he failed to have entered. There was Mrs Slocombe, who came with great regularity, but never took out a book, her standard being so high and particular that no author could entice her. The Sunday newspaper reviewers enraged her with their weekly eulogies over new master-pieces written by their friends. "They should be barkers for a circus," she said. But she was a glutton for P. G. Wode-house. And always late, with steady unpunctuality, came the *Reverendo*, transported by his wife in their small station-wagon. They consumed a dozen books a week, not one of them theological. No British community ever had a more darling honorary chaplain. On the verge of eighty, he preached every Sunday to the same twelve faces in a church designed for five hundred. The word 'preached' is not quite correct. When he arrived in Alassio he told his parishioners that he was there to please them. "Do you want sermons?" he asked. "No!" they replied spontaneously. So sermons they never had. His wife, in the gallery, chauffeur-cum-organist and renowned lampshade-maker, played the hymns.

They had a special claim to fame. They were intrepid motorists. Every summer, with flimsy courage and no sense of direction, they set out over the Alps for their beloved Scotland. Somehow they always arrived and always re-turned, but no one ever learned how, for they could never remember their route. They had never looked under the bonnet of their car, knew neither its speed nor its petrol con-sumption. Ice, snow, rain, blizzards and avalanches were all alike to them. Probably they had made every possible crossing of the Alps, if only they could have remembered what crossings they had made in the course of years. Their courage was quite unconscious, their adventurousness had an undefeatable innocence. "But which Channel crossing did you make? Calais to Dover or Boulogne to Folkestone?" I asked. The *Reverendo's* eyes twinkled. "Well, my wife would know—which crossing, my dear?" "We flew our car over!" she responded with vague triumph. "Your papers—your licence-plates, insurance, carnet, transport?" I asked, wanting useful details. "Oh! Oh, we get Galleani to do all that."

Dear, indispensable, omniscient, inexhaustible Galleani, who pays rates, effects bank transfers, offers exchange, calls in the plumber, reserves your sleeper, lets your villa, stores your furniture, registers you with the police, pays you six per cent. on your bank balance, gets the *permesso* to send home a family painting, to bring out a silver tea service, and who, though he cannot marry you, will arrange your burial, Protestant, Catholic, choral or plain.

The *Reverendo* has another gift besides automobilism. He paints exquisite water-colours. Enchanted with these, extracted one day from his portfolio, I stunned him by seeking to purchase four of them. For a moment he doubted my sanity, and then blushed at the thought of anything so commercial. I don't know whether he suspected me of trying to help the church, but I persisted and left with four treasures. When I had had them framed and had hung them, I invited him to tea. His suppressed pride was touching. He took my cheque to Scotland with him, unable to believe that it represented payment for art. I was relieved to find in due time that he had cashed it.

He lives in a large villa which he built thirty years ago. It is precipitously perched, high over the bay, and has incredible views from all its windows and terraces. He and his wife love to be called on. In winter they sit with their two cats before a log fire, eating buttered toast, while the sunset throws a veil of rose over the bay below. He loves his fellows, including an old infidel like myself. "Do come on Tuesday to tea and meet the Bishop of Gibraltar. He would love to meet you," he says as I go out.

In a little room adjoining the library is found another member of the colony, an octogenarian, half-advanced towards nonagenarianism. I was a long time discovering this, for a youthful smile disguises her. She is the library's hospital matron. To her come all sick books, those torn and tattered, with broken backs and dog-ears. Here she sits amid sheets of coloured binding linen, variegated end-papers—lovely *carta di Varese*, finished in blue and crimson with the Florentine lion, the fleur-de-lys and the Venetian anchor—gum and paste pots, scissors and sewing thread. She is alone in her cell like an eremite. Nothing deters her. I have found her in the bitterest cold, with no heating, her hands blue under the mittens she wears in winter, and in the great heat of the summer, working steadily on a pile of battered books. It is a labour of love and of great utility. I often wonder what she thinks about. Does she review a long life begun in far-away Australia, her girlhood, youth, courtship, marriage and the loss of two sons, one killed in the First World War, the other, having passed unscathed through the Second World War, killed in a street accident? Perhaps she thinks of nothing at all, and finds happiness in her task, for there is always a smile when I interrupt her.

One dark winter's evening shortly after tea-time we had a caller. I did not know his name and had not seen him before. When he was shown in he apologized for his intrusion, but as I was a new-comer he felt that he should call. He was slender, tall, with an attractive diffidence in his manner. His name was Neame, he said. It transpired that he had lived in Alassio for many years. After a while he confessed to one venture in authorship. He had written a book on the flora of Northern Italy. On expressing a wish to see it, he hesitatingly said he would lend me a copy. He departed into the night. I would not have let him go alone down the dark *salita* had I known what I learned later, that he was, for all his youthful appearance, a man of eighty-four!

A few days later he left the book, *Among the Meadows and Alpine Flowers of Northern Italy* by J. Armstrong Neame, and I had a great surprise. He was not only a man who loved flowers, with a botanist's knowledge of them, but he was also a gifted artist. His book was illustrated with fifteen coloured plates from his own exquisite water-colour studies. He had published the book, obviously a work of love, in 1937.

It was dedicated to his wife, "my constant companion". He lost that companion while in England during the war. They had had a comfortable income. His junior, and not expecting he would survive her, she left her money to relations. He was reduced to a small annuity. He now lived a lonely life in a pension on his minute income. He had been in early life a

New Zealand schoolmaster. Those must have been very happy years wandering with his wife through the Northern Italian Alps. He chose Alassio or Levanto as his head-quarters, declaring the former to be the best wild-flower centre along the Italian Riviera. He travelled near and far with his wife, following his passion. "Such a complete change of scenery is made in travelling from the Riviera coastline that within ten minutes of leaving Ventimiglia northwards it is as if one had passed through a door into another room," he recorded.

He had an eye for other things than flowers, and noticed in the towns and villages of south-west Piedmont that the sign over the baker's shop was a trophy of loaves and rolls in heraldic form. He penetrated to the Argentiera Pass between France and Italy, where, it is now believed, Hannibal made his famous crossing of the Alps. He was delighted to find by Lake Maddalena a little white flower, half-anemone, half-narcissus, and its companion, the yellow violet. He went on to Saluzzo and stayed at the 'Corona Grossa', for an excellent reason, "because the name sounded so attractive". The town had other claims to fame. Here was born, in 1740, Giambattista Bodoni, the famous typographer—his type is often used on our visiting-cards—and in 1788, Silvio Pellico, the poet, who was so cruelly imprisoned by the Austrians. After being sent to the notorious Piombi in Venice, he was condemned to death. The sentence was commuted to fifteen years' imprisonment. When released after ten years, he published an account, *Le Mie Prigioni*, which won him world-wide fame and is now an Italian classic.

Saluzzo was made famous by two marquises of that name. Ludovico II in the fifteenth century gave the town such advanced sanitation that it escaped the terrible plagues. He also made a short tunnel near Monte Viso by which he could transport salt from Grenoble in France to his marquis-ate. At a height of nine thousand feet he cut a tunnel six feet high and eight wide that would allow the passage of mules. It was used later for general transport, and is still kept open by the Italian Alpine Club. An earlier marquis, Walter, gave the place world-wide fame. It was he who took to wife

Griselda, the beautiful daughter of a Piedmont peasant, and to prove her submissiveness and loyalty subjected her to cruel tests. He took from her their two children in succession, making her believe they were dead, and sent her back to her humble home pretending that he was taking another wife. To all this she responded with such humility that she became a pattern and 'the flour of wyfly pacience'. Her story was immortalized in literature by Petrarch in 1373, who sent his Latin text with a letter to Boccaccio, saying that the story had pleased him when he heard it many years before. Boccaccio made it the last and tenth story of the tenth day in his *Decameron*. The most widely known version occurs in Chaucer's *Canterbury Tales*. The Clerk reports that he heard the tale at Padua from Petrarch's own lips, and it is probably true, for Chaucer was in Italy on the King's business from December 1372 to November 1373. Griselda's house is now a museum in the little town she made so celebrated. Any husband attempting the marquis's line would get a shock today!

From Saluzzo, Neame went on to Torre Pellice. Its name means little to us and yet, with its neighbour Pinerolo, it once made history. For the former was the capital of the Waldensians, those "slaughter'd Saints, whose bones lie scatter'd on the alpine mountains cold", as Milton's magniloquent sonnet proclaimed, calling on God for vengeance. These followers of Peter Waldo of Lyons, who raised the Protestant flag in the twelfth century, long before Luther, were a kind of early Quaker. They advocated poverty and simplicity. They were anathematized at Verona in 1184, terribly persecuted, massacred and burnt by the Inquisition in France, above all in Piedmont. Fire, sword and confiscations failed to quell them. They were smoked to death in the caves in which they sought refuge. Francis I burnt twenty-two of their villages and massacred four thousand souls. A hundred years later, in 1655, a particularly brutal massacre in the Piedmont valley, near Torre Pellice, called forth Milton's noble sonnet and Oliver Cromwell's protest. He sent Sir Samuel Morland to negotiate a settlement with the intolerant Duke of Savoy, and the Peace of Pinerolo was signed. Nearly two more centuries of persecution followed, but the Roman Church failed in its purpose. Then a curious thing happened. Colonel John Beckworth, who had lost a leg at Waterloo, read a book written by Canon Gilly of Durham, *Visit to the Valleys of Piedmont*. Moved by the sufferings of the Waldensians, he settled among them at Torre Pellice, married a peasant girl, and for thirty-five years carried on a mission of relief. He brought to success the Waldensian College initiated by Canon Gilly, founded a hundred and twenty schools, and died in 1862. The town has never forgotten him. The names of Cromwell, Milton, Gilly and Beckworth are commemorated in the names of streets and public buildings. It was a strange thing for Neame to find in a remote Piedmont valley town the names of fellow countrymen and an echo of the Miltonic thunder.

Neame's flower quest led him to some odd places for strange reasons. Alpine clematis had called him to Torre Pellice, where sprays of purple cranes'-bill swaying in the soft air, campanulas, pink torches of knotweed, and leopards' bane carpeted the fields once bloody with massacre. A rumour of pink dianthus, tiger lilies and spiræa sent him posthaste in May to Gravedona at the head of Lake Como. Another rumour that Chiesa, high under the ramparts of the Engadines, was the centre of Laburnumland speeded him north. He was well rewarded—

"Through the wide expanse of forest, clothing to a great extent the hillside opposite Chiesa, we noticed what from afar looked like veins of gold, gathering here and there into little pools of the same yellow glory. On closer examination we found that these veins were laburnum trees in full flower. They took from the woodland all of its sombreness and monotone, and added a very unusual charm to the view. It was, of course, only on such a slope that the brilliance of the laburnum blossom could be seen, because in the shade of the surrounding trees the gleam of it would be lost."

He had a bonus for his journey. He found the little frontier village full of Italian Alpine troops on manœuvres. An officer, seeing him sketching on the terrace of the hotel became suspicious, but the painter's simplicity soon charmed him. In turn the artist became inquisitive. On their marches through the mountains did they ever come upon the alpenrose? "No," replied the officer. Two days later, a shy private was shown up to Neame's loggia bearing an armful of magnificent alpen-roses, with the officer's compliments. Then one evening, going out to buy milk, he found the village high street had become a bower of gold. Whole trees of laburnum had been brought from the mountains by the happy soldiers to decorate the village in honour of the Capitano's birthday. "Every door was festooned with the gay blossom, every window was 'dropping veils of fire', while plainly written in chalk upon the walls ran the legend *Viva il Capitano!* It was to be a Fiesta. . . . Later the revelry was transferred to flower-decorated cabarets and dancing halls, where for want of a sufficient number of village maidens men danced together, and very rhythmically too."

Neame explored the Adige Valley, lingering at the old town of Malcesine on Lake Garda, once the stronghold of the Captains of the Lake. But it was not to see the castle of the Scaligeri, with its Ghibelline battlements, that he went. His quest on the heights above was patches of blue *Globularia cartifolia*, "which spread like Egyptian pectoral ornaments studded with grey-blue jewels", the salvia that stained the grass meadows a deep purple, and the glorious bee-orchid with its magenta sepal wings. His brush was busy copying these treasures. From Garda Neame went to the Dolomites, a flower-covered paradise in the spring. His book has an exquisite water-colour of the rosy peaks and the meadows of dark gentians and anemones. "The colour almost iridescent as it seems to change with the movement of the sun from dawn to dusk," he noted under a sketch made on Tre Cime del Lavaredo.

He had been in the lesser-known Brenta Dolomites, above Molvena, enchanted there with the pilgrim peony. But it was at Misurina, the lake near mighty Monte Cristallo at Cortina, that he was wholly ravished.

"We had seen in a good many places wide expanses of wild flowers in the gay bushland of Western Australia, in the bluebell, anemone and primrose woods of England, on the slopes of the meadowland in Switzerland, and on those of the eastern Alpine ranges of Italy itself—but never had we come upon so entrancing a vision of iridescent colour, for a light breeze was brushing delicately over the surface of the meadow and swaying the flower heads in waves of changing blue. McWhirter's great painting of a Tirolean meadow is the nearest reproduction of such a picture as Nature had put before us here. But no static impression can convey the life, the scintillating radiance or the delicacy of the colour, brilliantly yet with restraint distributed over the whole slope of the meadow."

On one more occasion I saw the lover of flowers who had called on me that dark winter's evening. It was on a hot day in spring just before I returned to England. I confess he created in me a spirit of mirth, for he was indeed a surprising and eccentric figure. He advanced down the blazing street, a tall thin figure, with a large yellow, green-lined parasol over his head, and wearing an enormous Sicilian straw sun-hat from whose brim a muslin veil hung down upon his shoulders. He was dressed in a white suit, and seemed attired for a butterfly hunt in the high Himalayas. A well-known figure, he created no attraction except for myself. He greeted me graciously and passed. Alas, I did not know I was never to see him again or to realize his particular quality until it was too late. When I returned to Alassio two years later I heard that he was ill and had been taken to a nursing-home, a first-class establishment that received him at a reduced rate with a kindness Alassians frequently show to old English residents fallen on evil days. Here peacefully he lapsed into oblivion. He was eighty-six. There was barely enough to bury him. His few possessions, his books and paintings were displayed for sale at the English library. It transpired from his books that he was a great lover of poetry, especially Tennyson and Browning. In a volume of the latter he had marked the last lines of *Prospice*:

And the elements' rage, the fiend voices that rave,
Shall dwindle, shall blend,
Shall change, shall become first a peace out of pain,
Then a light, then thy breast,
O thou soul of my soul! I shall clasp thee again,
And with God be the rest.

He must have been thinking of his lost companion on the flowery slopes.

I bought some of his books, the very volume that he had lent me, and a dozen exquisite flower paintings from his portfolio. There was a strange oddment in this cluster of his things, a battered little silver teapot and sugar-bowl. I had them valued and bought them. Repaired, they are a shining memory of him when I have breakfast on my terrace overlooking the hills where he gathered his flowers. From the sale of this small estate there was enough to provide a headstone and curb for his grave. He lies buried in the little valley cemetery at the foot of the mountains looking on the sea. It is beautiful, with dark cypresses, eglantine, and the silvery olive trees on the terraced hills. On the spring day that I went to find his grave some roses planted by a friend were in full bloom above the resting-place of the man who loved flowers.

CHAPTER FOUR

PALAZZO VAIRO

I

THE months slipped by at the villa. The winter was almost gone, and with it my six months' tenancy drew to a close. In March the spring leapt upon us. There were days of summer heat, the sea a radiant blue, with butterflies hovering over the early roses. Swiss and Germans, earliest of visitors, were already splashing in the sea, to the aloof amusement of the natives observing these mad creatures.

One morning while up a ladder picking the last of the tangerines—it is only bitter oranges that linger on the trees in the streets through all the summer—I heard a mysterious music floating over the garden. It came from a distance, now clear, now faint. I discovered that it came from the little church of Solva that stands high on a ledge of the mountains, very picturesque with its slender campanile. This music was the preliminary of a festival of the Madonna to be held that evening. What seemed curious to me was the clarity with which the music descended from a church so far off.

Soon after six o'clock I mounted up the *salita* from the town to make a closer investigation. The way led through terraces of olive groves, above scattered villas, with wonderful views of the bay below. It was a lovely evening, the path was hung with flowering wistaria, and the perfume of spring flowers loaded the air. The peach trees were clad in pink blossom, delicately vivid against the sky. As I mounted higher, the music from the church above became clearer. I now learned the exact nature of this music which had a distressing dissonance at moments, for the voices were quite extraordinary as they sang or chanted, making one wonder what kind of choir the priest had recruited for this festival. But now, in sight of the church, I knew. In the belfry of the campanile there were clusters of trumpets out of which

71

issued music. They were broadcasting church music from
gramophone records! The Italian passion for *modernismo* had
reached the church on the mountain! Gregorian chant and
Pergolesi came upon the air with a scratchy brassiness
familiar at the cinema. The frightful noise shattered the
serene evening. I drew near to the little piazza so loftily
placed in front of the façade just in time to see an approaching procession. It might have been inspiring, but with that
music it became tawdry. A bedraggled choir of acolytes and
old men chanted an anthem. They competed hopelessly with
the unrelated music braying from the campanile's broadcasting trumpets. The Madonna, swaying on a platform
carried by four men, had been taken out for an airing. I was
informed that this was her four-hundredth festival. She
looked like it, a tawdry, ill-carved, gaudily painted image.
As the procession passed, some of the crowd fell on its knees,
but by no means all. I saw something like a cold stare from
what may have been a cluster of village Communists,
though their Communism is of a curious quality. Odd members have been known to plead for the honour of being one of
the Virgin's bearers, deeper, older instincts triumphing over
their new scepticism.

There followed a bishop of venerable years. He was
brilliantly apparelled, with a gold mitre on his head, and
hands encased in great gloves. He carried a jewelled pastoral
crozier. He was preceded by a large crucifix, and followed by
two rubicund priests, a boys' choir in surplices trimmed with
white lace, and an undisciplined drift of old women and
children. It all struck a bright note in the tranquil spring
evening on the mountain. The procession slowly passed into
the dim church, but not before the campanile had brayed
forth Schubert's *Ave Maria*. Whether because this was considered inappropriate or was not properly co-ordinated with
the proceedings, it was suddenly switched off with much
needle-scratching, and a chant was substituted. Within the
church a sermon was preached, heard outside via the loud-
speakers. Meanwhile I had moved into the thronged church.
Although a village community, the Italian peasant seemed
to have disappeared. A war has left most of them prosperous.

The women wore nylon stockings and delicate high-heeled shoes, their cheeks were rouged, their lips painted red, their nails had been 'dipped in the blood-tub', as a friend of mine calls the incarnadine fashion in manicure. The young men, almost without exception, wore suits that would have done credit to a Savile Row tailor, helped out by athletic figures. I observed, as often elsewhere, how well-dressed are the young Italians today. Their clothes are well cut, their linen is always spotless. How long will the myth that Italians are dirty, widely held in England and America, persist? Almost every window in the poorest community will have its mattresses put out to air, after which they are beaten almost to tatters. The frequency and colour of the washing on the line often add to the gaiety of the landscape. And here in the church I observed how the elderly men, sun-shrivelled by years of labour in the groves, had remarkably fine features and intelligent eyes, and wore their clothes with much grace. They all had the natural good manners and courtesy of the race.

A little lower down, in the local school, there was a rival festivity. The young bloods were arriving with the maximum noise on their motor-cycles to attend the village dance. While Gregorian chant was broadcast from the campanile, the jazz band thumped in the dance-hall, the traditional Roman church music assailed by the negro rhythms of the New World. It epitomized a vaster struggle of protagonists in the sacred and profane worlds.

II

Towards the end of April I left the Villa Perdita for six weeks in Rome and the rest of the summer in England. After that I had planned to visit South Africa and Spain. I was sorry to leave Alassio, and did not know that I should ever see it again. Despite the ordeal of the cold, my memories of the place were wholly happy. With the aid of the library across the garden, I had finished a long book involving much research, and I had made some delightful friends among the English and Italian communities. The last few weeks were specially alluring, with a warm sea and a riot of flowers in gardens, falling over walls and cascading from those great terra-cotta jars that stand on terraces and under vine pergolas. I could not name the infinite variety of this blaze of spring flowers, which included mauve Judas trees in heavy blossom, jasmin, tulips, camelias, blue wistaria, bougain-villæa, early roses, and pink and scarlet geraniums falling like sheets of flame over old walls. I regretted leaving the balcony where I had breakfasted, with its view of the town on the bay and the silver sea where the moon, honey-hued, had risen. It had all been very pleasant, though I had not fulfilled my early dream of a home of my own in Italy, with a terrace and cypresses. Perhaps I was not destined to fulfil it.

How little we know what lies in the future! A year passed, spent in France, England and Spain. In the autumn I found myself in Bad Gastein, that Austrian resort which sits on a shelf in the amphitheatre of the mountains, and Delphi-wise looks far down to the distant valley. It was while I was there, towards the end of August, that I received a telegram from a friend in Alassio. I had seen another advertisement of a villa to let and asked her to look at it. It had not been found suit-able, but she had seen something to let that might please me. It was an apartment, not a villa. This was not at all my idea of life in Italy. You could not have cypresses in an apartment! While I hesitated, a letter followed the telegram. The apart-ment had a terrace! It faced the sun, and overlooked the sea and the town's piazza. There was also an option to purchase. As so often in my life, I took a risk and telegraphed to my friend to take it. We met in Florence ten days later, where I received a detailed description of this place I was destined to buy.

Later, when friends learned that I had gone to live in the Palazzo Vairo at Alassio, they imagined that, in jumping from a Chiltern cottage to an Italian palace I had contracted *la folie des grandeurs*. They did not know that I had taken only a floor of a palace. Almost every large building in Italy is called a palazzo. It may be the ancestral home of a prince or the offices of a bank. Byron lived in a palazzo in Venice overlooking the Grand Canal, but he occupied only one floor. Browning on the Grand Canal was a little more splendid, he occupied two floors of a vast palace bought by his son's rich American wife. Shelley, during a tragic sojourn in Rome when he lost his infant William, lived on the Corso in one floor of the Palazzo Vospi. When the guest in Rome of Prince and Princess Doria, I found that they lived on only one floor, though it contained a vast suite of reception rooms and a famous art gallery. Their palazzo is two-thirds the size of St Peter's and occupies a site that could accommodate both St Peter's and the Colosseum! "One often hears foreign visitors, ignorant of the real size of palaces in Rome, observe with contempt that the Roman princes let their palaces," wrote Marion Crawford, alluding to the Palazzo Doria. "It would be more reasonable to inquire what use could be made of such buildings if they were not let; how any family could be expected to inhabit a thousand rooms."

The Italian family is a very united one. These palaces were built in the age of grandeur to accommodate not only the father, mother and children, but also the grandparents, uncles, great-uncles, aunts, great-aunts, nephews, nieces, grandsons, granddaughters, married or single, and a large retinue of butlers, bailiffs, secretaries, priests and footmen, all under one roof. When the massive doors of the portal swung to they were like a small kingdom, unassailable by the outside world.

It transpired that my domain was one of thirty apartments in a comparatively modern palazzo built in the early twentieth century. It was a top-floor apartment. There was no art gallery, no vast entertaining rooms. It was a very manageable suite of seven rooms with a commodious entrance hall. There was a concierge on the ground-floor and a lift. My friend's account left me without enthusiasm. To live in Italy and lack a garden, a pergola, a vine, a cypress, seemed to me to be missing the very essence of the Italian scene. But I decided that I would give it a trial for a year. The attractions were really Alassio and its library, and a nice community. I took a tenancy from the following November with the option to buy. The place was furnished. Then I left for Rome, returning to England in November. While in Rome I contracted a poisoned foot—from the virulent dust of dead Cæsars stirred up during my incessant peregrinations of the Palatine, I wondered? I shall never know, but the foot was troublesome enough to keep me in hospital for a month. As soon as I could walk, I left for Italy. But for my foot I should have gone on a tour of South Africa, as planned. And here I was again in Alassio.

The owner was an Englishman who had lived in his own villa before the war. His brother had lived in the Palazzo Vairo and, dying, had bequeathed the apartment to him. Both villa and apartment had been occupied during the war. Like so many English properties in Alassio, the apartment had suffered from a succession of tenants. The owner did not think that it was furnished or equipped in the style I was accustomed to, but my friend, after a cursory inspection, had reported favourably. It was very manageable, with a large kitchen, good offices, on one floor and near the shops. The kitchen is to a house what the engine-room is to a liner, and if the chief engineer is disgruntled the journey is a trying one. That department seemed to be satisfactory, so I embarked hopefully.

I arrived in the early afternoon of a dreary December day. There was enough light left for me to survey my new domain. I found that the palazzo stood solid and unpretentious, neither in the antique nor concrete mode, facing the large leafy piazza. The rooms were all light and pleasant. The crowning glory was the long balustraded terrace commanding a splendid view of the town, the mountains, the piazza gardens, and the sea not a hundred yards distant. The elevation made the view extensive. Before us, south, beyond the town, was the great promontory of Capo Mele with its signal station, 715 feet high. The ridge of the mountains that swept in a semicircle around the town achieved a maximum height of nearly 2,000 feet, closing the bay on the north with the promontory of Santa Croce.

The terrace was really a terrace. The term is loosely used, so I had wondered whether it was open or closed in at the top, as is often the case in Italian villas. The word *terrazzo* in a strict

76

definition applies to a raised open walk. A roofed terrace is a loggia, typified by the well-known Loggia dei Lanzi, in Florence, near the Palazzo Vecchio, with its famous bronze statue of Perseus by Benvenuto Cellini. This loggia was named after the guard of German foot-lancers that the Grand Duke Cosimo had waiting near by, in case of trouble. My terrace, walled in at each end, had a marble balustrade with four Ionic columns, two in the centre and one at each end, that supported a pergola. It faced south-south-west and, being closed at the back and at each end, was obviously a sun-trap. It was sixty feet long and ten wide. I found that I could promenade on it like a captain on his bridge; to which it had this resemblance, it commanded a view of the sea a hundred feet below. The problem of warmth in winter, an important one, as the 'Villa Frigidaire' had taught me, seemed solved, for I was sheltered from the wind on three sides and exposed only on the south. I discovered later that the winter sun rose from the sea on its left, and set behind the mountain on its right. The terrace was even better placed than I surmised. In summer, the sun being high, it did not shine horizontally into the salon, with its glassed French door and long window, so that we were not baked in the summer sun. In the winter the sun, level, warmed the rooms.

Immediately below me was the public piazza, laid out with a fountain, trees and ornamental gardens. It was a large rectangular space between the main highway and the Corso Dante Alighieri. At one side rose the *Municipio*, a modern half-baroque building, with a parapeted roof and red pantiles. The piazza, the heart of Alassio, was a continuous delight. It had a great variety of trees, palms, araucarias, pines, magnolias, red and white oleanders, laurels, orange, cedar and jacaranda trees. The last, a tree of blue flame with which I was familiar in Florida, having had one in my garden there, has no correct name in Italy. The Italian vocabulary not only has no word for 'grandchild', using the same word as nephew, *nipote*, it also rejects the letter 'j' from its alphabet. It stigmatizes it as 'glottologically semivocal'. Since jazz has overwhelmed Italy, the 'j' has had to be admitted, but the word, and music, are termed *'d'importazione americana*', and the effect is rightly described as '*laceratori di ben costrutti orecchi*', lacerating the well-constructed ear! Since Italians have an insatiable passion for noise—the young pull out the baffle-plates of their motor exhausts to increase the noise—it is strange that, etymologically, they should stigmatize jazz in this manner.

But let us return to the piazza. It is a work of art with its well-kept flower-beds. Looking down from my terrace upon the ceaseless changes of flowers that border the lush green grass, watered each morning at 5 a.m., I appreciate the description of a friend of mine who boasted of 'an A.P. garden', meaning Another Person's garden, the best of all gardens, which he overlooked, enjoying it without labour or cost.

I have suffered much from gardens and gardeners, and often wonder if the delights balance the penalties. At Pilgrim Cottage I became wheelbarrow-driven. My leisure was menaced by a tremendous hedge that took six days to clip, by a lawn that became a menace if not mown every week. A month's absence, and an army of weeds took possession so that every holiday was clouded by the arduous labour that awaited my return. Nor was my lot lightened by those kind guests who, selecting the softest chair in the shade, congratulated me on how beautifully I kept the garden while I sweated behind the roller. I learnt the habits of jobbing gardeners, whose energy seemed most promising on the days when a downpour of rain frustrated them, and who in fair weather, somewhere in the garden, had a gift of disembodiment that a fakir might envy. One ancient specimen, a dear old man, adopted the rôle of a garden grotesque, with the immobility of an artist's model. Another, scarcely less somnolent, when I complained of the large clumps of Japanese anemones invading the grape hyacinth border, informed me that they had a habit of 'walking' down the beds! Another odd man had a vendetta against certain flowers, and gave them every inducement to die. Colds, lumbago, influenza, sciatica, rheumatism, all these waylaid my man in the press of spring-time. Along with my neighbours, I watched the skies on the eve of his day with us. Our solicitude for his health would have done credit to an orphanage. One eccentric, a genius with growing fingers, in great demand, had moods. He was apt to be seen on hot summer days attired in sandals and shorts as if leaving for the beach at Cap d'Antibes, and any symptom of illness touching his beloved dog entailed sudden absences. Perhaps he had the right philosophy of work, I reflected, as I filled in my income-tax form— enough to live on and not too much, whereas I worked eight months a year for the benefit of a confiscatory State.

In due time I made friends with the head gardener in the piazza. He was the kind that will always defeat us whatever our skills, for he belonged to the Order of Transitionists. I learnt about this Order many years earlier when returning at dawn from a London dance. Crossing St James's Park, near that glorious flower-bed south of the lake, I caught six gardeners burying pots of blooming azaleas transported from a nursery. They carefully scraped up the soil of the beds to hide the rims of the pots. With my umbrella I poked the bottom of a bending gardener. "Cheat!" I cried, to his astonishment. But now this subterfuge, enacted below me, gives me a wonderful floral display. No plant can wilt or be reluctant in blooming; as if on the sacred island of Delos, it may not die; at a sign of decline it is spirited away.

The piazza is amply supplied with benches, much patronized. When requiring respite from my desk or some information upon the town's activities, I have only to descend to the piazza, where I encounter some friend resting between shopping activities or merely sunning herself.

The terrace and its open vistas were not the only assets of my new dwelling. We possessed a small boiler that heated the whole apartment. It was designed for coke and proved highly efficient. Later an ingenious contrivance was added by which, instead of coke, we consumed, at much less expense and with greater cleanliness, a substance called *sansa*. This proved to be a utilization of the olive stones that had hitherto been discarded after the oil had been extracted from the olives. The stones, minced and dried, provided a fuel with a high calorific value, leaving no ash. *Sansa* came, after the olive harvest, from Stellanello, a village in the foothills. It was nice to think that the prodigious olive tree, the Italian's ancient friend, the oil producer essential to domestic happiness and health, gave back the heat of summer it had garnered on the mountain terraces to warm us through the winter. With an electric hot-water installation and power points in all the rooms, I felt we might defy the sudden bursts of cold that had made us miserable. Facing south, sheltered on the north, east and west, with a sun-trap terrace and our *sansa* boiler, we felt assured. When the test came our faith was confirmed.

III

On the evening of my arrival at the Palazzo Vairo, I felt very depressed. The apartment was dilapidated and badly in need of decoration. The lighting was miserable. The long salon possessed only one lamp, a cracked Chinese vase with a loose holder and a shabby silk shade that toppled off at a touch. The drab curtains hung on abominable poles with brass knobs. The poles swayed threateningly when the long curtains were drawn. The easy chairs were not easy, but were over-upholstered tubs long depressed by Victorian heavyweights. The passion for knobs was repeated in my bedroom. There was a monstrous brass bedstead, decorated with knobs in every one of which loose shot rattled on getting into bed. But the most hideous objects were on the walls. It is easier to live with another man's widow than with another man's pictures and furniture. These were, indeed, an ordeal. I was amid pictures and furniture descended from a rich Greek merchant of the Victorian era whose generous benefactions in the art world had made him a notable figure in London Society. He had been captured by the Pre-Raphaelite craze, and in particular by G. F. Watts and Burne-Jones. The former had painted many members of his family. Watts being then a fashionable artist of the day, the fees paid for these works must have been considerable. He was even transported by his patron to Greece to paint the portrait of a Greek Prime Minister. If the Greeks had a word for it, I could find no word for the inky daub afflicting my eyes. Out of a Cimmerian gloom and a mass of black whiskers two beady eyes fixed me. The Greeks, since the days of Odysseus, have been

The terrace faced the sun and overlooked the sea and the piazza.

Via XX Settembre, dubbed 'The Drain' by the English Colony.
(*Photo: Omniafoto—Torino.*)

renowned as wily fellows. I could have believed anything of this gentleman's political slipperiness.

It was particularly unfortunate that the artistic deity of the palazzo was G. F. Watts. I had been de-Watted very early. When a schoolboy I had been taken in a class to visit a special exhibition of the great artist's works. They were commended for their high moral 'message'. For some reason works painted with a moral message always demoralize me. It was so with the early works before which our art master was almost prostrate. There was a gloomy picture called *Hope*. It showed a loose-gowned woman, bowed in despair, sitting on top of a dark globe, plucking a harp whose strings were broken. We were told that this symbolized the great virtue of hope. There was also a very large woman with a rent in her dress, in which a number of amorphous naked infants crawled over one another; this, I learned, symbolized the spirit of Christianity. Yet another enormous canvas depicted a gluttonous giant with bulging eyes which symbolized Mammon. They all alike seemed to be conceived in a swirling mist of dark paint. I was intrepid enough to say that I thought the pictures morbid and fatuous. I was banished from the gallery by my indignant master and held up to the class as a little monster of depraved taste. Some twenty years later, I met at Philip Gibbs' house in Surrey a rather depressed young man, just out of the army after the First World War, who had obtained the post of curator at the Watts Gallery. The widow of the artist had added to her Surrey home a gallery for the public exposition of her husband's work. To this the young curator invited me and my host. He seemed to crave companionship. With great misgiving I went, and all my fears were confirmed. I understood his depression. Yards and yards of canvases, covered with thick dark pigments, portrayed some aspect of moral significance. An odd portrait here and there had merit, but mostly it was a nightmare of uninspired works.

Fashions in art are as transitory as those of dress. Who can endure the architectural confections of Alma Tadema, the draped effigies that Leighton grouped in simulation of the glory that was Greece? Yet these artists were powers in their day, anticipating their immortality. George Frederick Watts loomed large in life as in paint. He survived a disastrous marriage with young Ellen Terry. He made a large fortune. The Order of Merit was bestowed upon him. He twice declined a baronetcy. Living to a venerable old age, he looked like an Old Testament prophet. An art critic spoke of "his magnificent pictorial moralities, emblems of profound and subtle import". By an ironic twist, his fame chiefly rests today on a piece of statuary, his *Physical Energy* marking the Cecil Rhodes Memorial at Rondebosch, Cape Town, of which statue there is a fine duplicate in Kensington Gardens.[1]

One other artist, a contemporary of Watts, also captured the Greek patron, a man once in much fashion, Burne-Jones. The walls were gloomy with signed engravings of his paintings of woeful young women, thick-ankled, bare-footed, goitre-throated, dull-eyed, and loosely gowned, who trooped up and down winding staircases holding lilies or musical instruments of archaic design. Just what they symbolized it was difficult to conceive. There was one particular painting, possibly sensuous in intent but flaccid as a dead fish, that showed a melancholy nymph rising out of a weedy lake and having her head patted by an equally melancholy young faun. This sexless idyll, far removed from the customary erotic rapture of *L'après-midi d'un faune*, had a great vogue. Nearly all these sad-eyed damsels had the pomegranate mouths favoured by Rossetti and the P. R. B. School.

The general depression induced by these Victorian *chefs-d'œuvre* was so great that after a week I banished them all to a cubby-hole. They were hung in enormous gilt frames, so heavy that they required double chains from the cornice rail. But there was one painting, a Watts, that I could not banish. It was eight feet by five and hung in the hall. This was a painting of the Greek patron's wife. It showed a bosomy young matron in Greek national costume, with her three children, a small girl, a little boy dressed as an *evzone*

---

[1] Two of Watts's heavy allegories hang in the nave of St Paul's Cathedral. Like much of the memorial statuary there, they would have difficulty in gaining admittance today. Watts has for companion Holman Hunt's allegory *The Light of the World*, another dismal and gaudy work. One wonders why they were ever considered to be appropriate or to merit this honour.

in gold jacket and white fustanella, and, gurgling on the mother's lap, a very small, naked, coral-pink infant.

In the course of time we were called upon by a Franciscan monk, collecting alms. Bearded and rotund, he was agreeable and childlike. He came from the Franciscan church near us, before which stood a fountain with an exquisite bronze effigy of St Francis holding out his hand to the birds sculptured on the basin's rim. The Franciscans lived in a retreat built on to the church, with a roof-garden full of bright pots of flowers and a vine that they had trained over a pergola. It was not until the picture in my hall had been removed that the Franciscan expressed his relief. The luscious nakedness of the sprawling infant had so embarrassed him, he said, that he had found calling upon us, for all our kindness, a severe trial. Now he could visit us with unclouded pleasure. "*Troppo nudo! troppo nudo! terribile!*" he murmured. Had we put a nimbus on this infant and called it *Madonna and Child*, he would have thought it beautiful and holy.

When ultimately I purchased the apartment, together with the furniture but not the pictures, the Watts in the hall presented a formidable transport problem, and, transported, what modern house could find it wall space? Finally, I suggested, since the four figures were closely grouped, that it should be cut down. I volunteered to perform the task. The owner agreed. It took two men to lower the massive frame. Flat on the hall floor, I cut into the giant canvas with a bread-knife, separating the family from yards of black landscape. The shade of Watts must have wilted, but when I had placed the fragment on a small stretcher, the owner was delighted, for his ancestors seemed much enhanced by reduction of the picture. Moreover, they were now transportable.

The morning after my arrival, rising from the rattling bed, pulling back the wobbly curtains, and running the gauntlet of dark Greeks, melancholy maidens, surly fauns and the 'Unholy Family', I walked through the French window of the salon to discover a breakfast-table sparkling in the sun on the terrace, and a wide world of blue sky and sea, mountains and palms, spread before me. I forgot the chimeras of the

night, the rattling brass knobs, the portraits, the cracked
lamp, the shabby chairs and the feather bed in which I had
been immersed. I looked at the terrace, the view, enchanted.
There were two derelict plant tubs, a faded, torn awning, a
box of half-dead geraniums, and long shutters from which
the paint had peeled. But nothing could disguise the fact
that here was a bit of paradise under a radiant dome. It
made me believe that when God finished building the
heavenly mansions, He had a piece of blue glass left over
which He gave to Italy for a sky.

CHAPTER FIVE

THE ENGLISH ARRIVE

I

YEARS of neglect and misuse at the hands of temporary
tenants so depressed me that I set about renovating the
apartment. This was no hardship but a pleasure, as I have
ever been eager for an excuse to neglect the writing-desk.
The first thing that I invested in was a set of tools, a step-
ladder, brushes and paints. Although I had not then decided to buy, and had the apartment on a yearly lease, with
an option, the owner seemed delighted to have a tenant who
took an interest in it. Moreover, he placed at my disposal a
sum of money to make repairs and improvements, the sum
to be offset against the purchase price if I decided to buy. I
tackled the brass bedsteads first and spent a considerable
time deknobbing them with a metal hacksaw. It was not until
after many hours of labour on the terrace that I had an
inspiration. The bedsteads were of a Victorian solidity that
would have carried an elephant. On the top of their iron-
lathed frames were substantial box-spring mattresses. One
day in the cubby-hole I came across a pile of wooden
pedestal knobs, detached from some article of furniture. It
was a gift from Providence. I discarded the iron bedsteads,
attached the wooden pedestals to the box mattresses, and had
modern movable divans in the place of the brassy horrors.

The windows required urgent treatment. All the putty
had left the frames, and the glass was in danger of hurtling
down into the street. There were eleven double windows. It
took three weeks to putty and paint them. The wooden-
latticed shutters were a more formidable problem, twenty-
two in all, four of them ten feet high. Sun-blistered through
at least a dozen years, they required burning-off and painting—a two months' job. By this time I had ceased to be
an object of curiosity and had become a firm friend in an

85

ironmongery shop down the Via Corso Dante Alighieri. I knew no technical names of the things I required, but the quick Italian mind comprehended my pantomime. In this way I enriched my vocabulary and had much delight in the process. A screw was a *vite* (vītee), and a screw-driver, I found in Italian, does not drive a screw but chases it, and is a *cacciavite—caccia* being 'to chase or hunt', whether it be screws or foxes. But there came a day when we were quite defeated. I had started war on woodworms in an inlaid table and wanted a woodworm-killer. The dictionaries failed me. They gave me the Italian for wood-nymph, *ninfa dei boschi*; for woodpecker, *picchio*; for woodbine, *caprifoglio*; but never woodworm. I tried putting the two words together *legno*, wood, *verme*, worm, with no result. Wormwood is *assenzio*, but one cannot reverse it. *Zio Assen* means Uncle Assen. I could not demonstrate a woodworm, it makes no noise, its motions are unseen. By this time all the shop was interested in the slightly mad Englishman who haunted the place for the strangest things. Three assistants, two counter-boys and four customers—a carpenter, a painter, a metal worker and a plasterer—all joined in the hunt for the required word for the article. The quest produced a piece of rubber tubing, a nickel towel-rail, a brace-and-bit (induced by the screwing motion), and a tin of D.D.T. for garden pests, the nearest I got to the worm category. Defeated, deafened, exhausted with counter gesticulations, I departed and returned with a piece of wood that had worm-holes in it. There was a shout of triumph. *"Ecco! Tarli!"* they cried, twiddling their fingers, *tarli*—woodworms! I then said I wanted a bottle of woodworm-killer.

Now, for two months I had been unable to ask for anything that this incredible shop did not have, but at last I had defeated them. They had never heard of a woodworm-killer. Woodworms, they assured me, were unkillable. "Yes, there is one way, *signore*," said a little old man in blue overalls, buying a chimney-cowl. "You soak the wood in the sea for a week." I protested that I could not soak an inlaid table in the sea. They were all very sorrowful. There was nothing to kill woodworms in Italy. So I wrote to a friend coming from England to bring with him a bottle of woodworm-killer.

The wooden shutters produced another difficulty at the ironmonger's. I wanted a blowgun, another elusive word. Finally I mounted ladders and examined a hundred pigeon-holes that went up to the ceiling. I found my object, a *cannello*. There were ludicrous moments also. Muddling my vowels, I asked for a litre of *tramontana* (north wind) instead of *trementina*—turpentine. My advent in the shop always produced a joyous greeting and a general suspension of work while assistants and customers, all joining in the vivid gesticulation, succeeded in supplying my wants. And what strange things he wanted, this *signore molto elegante*. Finally one of the partners stopped my housekeeper in the street and asked the real nature of my profession. Could it possibly be true that the Signore was a famous English writer? If so, why did he buy putty, chisels, paint-brushes, etc.? "He enjoys himself that way," she explained. Although I am a steady customer in that indispensable shop, I am regarded as an *eccentrico*—nothing rare among the English in Alassio.

Lattice shutters, painted green or brown, are a feature of the windows of an Italian villa. These *persiane* are as essential as they are beautiful. In the heat of the Italian summer they are closed all day to keep the rooms cool, and are folded back in the evening. Alas, the utilitarian roller shutter, requiring less maintenance, is now being installed. Its name *saracinesca* is as lovely as *persiana*, but the object itself is ugly, making private villas look like shops and banks.

For two years I tinkered happily. Carpenters, electricians and plumbers accepted me as a 'mate', and thus I learned something of their trades, language and lives. At the end, when I had installed electric points, an electric boiler and cooking-stove, when keys turned in locks, doors no longer squeaked or windows rattled, I turned my attention to the furniture. I designed bookshelves for the end of the salon. From the shelves of a rickety whatnot that was not what it had been, I made a two-leaved, folding, gate-legged table. One Christmas in Rome I bought twenty yards of gold damask and webbing, and reconditioned and re-upholstered four chairs. With a green silk damask, I re-covered two delicate gilt salon chairs. I was thrilled, when I stripped them down, to find stamped on their canvases the name of a Paris furniture maker, and the date 1822. I played with the idea that Madame Récamier might have sat on them, for surely she sat as well as reclined? My publisher was reproachful at being kept waiting so long for a new book. I had surely lost much income with this desertion of my desk, but I had been happy. Much of my labour had been performed on the terrace in the sunshine, paint pots and brushes and saws all around. At last I approached the end of my labours.

There remained the terrace. I demolished the rotten plant-boxes. I designed and had new traverses made for the pergola. I cleaned the four Ionic stone columns supporting it, and repainted the lattice work on each end wall. The long roller awning was renewed. But the terrace was bare. I searched the town for terra-cotta jars and stone troughs, which I found after much journeying. One day, passing a foundry where hammers were plying and sparks flying, I discovered an artist in metalwork who was making some beautiful chairs. He told me he was supplying hotels in Capri. I gave him the measurements for three chairs and a glass-topped table. He delivered them a month later. It was characteristic of the Italian's innate love for anything beautiful that when he brought them he seemed to forget all about his handiwork and stood entranced with the view from my terrace. "*Che bello!*" he exclaimed.

Lastly there was a matter of plants. A bougainvillæa and a jasmin were bought for each end wall, a rose tree for the central trellis. All three plants dashed my hopes, and rapidly turned into withered sticks. Again and again we were on the point of discarding them. A year later they had a marvellous resurrection with the coming of spring. The jasmin put on new leaves and burst into a mass of yellow flowers, the bougainvillæa covered the other end wall with purple glory, and the rose tree, long a stick, not to be outshone by its companions, budded and put forth eight vermilion roses.

But the crowning feature, the consummation of my youthful dream, was missing. I waited until I had signed the deed that made me the owner of this Italian home. For a decision had been made. I was at an age when a man retires from his life's work. I had written thirty books, having published my first at twenty. It was time to compose myself, to travel as I wished, and to rebuff the possessive *daemon* that had so long driven me whenever I sought to desert my desk. Here under a lovely sky, in a land inexhaustibly rich with treasures of art and architecture, I had come to port, after a voyage of rich experiences. Active in mind and body, and still animated by an unquenchable curiosity to see and learn, I would hope for that last decade promised to us by the Psalmist. The atom bomb, the everlasting wrangles at Geneva, Washington, Paris, London, Berlin and Moscow, the daily horrors served up by the Press? I came to observe them distantly. "Man that is born of woman is of few days and full of trouble", for "our days are swifter than a weaver's shuttle". I would enjoy the full flavour of each remaining hour and be grateful. So I bought my part of Palazzo Vairo and prepared the crowning act of my new life.

Among the many amenities of Alassio there is an English Tennis Club, beautifully situated and housed, again a monument of Hanbury munificence in the days of the dominating English colony. It has a large terraced garden, including a long line of cypress trees of all sizes and ages. When I began to quest around for a cypress tree, the wife of the club secretary supplied my want. I had much to learn about cypresses, for if they were to decorate my terrace there was the question of their height and the proportionate depth of root, since I could only accommodate them in small vases.

The cypress has several species, the horizontal, and the perpendicular with appressed branches like a Lombardy poplar. It is a native of the Mediterranean countries. Everywhere in Greece and Italy its dark green spears, almost black in the mass, make a dramatic note in the landscape. Since classical times they have been associated with death, and were planted around tombs and temples. Its twigs were put into the coffins of Greeks and Romans. Turkish cemeteries are particularly fond of the cypress. But it is something much more than a symbol of mourning. If the oak is the national tree of England, the cypress is the national symbol of Italy. No artist can refrain from placing one in his Italian landscape. As its Latin name *sempervirens* denotes, the ancients regarded it as indestructible, since its high resinous content enables it to resist the action of water. Insects will not attack it. Its oil was used by the ancients for embalming. Mummy cases were made from its wood. Being of a beautiful colour and easily polished, it was long esteemed for fine woodwork. Cupid's arrows, according to tradition, were made of cypress wood. It has been identified as the gopher-wood of Noah's Ark. They made the first doors of St Peter's at Rome, opened in the presence of the Emperor Constantine, of cypress wood. These lasted eleven hundred years, and were quite sound when removed to give place to brazen ones; brazen in both senses of the word, for the new doors are engraved with pagan myths including a vivid portrayal of the rape of Leda by the swan.

I was surprised to learn, when selecting two young cypresses, that there are male and female species. The former is compact, the latter grows bushily. It seemed proper to select both varieties, they might feel less lonely on my terrace. The roots grow to one-eighth of the total height, which can ultimately be around a hundred feet.[1] Since my vases were eighteen inches high, I could not hope for the cypresses to attain much in excess of ten feet without dying. I would have to return them to the nursery at that height and select younger trees. When I imported my two young cypresses their height was four feet. In one year the lady grew six inches, the gentleman eight.

It was on an April evening when I carried them down the hill. In the half light a full moon was rising. As I walked homewards with my two green spears the bells in the campanile of Sant' Ambrogio broke into uproar. It seemed as if they were ringing for me, in joyous celebration of this day, delayed almost fifty years, when the wish of a small boy in

[1] The tallest cypress tree in Europe grows in the Hanbury Garden at La Mortola. It measures 160 ft.

the English Midlands had been at last fulfilled. Lord Henry and Lady Olivia were long dead, their Florentine villa with its terrace and cypresses had been bombed. Across all those years what a pilgrimage I had made!

II

After I had settled in, I began to look around at my neighbours. My apartment is reached by a lift. When it was temperamental, in the manner of continental lifts, I walked up a marble staircase. The Palazzo Vairo is situated on a small avenue of palms that goes from the main highway down to the sea. This is called the Viale Gibb, pronounced by the Italians Jibb. Who was this Englishman who, with Sir Thomas Hanbury, was immortalized in Alassio by having a street named after him? He was a wealthy Scot from Dunfermline who came here with his wife in 1875. In her late widowed years she kept a salon, ruled over the English colony like a queen, and quashed any gossip with a withering, "What you tell me may be true, but we never *say* these things in Alassio."

The Gibbs were accompanied by their friends General Sir Montagu McMurdo, his wife, the daughter of Field-Marshal Lord Napier, of Magdala fame, and family. The general was fifty-six when he arrived in Alassio with a brilliant army career behind him. He was with Napier in the Sind campaign, and at the battle of Meeanee in 1843 he killed three men in hand-to-hand fighting, a feat he repeated three months later in the battle of Hyderabad, where he was severely wounded. He saved the baggage of the column from capture, and was three times mentioned in despatches. Napier called him "An ornament to Scotland". In 1849 Napier returned to India as Commander-in-Chief and took McMurdo with him as A.D.C. These were the high days of Poona and Simla, soon to be immortalized by Kipling. His active service was by no means finished. The Crimean War found him organizing the chaotic transport service. When Sir Charles Trevelyan, Secretary of the Treasury, wrote to McMurdo telling him that he must limit his expenditure,

the gallant and fierce warrior shattered Whitehall by reply-
ing, "When Sir Charles Trevelyan limits the war, I will limit
the expenditure."

Such was General Sir Montagu McMurdo who descended
upon Alassio. It was then only a little fishing village set
among orchards, a stage on the drive along the famous
Corniche Road from Nice to Mentone, Bordighera, San
Remo and Genoa. Unlike these places, grown into popular
winter resorts, Alassio retained its primitive simplicity. The
Gibbs and McMurdos spent their first winter in an old
house on the beach, appropriately called the Pension des
Anglais. They fell in love with the place and decided to stay.
They bought land. On McMurdo's property stood an old
olive mill with a small house adjoining. He enlarged it and
called it the Molino di Sopra (The Mill Above), as it is still
called today. Gibb found on his land an old hermitage called
Fuor del Vento (Out of the Wind), whose name betrayed
Alassio's failing. Here on the side of a small hillside chapel,
now a ruin, he converted the hermit's retreat into a luxurious
villa. The railway had recently come. There was no broad
highway, traffic-thronged, cutting its way through Alassio.
All was tranquil, embowered in palms, orange and olive
trees, the only thoroughfare being the ancient Corriera, 'The
Drain'.

These two pioneers were the forerunners of the British
colony that created Alassio. It grew into a permanent settlement of over five hundred English living in their villas, and
swelled in winter to two thousand when, with dances,
theatricals, card parties, lectures and musical evenings, the
town took on a carnival air. Mr and Mrs Gibb have long
been buried in the hillside cemetery at Alassio, for Dunfermline knew them no more. They little knew what they
had started. When Signor Vairo erected the first skyscraper
in Alassio, forty years after Gibb's death, to which he gave
his own name, he built it on the Viale Gibb. Three years
after Gibb's advent, the English Mæcenas, Sir Thomas
Hanbury, arrived. He saw the possibilities of the little town
with the glorious sandy bay. The boom had begun. The few
Italians who had known Alassio only as a summer resort were

overwhelmed by an avalanche of English, many of whom had lived in India. Maids and gardeners were ten-a-penny. Ladies of small means lived in little pensions for four shillings a day, and, becoming possessive, were heard to complain that there were too many Italians in the summer season. The majority of the English colony migrated to England from May until November. A heavy sleep fell on the place, sustained by good golden sovereigns garnered through the winter season. Soon there was a demand for an English church, an English library, an English club. A chaplain was imported. All types lived in the utmost congeniality. It was characteristic that when an Anglican church became necessary the site was provided by a Quaker, and much of the building money by a Presbyterian.

Alassio had some early notabilities, Richard West, R.A., who painted many local scenes, and Margaret Roberts, authoress of *Mademoiselle Mori*, a novel famous in its day. Then two moneyed families joined the community, a Rathbone of Liverpool and a Lamport, shipowners. The former was a blessing to honeymoon couples. He lent his villa to them over a hundred times. Italian society was represented by the Marchese Ferrero Ventimiglia, one of the old families of the Riviera, domiciled in their large palazzo in the centre of the town. It still houses the same line, its old grounds now traversed by two new roads and a railway. The Marquise Montalembert, born a Choiseul,[1] built a French château, giving it an Italian name, the Villa Romana, again truncated by the railway. Retired admirals, generals, ex-governors, judges, Indian civil servants, clustered in sufficient force to administer a small kingdom.

Alassio's sudden expansion was due to the breaking of its isolation in 1864 by the coming of the railway. Since Roman days it had been accessible only by horse-drawn vehicles. All along the Riviera there were posting-stations, and many of the little towns were walled and gated. The Palazzo Valro had risen on ground by the northern wall of the town, and a

[1] She was the daughter of the Duc de Praslins (1804–1847) who, falling in love with his children's governess, had the Duchess murdered. A sensational trial was stopped by the French Government for political reasons. The story is brilliantly told in *All This And Heaven Too*, by Rachel Field.

few yards from my door stood the ancient Porta di San Vincenzo, with its Madonna over the arch, a city gate flanked by a blacksmith's forge and an inn. By the city wall ran the Rio Cardellino, the Goldfinch River. It still runs by my door, but underground along the Viale Gibb to the sea. The bastion, wall and gate disappeared in 1890, but the road, the ancient 'Drain', remains, and the Madonna has been built into a niche in the first house on the left. Alassio, as so many other places, did not realize then the tourist value of ancient walls and gates. It ruthlessly swept them away.

Losses are balanced by gains. We should all quail before the appalling hardships of travel along this coast in the eighteenth and nineteenth centuries. Smollett wrote from Nice on January 1st, 1765:

"Rome is betwixt four and five hundred miles distant from Nice, and one half of this way I was resolved to travel by water. Indeed, there is no way of going from hence to Genoa, unless you take a mule and clamber along the mountains at the rate of two miles an hour, and at the risk of breaking your neck every minute. The Apennine mountains, which are no other than a continuation of the Maritime Alps, form an almost continual precipice from Villefranche to Lerici, which is almost forty-five miles on the other side of Genoa, and as they are generally washed by the sea, there is no beach or shore, consequently the road is carried along the face of rocks, except at certain small intervals, which are occupied by towns and villages. But as there is a road for mules and foot passengers, it might certainly be enlarged and improved so as to render it practicable by chaises and other wheeled carriages. . . . What a pity it is they cannot restore the celebrated Via Aurelia which extended from Rome by the way of Genoa. The truth is, the nobility of Genoa, who are all merchants, from a low, selfish, and absurd policy, take all methods to keep their subjects of the Riviera in poverty and dependence. With this view, they carefully avoid all steps towards rendering that country accessible by land; and at the same time discourage their trade by sea, lest it should interfere with the commerce of their capital, in which they are personally concerned."

The same conditions prevailed thirty-one years later when Napoleon marched his army along this difficult route, and were little better even a hundred years later. The carriages shook their occupants to pieces. If not badly shaken, the travellers were unnerved by the frightful precipices and deep chasms perilously bridged. From 1827 to 1834 tunnelling began under Capo Mele and Santa Croce; these two barriers were pierced, but it took another thirty years before the railway-line was opened. It cut its way through the grounds of beautiful villas at the back of Alassio. Elsewhere, as at San Remo, it separated the town from the beach. There was no doubt a contemporary Alassian who said it was the end of everything, just as Ruskin declared it was the end of Venice when the steamboats ran down the Grand Canal. They were both right. Something has been lost for ever, but unforeseen prosperity lay ahead. Ten years after the opening of the railway, a train brought in General McMurdo and Mr Gibb. The trail had been blazed. Through the soot and sulphurous fumes of suffocating tunnels the English poured in. When Smollett journeyed this way, he went by a boat, which he called a gondola, from Nice to San Remo, and then passed Alassio by sea, for the roads were execrable. He landed for the night at San Remo.

"We were conducted to the Poste, which our gondoliers assured us was the best auberge in the whole Riviera of Genoa. We ascended by a dark, narrow, steep stairway, into a kind of public room, with a long table and benches, so dirty and miserable that it would have disgraced the worst hedge almhouse in England. Not a soul appeared to receive us. This is a ceremony one must not expect to meet in France, far less in Italy. At length the landlord arrived and gave us to understand that he could accommodate us with chambers. In that where I lay there was just room for two beds, without curtains or bedstead, an old rotten table covered with dried figs and a couple of crazy chairs.

95

The walls had been whitewashed, but were now hung with cobwebs and speckled with dirt of all sorts; and I believe the brick floor had not been swept for half a century. We supped in an outward room suitable in all respects to the chamber, and fared villainously. The provision was very ill-dressed, and served up in the most slovenly manner. You must not expect cleanliness or conveniency of any kind in this country. For this accommodation I paid as much as if I had been elegantly entertained in the best auberge of France or Italy."

He fared even worse at his next coastal village, Noli.

"The auberge was such as made us regret even the inn we had left at San Remo. After a very odd kind of supper, which I cannot pretend to describe, we returned to our repose: but I had not been in bed for five minutes when I felt something crawling on different parts of my body, and taking a light to examine, perceived above a dozen large bugs. You must know that I have the same kind of antipathy for these vermin that some persons have to a cat or breast of veal. I started up immediately, and wrapping myself in a greatcoat, sick as I was, laid down in the outer room upon a chest, where I continued till morning."

We complain today of the roaring traffic, the hideous road advertisements, the concrete apartment houses, but Smollett, coming ashore to find these clean pensions and hotels, with their spotless linen, gay flowered tables and excellent cuisine, would deem himself in paradise. I am the first to rail against the hideous chasms of concrete that shut out the views on either hand, so that neither mountains, sea, nor orchards are visible, and I hate the stark utilitarian breeding-boxes of modern housing schemes, but I confess myself appalled, on close inspection, by the 'picturesque' houses of fishermen and peasants, mostly insanitary hovels devoid of light or convenience. If only the passion for destruction and construction were devoted to reconstruction!

The Palazzo Vairo was well planned, with three lifts and

Capo Mele with the road to France, and the noble bay of Alassio.

(*Photo: Omniafoto—Torino.*)

The night scene from the terrace.
(Photo: Rotalfoto—Milano.)

three marble staircases serving some thirty apartments. The ground floor was occupied by shops and a bank. Our own staircase had ten apartments, five north and south of a central staircase. Each apartment was reached by a small open bridge that looked down on the inner court. These bridges were gay with pots of geraniums, azaleas, cinerarias, lobelias, daisies, and cyclamen. Each bridge had a high wrought-iron gate, like a portcullis guarding the entrance door. I was amused by the names on my neighbours' doors. On the first floor lived an English doctor who, like my predecessor, had bought his apartment as soon as the palazzo was built. He recalled my own country by something else besides his name. He owned a sturdy foxhound. When its tail wagged at my approach I was back in Leicestershire with the Quorn in full cry. On the second floor was Signor Topo (Mouse). On the third floor Signor Quadri (Pictures) confronted Signor Lupi (Wolves). On the fourth was Signor Vacca (Cow). On the top floor, my opposite, was Signor Calandri (Meadowlarks).

We were all watched over by a fatherly concierge called Giovanni. He had a small office opposite our lift in which he sorted the mail and received messages. It was he who shut the great doors at night and prevented errand-boys from playing games in the hall. He was seldom in his office. His real one was out of doors. Fortuitously the authorities had placed a large bench under the palm trees exactly opposite the palazzo entrance. Here Giovanni passed much of his time, smoking his pipe and conferring with the retired elders of the town. Not a thing missed him, going in or coming out. He was a super-watchdog, but with a paternal benevolence rare in concierges. We won his heart very early by treating him as a venerable figure, which he was physically and mentally.

In time I learned some biographical details. His father was a cooper. At the age of seven, adventure in his blood, Giovanni got aboard as a stowaway in the boat on which his father worked. A child of seven was an embarrassment in a rough boat bound for the tunny fishing around Sardinia, so the vessel called at that island and found a temporary post for the stowaway. Giovanni was clad in a small white jacket and trousers, and found himself a page in the house of a Sardinian Marchesa. Thus began a friendship between mistress and boy that lasted for over twenty years, during which time Giovanni made periodical visits to the Marchesa in Sardinia. From seven until sixteen he worked in a cooper's shop, making the barrels that stored the tunny fish. At seventeen he shipped as a hand on a boat sailing for Buenos Aires. He made over twenty crossings of the South Pacific and spent two years on the Rio Paraguay and Rio Parana. He also sailed to the ports of the Mediterranean, and to Portugal. Then, in middle age, he became a postman in his home town, and when the Palazzo Vairo was built, its concierge. He is now a grandfather with two beautiful daughters and two grandchildren. He has achieved the ambition of all Italians. He possesses a little *podere* (farm), up in the hills behind Cervo, the near-by village that hangs on a precipice overlooking the sea.

Giovanni has never recovered from his astonishment at the size and diversity of my mail, a subject for discussion between the postman and ex-postman. There is no emergency to which he is not equal. He employs his leisure painting doors, making ladders and boats. On local history and personalities he is a mine of information, for the Natteros, his family, have been in Alassio for over five hundred years. One of them, Ippolito, was a famous soldier of fortune whom Philip of Spain made Captain-General of Gibraltar. Another has his name over the door of the parish church of Sant' Ambrogio, in association with two colleagues who assisted in the erection of its new western entrances in 1511.

III

From my terrace I have a bird's-eye view of the town and bay. It is a very different scene from that which greeted the eyes of those pioneers, McMurdo and Gibb. The palazzo, rising near the site of the old town wall, is situated on ground once covered with orchards. The piazza gardens are almost all that remains of that open space. Where the Town Hall now stands there was once the old grey convent of Santa Chiara. It then lay within the north-east angle of the city wall, with an orchard behind that opened on to the street now the Corso Dante Alighieri, and thence through an alley, still called S. Chiara, that led to the main street, 'The Drain', and the sea.

The history of the nunnery is a long and stormy one. Two ladies of Alassio, Chiara and Angela Martini, entered the Franciscan Order and in 1609 began to build the convent. They ran out of funds, so the town wardens took over the operations and finished it eleven years later. The town granted the nunnery an income of three hundred *scudi*, collected mostly from the prosperous coral fishers and merchants. Alassio was a flourishing community in 1609 and had produced three bishops, an historian, a Genoese ambassador to France, some distinguished lawyers, two navigators and half a dozen poets of renown. Alas, too much of its energy was consumed in a perpetual feud with Albenga, the ancient and powerful town four miles up the coast.

Within a hundred years the convent of Santa Chiara was in financial difficulties. That master looter, Napoleon Bonaparte, descended upon Liguria. He billeted soldiers in the convent. The British bombarded the coast, attacking his line of supplies. In 1810, incorporating Northern Italy into the French Empire, he suppressed the monasteries and convents. In 1819, Alassio having fallen into the domain of the King of Sardinia, the mayor and citizens petitioned him to restore the convent, but some Dominican monks had moved in, and it was not until 1828 that a Pontifical Brief put the nuns in possession again. In return for civic support, they undertook to educate the daughters of the citizens, but later the nuns went back on their contract, saying that teaching was none of their business. The town withdrew its grant. By 1860 the convent was in a bad way. The town took over the building, and after the earthquake of 1887 lodged derelict orphans in it. Six evicted nuns moved over to a palazzo across the railway, and there today the Order is cloistered. In 1889 the authorities pulled down the old convent, and built on its site the ochre-coloured Palazzo Municipale, which I observe from my windows. It is rimmed with lights on festive occasions, and is altogether a pleasing object in the piazza gardens.

Nothing remains in the piazza of the ancient town wall, built by captured Turkish pirates, nor of the gates, but Richard West, R.A., was here just in time to leave a pictorial record. He was here, too, with the small English community, when an earthquake, not the first, wrecked the town. This happened on Ash Wednesday, February 23rd, 1887. There were forebodings and premonitions. The atmosphere was sultry, the fishermen would not go out to sea fearing a tidal-wave. A fox from the hills suddenly took refuge among them. The horses and the cattle were restless throughout the previous night. But General Sir Montagu McMurdo, that sturdy Scot Mr Gibb, and others, thought it all Italian hysterics. They went off to a carnival ball thronged by the English community. It had scarcely ended and merged into the Lenten services when, in the early dawn, a heavy rumbling was heard, followed by something like an explosion. The chancel arch of Sant' Ambrogio opened an inch. Revellers in costume going home were joined by a panic-stricken public rushing from churches and houses. The shrieking population emptied itself into the streets. A second shock followed at 9 a.m., equally intense. Nevertheless, the English community met in church an hour later and held their customary Ash Wednesday service.

The loss of life was small, but the poorer community lost their homes. It must be recorded that one person spoilt the sangfroid of the English colony. An old lady, Miss Robinson, was living at the Hôtel di Roma with a paid companion. The hotel was badly damaged and Miss Robinson, being bedridden, was brought out in her bed and deposited in a neighbouring garden until accommodation could be found for her. She was deserted by her terrified companion, who fled to Rome. The old lady was not known to the English colony, and by a mishap was left in the open for two nights before help came. It was too late, and the poor woman died of shock and exposure. The companion never showed her face again in Alassio. Against this let us record that the aged

English chaplain, Mr Hayes, leading his fellow countrymen in rescue work, died of exhaustion. General Sir Montagu McMurdo had at once gone into action. He erected a large bakery and supplied the semi-starving population with bread.[1]

A prudent gentleman, about to build himself a villa in Alassio, thought he had better make sure of his ground. He consulted the Seismological Bureau at Rome. It informed him that from records covering two thousand years of Liguria major shocks had occurred at intervals of about four hundred years, with minor negligible ones every thirty-three to forty. Since four hundred years from 1887 carried him into 2287, the prudent gentleman felt safe in building his villa. When I look over the town I see that about half the roofs are tiled with grey slates and the other half with red pantiles, used for repairs after the earthquake. I like the gay note that these add to my vista and feel indebted to that catastrophe.

There is another legacy of that event. Enterprising Miss Lamport bought two of the wooden huts erected to house the earthquake's victims, and used them for the growing library of the colony. Ultimately this public-spirited woman built a spacious library with a lounge, and presented it to her countrymen.

IV

The night scene from my terrace is wholly delightful. The long Corso Dante Alighieri is in direct view stretching across the town. To the left I can just detect the red light on the end of the pier. Along the right side of the piazza runs the Viale Hanbury, parallel with the Corso. Both these long avenues are nightly lit by the town's lamps and are given a carnival air with coloured neon signs displayed on the fronts of restaurants and cafés, doing business beneath me. Also there are the lights mounting the foothills and, higher up, those of the scattered villages. There is a wall of light which

[1] I would not like to give the impression that General McMurdo was an early 'Blimp'. To gallantry he added wide interests. In the National Gallery, London, hangs his bequest, a portrait by Sir Henry Raeburn of his grandfather, Lieut.-Colonel Bryce McMurdo.

belongs to a large hostel built above the town by a rich in-
dustrialist for his work-people and their children. It sparkles
like a diamond brooch on the dark mountain-side. Then,
farther on, shine the moving lights of automobiles rounding
the road on the great promontory of Capo Mele as they
gradually descend into the town. Lastly, there are the lights
of the piazza garden immediately below me, clusters of
triple white globes pendent on standards that carry iron
baskets for flowers. And there are still other lights I must
particularize because they have become part of my life in
the Palazzo Vairo. On the corners of the piazza below me
there are café-restaurants. They involve one in endless
speculation on their means of existence. Every morning at
six they open. On the pavements before them are set out
their tables, with gay cloths, cutlery, napkins, flowers, and
always a symbolic bottle of wine. They are all ready for
business. Over these tables are drawn coloured sun-awnings,
green and white, or plain blue or purple. At night when the
lights go on they glow with a carnival air. In addition, there
are vivid sun umbrellas, and all around stand terra-cotta
urns of flowers, and painted tubs with dwarf orange trees,
oleanders and palms. For nine months of the year there are
practically no customers. The former large English colony
having vanished, Alassio has no visible means of support
through the winter.

Owing to its gaiety, we call the café nearest to us the Café
Bohème. We like to think that Mimi and Rodolfo go there,
as well as the Marios and Marias. We are always on our terrace, peering anxiously down on the tables so beautifully
set out, in the hope of seeing a customer. Very occasionally
we are rewarded. Then one of us rushes indoors and shouts
"They've a customer!" There is some selfishness in our con-
cern about these *al fresco* restaurants. We are afraid they will
go bankrupt and that we may lose these gay spots. That
might involve us in disaster, for if our left-hand restaurants
failed, a monstrous concrete five-storey apartment house
might go up, blocking most of our glorious view over the sea
to Capo Mele. We utter prayers for the prosperity of the
Café Bohème. We are told it is quite unnecessary. We are

assured that all these cafés and restaurants, there must be two hundred of them, do such a roaring business in July and August that they can live for the other ten months. Somewhat incredulous, one year I postponed my usual migration to England at the end of May to observe what really happened. I was warned that the crowds, the traffic, the pandemonium from café orchestras, open-air cinemas, night-club jazz bands, itinerant loud-speakers announcing events, motor-buses, motor-cycles, etc., would drive me insane. I was warned that I would never sleep, for Italians on holiday never go to bed until 4 a.m., that at 5 a.m. the pavements were all washed down, for not a speck of dust is allowed to lie on the streets, and that for eight weeks a town of fifteen thousand would swell to one hundred thousand. A neighbour told me that when she let her apartment with five beds, a family of twenty camped in it. Bathrooms went out of use to provide bedspace. Kitchens were subdivided with curtains to make bed alcoves for maids. I had seen Coney Island in the month of August, and Miami Beach in the month of January. I was told I had seen nothing.

The signs began in the first weeks of June. Alassio became a stage getting ready for a gala performance. All day long youths pushing barrows went streaming down to the beach. They were transporting collapsible bathing-huts, chairs, umbrellas. The huts began to go up along the front promenade, obscuring the view of the sea. Everybody began frenziedly splashing blue, green, red, yellow and white paint on lamp-posts, railings, chairs, benches, balustrades, café tables, bathing-huts, boats and canoes. *Rosella* appeared, the boat with an auxiliary motor that made excursions to the island of Gallinaria, her little mast aflutter with coloured bunting that paid tribute to all nations. The sign-writers, amateur and professional, were flamboyantly industrious. One sign on a stand before a café announced Snak-Bar, to which a wit added an '*e*'. There were giant flamingoes from whose beaks were suspended baskets of flowers. The cafés flowed over the pavements, filling them with tables and chairs. Pianos came out into the open air, and along with guitars and drums were assembled on platforms. Battalions of brown-legged boys rushed about on bicycles carrying parcels. In the Corso Dante the awnings grew gayer and gayer. I looked down on blue, mauve, crimson and green shades, lovelier by night. Under them gathered young waiters in white jackets and shirts, with bow-ties and black trousers. The shops began to fill their windows with an amazing wealth of goods. For months I had been almost the sole customer, now they produced fashionable goods, jewels, leatherware, and costumes that began to make the place appear like the Rue de Rivoli. When all the beach umbrellas were opened it looked from the hills above as if Alassio had been invaded by a coloured Parachute Division; when they closed at dusk they looked like beds of grape hyacinths. The sand was obliterated by bodies. My housekeeper went forth at seven to shop to avoid the crowd. The prices rose. We began to believe Alassio might live on these three months.

There was no exaggeration about the noise, but somehow in the infectious gaiety of the scene I became indifferent to sleep. Or was I becoming attuned to the noisiest nation, with the fastest speech, after Chinese, in the world? The café chantants bellowed, the jazz bands brayed, the guitarists strummed madly, the motor-cycles roared, and fifty thousand vivacious voices turned the town into a parrot-house. And fittingly there arrived one day an itinerant aviary. It was an automobile piled high with cages containing hundreds of parakeets, all a-twitter, bright blue, yellow, pink, mauve and green. The vendor sold these chattering birds, with cages, to delighted Italians who achieved one more noise for their pleasure.

There was one short space of quiet. At noon the beaches and streets emptied, the crowds departed to hotels and pensions for lunch. Then came the 'spaghetti-stagger', a sleep in close-shuttered rooms, the sun beating down on a silent town in which not a cat stirred. At four o'clock the shutters were thrown open, the siesta was over. One more garment was added to the only one retained, and then off they went to the beach again, and after the beach the cafés, until the sun rose on a new day.

On the last day of August the town emptied as fast as it

had filled up. The Italians vanished. It was now the turn of the foreigners. They arrived steadily, the pale English, quietly sad, or appearing so, the white Swiss, solid and imperturbable, the flaccid Germans, with their organized games, their complete list of accurate prices for everything, and their militant batteries of cameras. In October back came the resident English, with the air of park-keepers when the picnickers have gone. There was a homeward trek of bathing-huts, umbrellas and mattresses moving from the closing summer pensions. The beach was again visible, a cup of coffee fell from one hundred and twenty to eighty-five lire. Enrico, the old porter, greeted the returning 'residents' on the platform; Dante, the postman, was all smiles when they stopped him in the street for their mail; and there was no mob at Galleani's Bank when they went to cash their monthly cheques. Alassio was theirs again, sane and tranquil. They all hoped that everyone had made enough to keep like that for another nine months.

CHAPTER SIX

A LITTLE HISTORY

I

AFTER I had settled in at the Palazzo Vairo and might consider myself a resident of the town, I began to look into its history. From birth I have suffered from an unquenchable curiosity. I must go to the top of any height I see or look around the next corner. I once had a friend who contrived to stay in Zermatt for four months without ascending the Matterhorn. To me that was an intolerable thing. Every morning when I arose and opened the window in my hotel, there it was with its sinister, provoking peak. I am also a merciless inquisitor, and I have to exercise firm charity towards some people whose mental flabbiness, concerning things that surround them, seems deplorable. I am aware that it is a tiresome thing not to be able to live in a house without wondering how old it is, what scenes it has witnessed; nor to travel on a ship without knowing the yard it came out of, its tonnage, the size of its decks and its propeller. Nor am I satisfied with 'round about', 'nearly', 'I should think', 'at a guess', or 'probably'. I like firm facts. I find everyone worth talking to; the most opaque mind is often the unconscious repository of some jewel of information.

I was merciless with poor Giovanni. Going out or coming in, conscious of a mine of local history, I dug into him, trading on his infinite patience. The barber across the piazza, whose chairs were cunningly placed so that as you sat in them you saw reflected in the mirror the fairyland of palm trees, flower-beds, emerald grass and the highway traffic behind you, knew well the Austrian, now the Italian, south Tirol. My banker's son was a man whose nocturnal hobby was flare-fishing with the fleet from Laigueglia. Why were fish so silly as to be attracted by flares, why didn't they rush away from them? I learned that there was something in the construction of a fish's eye, like that of a moth's, that impelled them hysterically towards the light.

The ground upon which I live at Alassio had been Ingaunian, then briefly Carthaginian, Roman, Visigoth, Burgundian, Saracen, Lombard, Spanish, Genoese, French, Sardinian, and finally Italian after Garibaldi and Cavour had created a united Italy. The Italians are often condemned as turncoats. If they had not learned to turn their coats quickly, they would have had no coats left. The whole history of their city-states teaches us that. For over fifteen hundred years once, twice or thrice in a century, the invaders swept over Italy, from the Goths in A.D. 408 to the Allies in 1944. In the Piazza Municipale there is a marble plaque in memory of five Alassians, 'defenders of liberty fallen in the battle against the Nazi-Fascists'. The small street immediately across the way has been renamed the Via Giovanni Minzoni, 'martyr for liberty, August 23rd, 1923'. He was a Fascist priest! Similarly a plaque commemorates the Day of Liberation, April 25th, 1945. Liberation from whom? From the Germans invited in as allies when Fascist Italy declared war on her oldest friend, England.

Every nation has its political inconsistencies. We officially 'loved' the Russians in 1944, after they had massacred our Polish allies. An island race, we have hitherto been preserved by isolation from swift changes of face. Constancy has been a virtue born of our security. Alassio, like most Italian towns, had no security for a thousand years. She had to build a defensive wall and gate as late as the sixteenth century against the raids of her neighbour, Albenga, four miles away.

Wherever one goes here, whether from Genoa, along the Italian to the French Riviera, over the crests or down the valleys, again and again one stumbles upon the Roman road. It is often a mule-track or a highway nearly obliterated, many times lost for long stretches, and then appearing again, much like the roads the Romans built across their British colony. This road is, in fact, all one. It was the means by which the centurion guarding the Great Wall, or building a bridge at Newcastle, received his instructions and authority from Rome. It is naturally much obliterated by time and change. There is much confusion as to its exact site. An old Roman road existed up from Rome and through the Province of Liguria into Gaul long before the Via Aurelia, whose name still marks the principal route through Alassio.

The ancient Liguria, the name given to the province bordering the northern Mediterranean coast, was much larger and wider than the present strip of land. Fréjus on the French Riviera was almost a halfway-house, for Liguria extended from the Rhône in the west as far east as Piacenza and the Apennines. In Gaul it reached as far inland as Grenoble and the Isère, and in Italy it was bound by the upper half of the Po running through Piedmont.

In early times the Iberians and the Ligurians divided between them the north-western Mediterranean coast before the coming of the Celts, a domain running roughly from Barcelona to Pisa. A Carthaginian sailing those waters in the fourth century B.C. reported the Rhône to be the dividing line between the Iberians and the Ligurians. The Celts coming south down the Rhône valley had not yet reached the coast. When Herodotus lists the Iberians and Ligurians among the mercenaries collected by Terillus, Tyrant of Himera, in an effort to recover his throne, 480 B.C., there are no Celts in the lists. The Romans conquered Provence in 122 B.C., but long before they arrived the Phocæan Greeks had formed a flourishing colony at Massilia (Marseilles), on the site, it is alleged, of an earlier Phœnician settlement. The Greeks, according to Timæus, founded their colony in Liguria one hundred and twenty years before the battle of Salamis; that is, about 600 B.C. Aristotle held up their constitution as a model for the admiration of the world. Happily for the Massilians, the conquering Romans became their warm allies and increased their prosperity. This was so great that the Greek colony had its own Treasury at Delphi. During the Punic Wars they were the closest allies. When Rome was attacked and burned by the Gauls, Massilia made a collection for the Romans. Lord Mayors' Funds are not an innovation.

The sacking and burning of Rome after the defeat of the Romans at the battle of Allia in 390 B.C. began an eternal

feud between the Romans and the Gauls. There was always
the nightmare of another invasion from the north. The
Romans put aside money to meet these occasions, dispersed
only when Julius Cæsar gave it to the mob, confident that his
Gallic War had ended the menace from the barbarians. In
218 B.C. there was the greatest alarm in Rome. The second
Punic War had opened in Spain. Scipio was about to em-
bark for Spain when grave news came from the north.
Hannibal had frustrated Scipio's hope of challenging him in
Spain, had crossed the Pyrenees, reached the Rhône, and was
recruiting the Gauls. He had again by-passed Scipio, who
was at Massilia on his way to Spain. From the Massilians,
excellent spies by reason of their extensive trade, he learned
of Hannibal's arrival on the Rhône. Scipio had hoped to
block his way, but was too late. The wily Carthaginian had
won over the Gallic chieftains, who provided rafts for
crossing the river. The transport included thirty-seven elephants. While effecting this crossing Hannibal sent his
Numidian cavalry south to check Scipio. The Numidians
failed and were driven back. Undaunted, Hannibal faced
the formidable crossing of the Alps, guided by his allies the
Cisalpine Gauls, who had just made the crossing westwards. He was one hundred and twenty miles north of the
Rhône's mouth, near Orange. Soon he was in the gorge of
Donzère. Behind him lay the almost African plain that saw
the passing of this Carthaginian army with its dark Numidians in white burnooses, its turbaned Africans, its ponder-
ous elephants. The army had to cross the Alps before the
weather broke. In the fourth day's march Hannibal was at
the confluence of the Rhône and Isère. Three days after he
had left, Scipio arrived at the Rhône camp in pursuit. He
was too late to overtake the Carthaginians. He turned back
to the mouth of the Rhône, re-embarked his army, and sent
it to Spain for his brother's use, enabling him to cut off Hannibal from his Spanish base. Then by ship he sailed for Genoa
on the Ligurian coast. His hope now was to stand in the
Po valley and intercept Hannibal on his descent from the
Alps.

Where did Hannibal cross the Alps? He was thirty-one,

son of the great Hamilcar Barca, conqueror of Spain. He
commanded an army of 50,000 foot, 9,000 horse and
thirty-seven elephants. It is said that he crossed the Alps by
the Little St Bernard Pass. This is pure conjecture, for the
only contemporaneous historian of the march, Polybius, is
maddeningly vague, omitting all place-names, despite his
assertion that he had questioned all eye-witnesses and had
himself gone over the Alpine pass to check the facts. But by
which pass, he is obstinately silent. Livy, writing more than
two hundred years later, sends Hannibal doubling back to
cross the Durance. This route is rejected by Mommsen, who
carries Hannibal up the Rhône to Vienne. Other writers
have suggested the Pass of Mt Genèvre, but Pompey in a
letter to the Senate claimed to have opened up that route
later on his march to Spain. The claims of the Mt Cenis Pass
are strong. Livy's account best fits in with the Col de l'Argen-
tière, and Varro seems to support him.

Whichever the pass, Hannibal was delayed in getting over
it by necessary arbitration with the tribes whose support he
needed. He was a month too late when he started, the
weather had broken. Half his army perished in the attempt.
Of the 50,000 infantry and 20,000 cavalry only 12,000
Africans, 8,000 Spaniards and 6,000 cavalry reached the
Italian plain. He received no further supplies for two years
until after the famous battle of Cannæ. It would seem that he
gained his spectacular victories in those two years with
recruited Gauls and Ligurians. He lost 4,000 of the latter at
Cannæ. But a victory on the Trebia below Placentia
(Piacenza) made Hannibal the general favoured by fortune,
and 60,000 Gauls and Ligurians flocked to his standard.
Hannibal failed to take Placentia, and retreated back into
Liguria, where he passed the winter until the spring of
217 B.C.

Then followed ten years of battles fought by Hannibal,
now in central Italy. In the spring of 207 B.C. something
startling happened for the Romans. Hasdrubal, Hannibal's
brother, came out of Spain, crossing the Pyrenees and the
Alps. Arriving in the Po valley, he recruited 8,000 Ligurians.
He was on his way to assist his brother. There was con-

sternation in Rome. Luckily for the Romans, Hasdrubal
wasted time in a siege of Placentia. In the battle of the
River Metaurus he was defeated and slain. Mago, the
youngest brother, now appeared upon the scene, hoping to
relieve the pressure on Hannibal. He planned to create a
diversion in Liguria. With thirty warships and transports
carrying 12,000 infantry, 2,000 cavalry and some elephants,
he sailed from Minorca and made a swift descent upon Genoa,
which fell to him without a blow. He fired the town and
deposited his booty in Savona with his allies the alpine
Ligurians. He now made an alliance with the Ingauni, the
lowland Ligurians, and thereby opened a way to the Pass of
San Bernardo, north of Albenga, leading over the Apennines. He established himself at Albenga. The offshore island
of Gallinaria was also seized.

Mago was well placed. The fertile plain of Albenga, with
near-by Alassio, provided all the forage needed for his
troops coming in by sea from Carthage, for while his fleet
lay off Albenga a large expedition succeeded in evading the
Roman fleet as it came up the Mediterranean. Large numbers of Gauls and Ligurians now joined Mago. He held a
council of war, but Mago was disappointed in his allies. They
showed no eagerness to revolt against the Romans, having
had their fill of fighting against their own highland enemies.
Nevertheless, Mago marched on across the Apennines by the
San Bernardo Pass, twenty miles up the Albenga valley, and
appeared in the plain of the Po. There the Romans chal-
lenged his march with 16,000 Roman, 28,000 allied infantry
and 3,600 cavalry. The battle was fiercely waged, and for a
long time was indecisive. At the critical moment the desperate
Roman leader, Quinctilius, hurled the whole of his cavalry
on the steady ranks of the Carthaginians. The charge appeared to be successful until Mago brought up his elephants.
The Roman horses, terrified by these enormous animals, their
trumpetings, their smell, threw their riders and charged in
panic into the infantry behind. The Numidians followed and
slaughtered the disordered Romans. The day seemed lost
with the XIIth Legion now a skeleton but the Roman general
held the XIIIth Legion in reserve and now threw it in. Mago

brought up his own reserve of Gauls, but it proved useless. The Romans had feared the javelins of the Numidians more than the short swords of the Gauls, which they parried with spears. They faced the terrible elephants, discharging their pila into them until the wounded and enraged animals, out of control, trampled to death the ranks around. The XIIIth Legion drove the enemy before them, supported by a fresh cavalry charge thrown in by Quinctilius. Even so, the battle raged with even honours.

The day began to wane. The flight of the discouraged Gauls, and elephants trumpeting in their last agonies, had not checked the battle rage of Mago and the Carthaginian infantry around him. He might even then have gained the day with his brilliant tactics, but in a personal affray his thigh had been pierced. Faint from the loss of blood, he fell by his standard. At the sight of their fallen leader the ranks broke, and Ligurians, Gauls and Carthaginians took to flight. Darkness fell, Mago was carried by his faithful staff from the stricken field. It had been a fierce and bloody business, with 5,000 dead in the Carthaginian ranks, and 2,300 Romans, mostly soldiers of the XIIth Legion. But Quinctilius was victorious. There could be no hope now of Mago bringing up reinforcements to his brother down in Italy. The Romans were masters of Liguria and all the communications to the south.

The long and painful retreat of Mago and his generals was made in the night. They carried their sorely wounded leader up the valley of the Tanaro, back over the Col San Bernardo, 2,900 feet high, and made the tortuous and precipitous descent into the plain of Albenga, forty punishing miles.

One lovely spring day I went over this route in a car. Leaving Albenga we ran up the long valley, whose rich soil, covered with orchards and vines, has made the fortunes of the market gardeners of Albenga. We drove through a glory of apple and peach trees in white and pink blossom, by a river overshaded with slender willows and tall poplars in their spring colours. I do not think the scene has changed much since the days when Mago, after uniting the Ingauni

Laigueglia, the twin towers of the church.

(Photo: S. A. Fototipia—Berretta, Terni.)

The slender campanile of Solva on a ledge of the mountain.

(Photo: Rotalfoto—Milano.)

inhabiting the lowland of Albenga, and their enemies, the Epanteri on the heights above them, rested his men in the rich valley, until he was ready to take his allied army over the Col San Bernardo and challenge the Romans. Before we began to ascend the mountain road we passed the aerodrome in the valley from which enterprising Albenga flies its fruit and flowers to distant markets, so distant that one morning, in a greengrocer's in Henley-on-Thames, I had seen boxes of luscious peaches, tomatoes and pears stamped with the name Albenga.

The road to the pass began to climb precipitously, round perilous bends, high over the floor of the valley covered with olive trees. Old castles on solitary crags frowned down upon us. We ran through lovely mountain villages, under arches and over bridges spanning torrents that wore away rocky ravines. Past the medieval castle of Erli, rising from a small mountain plain, the road brought us to the barren Pass of San Bernardo. From it we surveyed the snow-capped Alps around us that walled off the Ligurian coast from the plain of Piedmont and the River Po. Here one could realize the stupendous task that confronted the Carthaginians in moving a vast army with all its impedimenta over what then could have been only mountain tracks, traversing unbridged ravines and torrents.

The Carthaginians succeeded in bringing back Mago to his ships at Albenga. Envoys from Carthage were awaiting him with grave news. The Romans were menacing Carthage and every soldier was needed at home. Grievously wounded and exhausted after his journey through the mountains, the imperative command from Carthage left him no choice but to sail for home. The Ingauni, finding themselves abandoned, began to enter into negotiations with the pursuing Romans. Hurriedly embarking his troops, Mago set sail, risking the interception of the Roman fleet. He was not fated to fall into the hands of the enemy, for he died of his wounds off Sardinia just before the capture of his vessels by the Roman admiral.

The blow was a heavy one for Hannibal, so near to complete success again and again, now waiting for the reinforcements that should make victory over Rome final. Four years had passed since he was acquainted with the death of Hasdrubal by his brother's head being thrown into his camp by the Romans. Now his younger brother Mago was also dead. Grave news coming from Carthage impelled him to abandon his strong position on the Lacinian promontory. He performed one act before quitting Roman soil. In the temple of Juno, standing on the utmost point, he hung a number of brazen tablets, inscribed in Greek and Punic, with the principal events of the long contest. It was these records that Polybius, the historian, saw, and by them modified the boastful claims of other Roman annalists. Then Hannibal, after sixteen years of struggle in Italy, sailed for Africa to suffer there the crushing defeat of Zamara, which finally erased the powerful rival republic of Carthage. The defeat was at the hands of Scipio Africanus, son of that Publius Cornelius Scipio who, sixteen years earlier, had failed to intercept Hannibal in the Rhône valley and prevent the famous crossing of the Alps.

The Romans now thought they had disposed of the Carthaginians and the Ligurians. Two years later they were dismayed to learn that the rebellious Ligurians and Gauls had risen under another Carthaginian named Hamilcar, one of the officers left behind by Mago. He threw his army on Placentia (Piacenza) in the Po valley, carried the city by storm, fired it and took 2,000 inhabitants captive. Rome's great stronghold in the north, which Hannibal and Hasdrubal had failed to take, was reduced to ashes. Hamilcar next arrived at the gates of Cremona and laid siege to it. Sieges were a slow form of warfare disliked by his Ligurian and Gallic allies. A Roman army advanced to the relief of the city. Hamilcar was killed, his allies melted away. The Cisalpine Province was once more recovered. For ten years some Gauls, the Boii, held out. Then they were finally crushed by Scipio Nasica. Most of them were exterminated with excessive cruelty. Scipio boasted that he had left only old men and boys alive. The Roman province of Gallia Cisalpina, which included Liguria, was finally under complete Roman rule.

II

That is sufficient history for a while. Let us go for a walk. I have just risen and breakfasted in the sunshine on my terrace, having watered the purple bougainvillæa, the rose tree with ten roses, the jasmin, the jars with pink and red geraniums, and the pots of vivid scarlet carnations and cinerarias. It is a morning of radiant June, the sky blue above, the calm sea azure below. Across the town, in the corner of the bay made by the long promontory of Capo Mele, Laigueglia is sparkling in the sun. The name of this old fishing village, Alassio's nearest neighbour, and almost absorbed by a long, new promenade built out towards it, is a tongue-twister for English tourists. But the three cheerful porters in print jackets and peak caps, who preside over all arrivals and departures at Alassio's flowery station, know where the visitors want to go to when they ask for Legooglia, which is, phonetically speaking, Leh-gwel-yah in Italian.

At breakfast I had been watching three gardeners down in the piazza planting a hundred hydrangeas around the boles of two palm trees. There is much to be said for a sunken garden, especially if sunk a hundred feet below, as this is. One gets a new sense of values. There are ten flourishing magnolia trees beneath me, and from my terrace above I have a rewarding view of their glowing white cups lifted to the sun, as also of the pink and white oleanders just coming into flower. At the corner of the Viale Gibb and the Via Aurelia (Viale Hanbury), hidden by the green luxuriance of palm-tree branches, the motor-bus from San Remo to Florence has just arrived. It leaves as another motor-bus comes from Genoa, bound for Cannes. They are almost soundless, unlike the monstrous motor-cycles which blast the morning air. Leaning over my terrace a little more, on the rising ground across the railway I can see the pink, red-roofed, blue-balconied villa that was my first abode in Alassio. The new Bishop of Gibraltar has just visited Alassio. He did not sleep in the bishop's room at the villa, but high up near Solva in the villa built by our transalpine-automobilist, the *Reverendo*.

On the pavement below, the café tables have long been

out, with their coloured cloths, bottles of chianti, flower vases, and cutlery for the tourists, who surely will be coming now after a nine-months' wait. Every day Alassio puts on more and more of a gala attire, so today I wear a suit of tropical blue worsted that a tailor in Algeciras made for me in one day from cloth bought in Gibraltar. As I descend, Giovanni is washing down the marble steps, one hundred and twenty of them. On emerging into the palm-shaded Viale Gibb I see on the right the English Club. By its steps crouches a symbolic British stone lion. He reminds me that it is exactly one year since I hung a wreath of roses around his neck and put a small Union Jack on a stick between his paws. The British colony was celebrating the coronation of its lovely young Queen with a cocktail party at the Tennis Club, and I felt that he should not be left out of the festivities.

But I am turning left this morning, down to the sea, already gay with striped sun umbrellas and some thousand painted bathing cabins now assembled in line like a regiment, for the opening of the summer bathing-manœuvres. The sand is firm and very clean, for a hundred cabin attendants have for days been digging and throwing it on screens to rid it of the winter's accumulation of stones. I have just reached the beach when there is a tremendous uproar in the morning air from the siren of a merchant ship unusually close to the shore. No, she has not run aground. She is on her way back to Genoa from a transatlantic trip. Her skipper is an Alassian, and this is the signal to his devoted wife that he is in home waters. She immediately packs her small bag, catches the next train to Genoa, and is there to greet him when the ship docks. His ship will take more time, of course, than the great Italian liners, the *Andrea Doria* or the *Vulcania*, making the reverse trip, *en route* from Genoa to New York, calling at Cannes, Naples, Palermo and Gibraltar for passengers. We can time these liners like express trains. They sail from Genoa at 11 a.m., and they are gliding across the bay at Alassio exactly at one o'clock, as we sit at lunch on the terrace. We watch them through glasses, gleaming white until, soft as a magic-lantern slide, they glide out of view behind Capo Mele.

We are now proceeding along the beach, not to inspect the umbrellas and bathing cabins, but to leave a note at an hotel almost under the brow of the Santa Croce promontory that blocks our view of Albenga and closes in the bay of Alassio. The mauve-grey snail, Gallinaria, is still motionless on the blue sea offshore. I pass a new apartment house that in a passion for *modernismo* has slanted balconies with magenta window-boxes. It looks as if the whole structure is falling backwards. I gaze up, mindful of one tenant who is coming to lunch. I call her the Renoir Marquise. Actually she is Polish, the widow of an Italian marchese. She speaks fluent Polish, French, German and Italian. She apologizes for her hesitant English, but I would not have it otherwise. The uncertain quality she gives to her words makes her English enchanting; she has the voice and manner of a bird trying its first notes, and a habit of raising her head in the air as if about to sing an unpremeditated phrase. She has all the allure of her countrywomen, that hesitant, insouciant air Napoleon found so captivating in Madame Walewska, under the veil of tragedy which is Poland's gift to her children. I call her the Renoir Marquise because her face, surmounted by one of the charming little hats and veils she affects, has the colour and vitality that illumine his canvases. I could expect to find her on a seat in the Luxembourg one spring morning, with the new leaves of the plane trees throwing patens of gold and green over her svelte figure. She is an omnivorous reader in three languages. Elsewhere, in another milieu and age, I feel that I might have been a visitor, in stock-tie, frock-coat and gloves, to her salon in the Rue de Varenne, and have found that the slim, brown-eyed young man with ash-blond hair and tapering fingers, whom she asked to play for us, was her fellow countryman, M. Frédéric Chopin.

We are proceeding along the beach to what was the fishing village of Coscia. It has been absorbed into Alassio, but it is very old and not yet rebuilt. I observe the houses fronting the beach, the endless variety of balconies, arches, alcoves, pergolas and alleys. I dive down these side-streets, by winding passages with outside stairways. One passage has an old vine that starts from a hole in the ground, ascends snakelike and leafless for two storeys, and then, crossing one of the brick arches, reaches an open dining terrace where, forming a pergola, it breaks into joyous spring leaf. By autumn this old veteran, climbing fifty feet out of darkness into sunshine, will hang rich clusters of grapes over the diners.

It is impossible to say where one house begins and another ends. They clamber over, round, under and through each other, Laocoöns of ancient masonry. Farther along, an old watch-tower on the shore has been sliced like a potato on the sea side to make a terrace for this stronghold converted into a villa. Once upon a time it was a defence against the Barbary corsairs. The beach here is particularly fine, wide and well-placed under the rising mountains, where the exquisite baroque campanile of Solva's church points a shining finger to the sky. The beach is suddenly vocal with young life. Out of an orphanage come thirty little girls all dressed alike, shepherded by four nuns who make a curious contrast on this coloured scene, with voluminous black dresses and dazzling white coifs. Their pretty little charges twitter like excited sparrows. We pass a villa with a picturesque octagonal gazebo in the shade of a giant stone pine, overlooking the promenade. And now we are at the Hôtel Beau Séjour, my destination, with its long pergola terrace facing the sea.

My message delivered, let us cross the garden to an adjoining villa, finely placed among the stone pines. It is an orgy of pointed windows, doors, towers and turrets. It is called the Villa Gothic. Strange that anyone should ever have wanted to build such a monstrosity, but with time it has taken on a pathetic aura. A proud owner once sat there, and peered out of its arched windows, possibly between plush curtains with tasselled borders. Let us not laugh at the place, mellowed now in its spiky dilapidation. One feels it is not long for this world of conquering concrete. It occupies a valuable building site with sea frontage. For the present it lingers, empty most of the year, an adjunct of the hotel that uses its drawing-room for a summer café-bar. Once this room was filled on a momentous occasion with excited Alassians come to present an address of welcome. For the Villa Gothic, amid its palms and pines, had its hour of glory, its four months of glory to be precise, from November 8th, 1880, to February 24th, 1881. Here dwelt for this period one of the fabulous figures of his age, Garibaldi, the liberator of Italy. It was a momentous year for the old hero. The marriage into which he had been trapped by an adventuress in 1859 was annulled. He had promptly married his peasant companion of many years, Francesca, originally nurse to his daughter's children. She had nursed him, now a helpless invalid, on Caprera, and her devotion to the old lion was at last rewarded. He was within eighteen months of his death, still one of the most famous and adored figures in Europe, the champion of Liberty and the Unity of Italy. His arrival at Alassio for the winter of 1880–1 was an event in the life of the town. Every house along the Ligurian Riviera where he stayed, if only for a night, commemorated the honour with a plaque thereon.

On his arrival at the Villa Gothic he received an address of welcome from the local notabilities, and then asked to be allowed his privacy. But all Alassio watched the venerable figure with the white beard, heavy cloak, scarf, and black felt hat jauntily set on his noble head when he went forth with his faithful Francesca to take the air on the sea front. He took one excursion slightly afield, as far as Laigueglia, to revive a memory of his boyhood. He had accompanied his father in his sailing ship when the treacherous *Libeccio* wind caught it off Capo Mele and dismasted it. Seeing the vessel in distress, four Laigueglian fishermen manned a boat. After a hard struggle in the wind-swept sea they succeeded in rescuing the Garibaldis and bringing them ashore. Now, on his visit to Laigueglia after so many years, he met and embraced the sole ancient survivor of that gallant quartette.

Let us make the return journey home, but first I have a mission at the other end of the town. We go by the narrow street running through old Coscia. It is a part of the ancient highway to Rome, a continuation of The Drain. Here we can see the narrowness of this ancient highway of Napoleon's time, only ten feet wide in places between old houses, with arched alleys off it offering blinding vistas of the sea. We come after a time into the small piazza where stands the Franciscan church, whence came that bearded monk in brown habit and sandals who was so scandalized by the dreadfully naked baby he had found in my hall. The church has a modern front of little merit. Modern also is the fountain facing its door, but altogether enchanting. Under a graceful pepper tree stands a bronze statue of St Francis, hands outstretched to five birds on the stone rim of a stepped fountain that makes soft music. The modelling of the great Franciscan is masterly and moving in its simplicity. The bronze birds are trustful of the saint that loved them. Around the fountain run the words of his exhortation—*Laudato Si Mi Signore Per Sor' Acqua La Quale E Multo Utile Et Humile Et Pretiosa Et Casta*—"I praise Thee, my Lord, for Sister Water who is very useful and humble and precious and chaste."

We are now near my palazzo. The flower-market where I wish to buy two pots of variegated geraniums is at the other end of the Corso Dante, which I can see from my terrace for half a mile, intersecting the town. Alassio these last few weeks has become such a festival place of bright paint and bouquets of flowers that I feel somewhat out of step. From the piazza gardens, on looking up, my terrace seemed devoid of decoration since our bougainvillæa and roses are set too far back. So I have bought two ornamental vases to put on the marble balustrade, and now I require plants for them. Then I shall feel I have made a proper contribution to the civic effort.

First, let us turn down the little Vico S. Chiara just past the Café Bohème, which I am glad to see has four customers. English, undoubtedly, from that tribal convention of grey flannel trousers, rolled-up sleeves of cricket shirts, and pipes. Their sunburnt wives wear large white holiday shoes. The husbands are silent, deep in English newspapers. I turn down the narrow Vico, where the ghosts of long-dead nuns from the vanished convent across the way still seem to pass under a low arch, and find myself in the cool, shadowy Drain with its tall houses and shops. It is gay with colour these days, with goods displayed on outside shelves and decorating doorways and windows—fancy summer and

beach shoes in blue, green, red and white, hats and baskets
of plaited straw, rubber floats and toys for children, yards
and yards of postcards, coloured and plain, skirt and dress
material and lovely silks from the Turin mills that tempt
feminine tourists. There is every known sausage pendulent
over the grocers' shops. *Man Spricht Deutsch* says a card, for
the Germans are back again—*Kennst Du das Land Wo die
Zitronen blühen?* Indeed, they do. They comprise again one
half of the total of sixty thousand visitors, the remainder
Swiss and English.

I call for my morning *Times* and *Telegraph*, flown in via
Milan. The newsagents' racks seem to cover all Europe and
the U.S.A. What do restaurants, bakers and newsagents do
with all their unsold food, cakes and papers, I wonder? And
who buys all these shoes, endlessly displayed, sufficient to have
shod Napoleon's army marching to Moscow? Here are my
three old friends, the railway porters. What are they doing?
They have a barrow but no baggage on it. Instead there is a
flat object, black and much too large, for the barrow creaks
under its heavy load which projects over each side and
almost blocks The Drain. They superintend their transport
with noisy amusement. I am given a clue by an upturned
three-legged stool on the top of the black object. It is a baby
grand piano! Have they gone into the furniture-moving
business? No, they turn up the avenue of palms by the
Palazzo Ferrero towards the station. Surely the owner will
not insist on taking it with him on the luggage-rack? Italians
have the habit of travelling with all their household goods.
By tomorrow I shall know the whole history of this piano-
moving. Alassio is of a size and disposition where life is highly
communal. Giovanni on his bench in the piazza will collect
all the details, or my housekeeper will return with them from
the 'Communist's'. The Communist is the name for the
owner of an excellent cake shop. The charge was made
against him by a rival baker, but the Italians, unlike the
Americans, do not get excited by such charges. Everyone
here has been everything for a trial trip, and may be again.

We are almost at the flower-market, and we must not miss
something in The Drain which few visitors observe. It is a

little church, with three demure doors wedged in between
the shops. It has a campanile with a pyramid dome like its
illustrious brother, Sant' Ambrogio. This quaint little
church was originally a chapel attached to the Ospedale della
Carità, a charitable body that assisted pilgrims. It was
founded in 1319, and it functioned until 1842, when the
large hostel became a bathing establishment. The chapel,
grown into a church, survives. It was a mark of the Christian
dispensation that man should not be indifferent to the
sufferings of his fellows. With the parable of the Good
Samaritan, Christ established a concept of charity unknown
to the pagan world. This church in The Drain was once a
Domus Dei, well-named God's House, one of the many
established in the twelfth century, generally in seaport
towns, for the reception of poor pilgrims going to famous
shrines or to Rome, the mother of their Faith. These hostels
also received travellers from overseas. The great scourge of
Europe in the Middle Ages was leprosy, brought from the
East by the Crusaders. It was to prevent the spreading of
this disease that pilgrims were given shelter and nursed in
sickness at the *Domus Dei*, situated just within the walls of the
town for convenient service. There was a large pillared hall,
divided into bays with beds, with an entrance porch at one
end and a small devotional chapel at the other. Its management was entrusted to a master under whom worked
brethren and sisters who performed the nursing, washing
and cooking.

The shape of the surviving church, the Chiesa della Carità,
is singular. Instead of being long and narrow with an altar
at one end, it is short and broad with three altars along
one wall corresponding with the three doors from the street.
Originally the entrance had been at the narrow south end,
with the altar at the north to which pilgrims had access from
the hostel, but later, about the beginning of the sixteenth
century, the chapel came into more general use. It received
the offerings of travellers to the patron saint who had pro-
tected them in their pilgrimages. Perhaps one door was cut
through from the street, then two others. On one there is an
inscription, still legible, carved on the black marble lintel,

with the date 1606. This date suggests a later opening of the third left door.

These three entrances are framed in black marble. Their lintels carry heads of saints. On that of the centre door there is a seated Madonna and Child, with attendant saints—St Catherine with her wheel, St John the Baptist, St Michael with scales and book, and St Christopher at the ford, with staff and child. The hostel building still exists. It carries over its entrance the word *Balnearia*, painted on the stucco façade, indicating that after the abolition of the hostel it became a public bath-house. It is now a *pension*, its rooms running through from The Drain to the beach.

Stepping inside the little church—it should be seen in the morning light—I was overwhelmed by the scent of flowers. The three altars on the opposite wall were covered with fresh Easter lilies, roses and carnations. Though heavy with baroque decoration, the altars are not garish in their many colours, their marble pillars and gilded encrustation. The centre altar has a baroque Virgin, with a garland of cherubs. The left altar is altogether charming. Here stands St Antony, with the infant Christ perched on an open Bible held in the saint's left hand. These are no painted plaster figures. St Antony wears a habit of real brown cloth, with a real rope girdle, and the infant Christ is dressed in a little white linen frock. The whole church, its pillars, its arches and ceiling, is hand-painted in *settecento* fashion. The total effect is charming, reflecting a pious affection for the little old church known to pilgrims through six centuries.

On emerging we are so far down The Drain that we might look at the little piazza by the sea, where the corner of the street is still part of the ancient town wall. The hotel on the beach near by is actually based on the solid foundation of the old bastion. The corbel of the wall is still visible, both on this foundation and on the corner house. I turn back into The Drain, and my eyes are caught by a riot of colour in the narrow strip of sky between the high houses. A roof terrace I have never noticed before presents one long façade of cascading pink geraniums, brilliant in sunlight above the shadowed street. It is while I am gazing up at this aerial garden, thereby inducing half a dozen passers-by to gaze up also, that I am accosted by Violetta, dark-haired and slender in a neat green costume. Four years in England have left her with the conviction that London, and not Alassio, is the true *paradiso*. Her life is one long aspiration to return, though all her family roots are deep in Ligurian soil. She is a creature of infinite utility. If your neckband is frayed, she can renew it. A length of damask is transformed by her into a cushion cover, a spare piece of silk becomes a lampshade. I am envious of a rose tree on a garden trellis. A cutting is on my desk the next morning. She tells me of a *salita* to Moglio, a village clinging with its baroque church halfway up the mountain, on the way to the Madonna della Guardia. She knows the names of the lustrous-eyed ten-year-old twins who come out of a little *vico* off The Drain, also that of the nun who, with skirts billowing, rides the Vespa motor-cycle, hurrying to give injections, free or otherwise, to the poor.

Just now I wanted her badly. She knew the names and the characteristics of the bewildering host of saints that surrounds one in art, architecture and literature in Italy. I had been unable to identify all the saints on the marble lintels over the doors of the Chiesa della Carità. So back down The Drain we went, and the problem was solved. Passing a door that was open, I darted in. At some time or another one finds all doors are open, so curiosity can be satisfied. Here, obviously, I had found a stately palazzo with a fine staircase and marble pillars supporting a vaulted ceiling. From The Drain, where I had passed it a hundred times, it looked nothing at all. Every little *vico*, with gardens hidden at the bottom on one side and brilliant vistas of a jade-green sea on the other, entices one from the main errand. I mentioned to Violetta the two hidden palaces in the 'Street of the Unknown Soldier', which led from The Drain to Sant' Ambrogio. One had a noble double door of green bronze with brass studs, behind which was a vaulted hall with a carved effigy of St George and the Dragon. This was not surprising, for St George is not only the patron saint of England but also of Genoa, and his bones rest on Ligurian soil in a little chapel at Portofino.

The other palazzo I had peered into in the same street was on the corner of the Corso Dante. It had a heavily studded door between two Ionic columns, with a marble balcony above. It was a *casa nobile* at one time, with its coat-of-arms in the arched entrance hall, and a fine staircase with polished marble pillars on two flights, but now it had a decayed look despite the motto over the doorway, "comfortable and hospitable"—a nice description for a home. It had been the palazzo of a distinguished old Alassian family, the Counts of Lengueglia. We hear of one of them, Count Marc Antonio, bringing up his serfs and leading them in the cause of the Genoese Republic to fight the Duke of Savoy, when Charles Emanuele II invaded the Republic's territory in 1672. For this gallantry the Count and three other Alassians were awarded golden collars with pendants by the grateful senate. The counts long held a seigniory in the Taggia valley under the Marquesses of Turin. This dated from 1162 when they were invested with it by the Emperor Frederick Barbarossa. They were also granted tithes in his diocese by the Bishop of Albenga, a grant sealed on April 13th, 1153, in a ceremony by which the Count received the kiss of peace and a golden ring.

"Is the family here still?" I asked Violetta, as we came to the palazzo.

"No. The line is extinct. I knew the last of them, Count Federico della Lengueglia. He was a charming old man, saintly and very quiet. He lived here alone. Then one day he stunned all Alassio by blowing out his brains, no one knows why."

It seemed a sad end for a family coming down from the twelfth century.

I parted from Violetta by the Palazzo Lengueglia, and turned down the Corso Dante to the flower-market. On the way I was greeted by Alberto on a bicycle. Around this season the boys of Alassio suffer a transformation. Alberto normally carried milk-bottles. Now he was arrayed in a spotless white uniform with a gold-lace cap. He had become an hotel page. With the advent of summer the local boys get into the shortest possible shorts and find a hundred tasks as cooks' assistants, attendants at beach cabins, painters, bill distributors and errand lads. Early in the morning from my terrace I see huge baskets of bread travelling in all directions by bicycle on the backs of urchins in flour-dusty shorts, vests and caps. The tourists in the pensions must have fresh rolls for breakfast. What happens to all the young girls I do not know, since almost a harem tradition keeps them indoors. Possibly they are cooking, peeling potatoes and mending linen.

Since we have been looking at the town wall let us cross the road and, on the farther side of Sant' Ambrogio, observe a large section intact. It is preserved, oddly enough, because about A.D. 1600 the confraternity of St Catherine built its oratory on the top of this wall, carrying its roof on to the parish church. The wall is a formidable affair. Behind part of it stands the campanile, which belongs to the church and not to the oratory. It is probably nearly eight hundred years old, and looks as if it might collapse at any moment with its pyramid and open arches, a hotch-potch of stone, bricks and crumbling plaster. It is a familiar object all over the valley, and is regarded with veneration. Out of it comes the tuneless jangling we should all miss, and out of it also comes the solemn sound of the 'passing' bell, for Alassio is not yet of a size that one can die unnoticed.

Let us now to the flower-market situated in the shady Via Torino. At one end we can see the Madonna in her new niche, to which she was transferred after the demolition of the South Gate, like the sister statue at the North Gate. At the other end of the street, high up above us, rises Monte Tirasso with the Madonna della Guardia chapel silhouetted on its crest, 1,920 feet above sea-level. The Via Torino is lined with stalls that make a vivid scene with their cherries, tomatoes, strawberries, oranges, asparagus and small branches of yellow lemons suspended with their leaves. Here is what I seek, stalls stacked with flowers and ringed around with flower-pots offering a bewildering choice. I was once tempted by the great white trumpets of the datura, but since, up at the Casa San Giorgio, Lady Rieu had told me that in India the natives' wives extracted from them a poison with

which they killed their sleeping husbands by administering
it through the ear, as in *Hamlet*, I was put off, though I have
no wife seeking my ear. Here are tuberoses, but again I am
not buying—remembering how in Palm Beach, Florida,
their overpowering scent invaded my bedroom at night with
a sickly sweetness. I content myself with two pots of variegated geraniums, a glorious mass of colour, and start homewards at last. In the Corso Dante the splendour of my pro-
gress causes an Italian lady to exclaim *Che bella*! I assure her
she can continue seeing them, for they will be displayed on
my balcony, visible half a mile down the Corso.

It is nearing the lunch hour and I am expecting the
Renoir Marchesa, but I am entranced as I pass the Palazzo
Ferrero by seeing through its high rails covered with masses
of yellow mermaid roses, a great bank of geraniums massed
around the trunk of a palm tree to the height of one yard.
The stately old palm looks as if it were dressed for a fancy-
dress ball, standing on a green carpet of emerald grass. And
there, bending, the natural position for all gardeners, is my
friend Adelio. He is of a vintage soon to be no more in our
midst. He was born in the service of his *padrone*, has passed
all his life in the palazzo, and has tended the garden for nigh
half a century. Within its prescribed area, for the town has
grown in on it, behind its high railings and ornamental gates,
it is a fairyland of trees, scented shrubs, blossoms and
exotic plants.

I have a few questions on gardening matters for Adelio, so
I open the catch in the great gate, of which I have the
secret, and go into his green paradise. I surmise, since
Italians lunch at noon, that the Marchese, in residence for
the summer, is indoors, so my intrusion will not be considered
a call. Adelio straightens himself, a garland of blood-red
roses in his hand. We at once go into conclave. Gardening in
Italy has linguistic difficulties for foreigners; our names of
plants are not theirs. The only possible base of understand-
ing is in Latin, and the most familiar plants can disguise
themselves under botanical nomenclature. There had been
an occasion when Adelio had a basket of strange berries that
he had collected to send to a friend of the family. They had

been plucked from a *Morus alba*, a great tree that dominates the garden. A *Morus alba*? We were hopelessly at sea. Adelio proceeded to steadily munch a leaf, but I was not enlightened. He made a concertina movement with his finger. I was still dumb. Then in a moment of inspiration he pointed to my silk shirt, *Per fare la seta*, he said—'for making silk'. Silkworms eating leaves! So *Morus alba* was the mulberry tree, and this was its fruit in his basket! I had gone round the mulberry bush and arrived at last.

It was not always so simple. In the cool hour of breakfast in the June morning, and sometimes in the evening, a delicious perfume is wafted up to my terrace from the piazza below. It is not the scent of the orange blossom or of the magnolias in flower, it is something more subtle. For a long time I could not find the exact source. And here was the scent again as I talked to Adelio. It led us to a stone pillar supporting the railing, covered with a white waterfall of blossom. Undoubtedly a current of air bore its perfume across the piazza to my terrace. What was it, I demanded. "*Pittosperum*, signore," declared Adelio, plucking me a piece. I was no wiser. I carried the question to Lady Rieu who, if she doesn't know always has a book that will inform you. "*Pittosperum*, yes. It's Parchment Bark, a shrub with white flowers and brown berries," she said.

I was a few minutes late and my guest, the Renoir Marquise, had arrived. She was surveying the terrace and the view. She could not forgive herself for not buying my apartment when she had the opportunity. She tilted her head, prettily adorned with a little toque of leaves, hydrangea-like, and exclaimed, "*Comme c'est beau! Je pleure, je pleure! Quelle bête que je suis!*"

The endless variety of balconies, arches, alcoves, pergolas and alleys.

The Bird Fountain of Saint Francis by the pepper tree.
(Photo: Brunner & Co.)

CHAPTER SEVEN

PIAZZA LIFE

I

AT the time that I moved into Palazzo Vairo there came a
new priest to the parish church of Sant' Ambrogio. Don
Ferrari was more than a new broom, he was a positive
vacuum-cleaner. Clouds of dust went up in the dingy old
church. The entrance doors were remodelled, the façade renewed, the interior reseated, the altar regilded, the glass
cleaned, the lighting revised. It soon became apparent that
a man of energy and zeal had descended upon the parish. He
let no *festa*, no saint's day go by unmarked. I noticed or
imagined a new vigour and piquancy in that campanological
jangling that goes for bell-ringing in Italy. Why is it, I often
asked myself, that in this land which has produced such
numbers of maestros and divas, to the delight of the whole
world, there is so much hideous noise that purports to be
music? What unlovely voices some of the Italians have, the
ear-piercing stridency of the crone, the croak of the men, the
throaty huskiness of the children. The chanting of the church
congregation lacks for me any kind of beauty—being a
metallic mutter punctuating the dreary monotone of the priest.

The campanile from dawn to sundown emits a harsh
agitated jangle, often like the rattling of a can. I can never
forget the lovely contrast when, leaving Alassio early one
morning, I found myself in the square at Bolzano in the
Tirol, and heard from its church belfry, and others on the
slopes of the hills, the exquisite peal of the vesper bells. I had
passed from cacophony to music. Yet how often, listening to
the clatter of Italian voices in the street and in church, do I
remind myself that one of these little black-eyed boys may,
miraculously, be transformed into a Caruso or a Gigli.[1]

[1] The Ligurians are aware of this jangle. Of a bad singer they say—*Canta
false come le campane Liguri*—to sing out of tune like the bells of Liguria.

Don Ferrari may not be able to change the singing or the bell-jangling, but he has a compelling touch in other things. Having cleaned up the parish church, his eye fell upon the ruinous edifice of the Madonna della Guardia. It is Alassio's most conspicuous sanctuary, silhouetted against the sky on the summit of Monte Tirasso, the great green wall that hangs like a backcloth to the town in the valley. The church is a kind of Noah's Ark, looking in shape and position as if it had settled there after the Flood. Beyond it, on the other side of the mountain, stretches the great fertile plain of Albenga with the village-dotted valleys of Arroscia and Lerone, and the great snow-capped ranges of the Ligurian Alps.

From dawn to dusk the Madonna della Guardia stands silhouetted against the blue sky, the constant companion of every Alassian. Founded at the end of the twelfth century, a sturdy legend assures us that its site was occupied by a Roman *castellum*, a military guard-house or posting-station on what may have been the early route of the Via Aurelia, or, if not of this actual road, of a track turning into the interior. The early church was built with a semicircular apse. It seems to have been enlarged and decorated in 1516. Solidly built on a narrow ridge, it has superb precipitous views. Alas, it had fallen into a semi-ruinous state, possibly because of its remoteness from human habitation.

Don Ferrari did not like this, far removed though it was, on the edge of his parish. But building restorations are costly, more costly if they have to be made on the summit of a mountain. Nothing deterred the *parroco*. It took seventy donkeys to haul materials up to the Madonna della Guardia. When he asked how much this would cost the answer was 'Nothing'. It was a present from the donkey owner. Don Ferrari was in luck in another way. It happened that his curate was a skilled interior decorator, an artist with his brush. He went to work on the walls, in that beautiful tradition of Italian fresco work seen in so many baroque churches. The restoration was finished at last. On a May day in 1954 the service inaugurating the restored church was held. The occasion was Ascension Day, and all night over the mountains and valleys came those who wished to be present at the dawn Mass held in the church once a year. It was a lovely spectacle to see the pilgrims' lights converging on this mountain shrine.

It happened that the church had an effigy of the Madonna, but she, too, was in bad repair. A new one was substituted. There were two gold crowns on the effigy, a large one for the Virgin, a small one for the Child. For a week before her journey up the mountain she was on view in all her glory in Alassio's parish church, surrounded by flowers, illuminated with votive candles, and the recipient of many prayers. Kneeling before her was the bearded figure of St Bernard, the patron saint of shepherds.

On the morning of the Virgin's journey up to La Guardia, all Alassio was early astir. The commotion began at dawn. I encountered the Anglo-Indian ex-judge in the street at eight o'clock, on a shopping expedition as usual, with basket and dog. He complained that the shops were shut. They were, indeed. For Alassio this was a *festa*. On these occasions the ordinary business of the day is brushed aside. The telegraph office closes, for what can be urgent when the Virgin or a saint has a celebration? No letters are delivered, no errand-boys arrive with provisions and vegetables. The shutters are down, the banks are closed. I marvel that they do not stop the trains on the main line. No one should want to go to London, Paris, Genoa, or Rome on such a day!

At 6 a.m. the pilgrims gathered in the parish church. After a brief service, four sturdy youths lifted the platform of the Madonna on to their shoulders and the procession began its march up the mountain. It was a God-given day. After the worst winter and spring known for twenty years, summer came with a burst of splendour. The sea was like a sheet of silk, the sky was unclouded blue. While the long procession climbed the mountain trail to the village of Vegliasco, the first stage, other pilgrims had congregated at the Madonna della Guardia for the Mass at dawn. At 8.30 a.m. they departed for Vegliasco to join the pilgrims escorting the Madonna.

I confess to making the journey more easily. From my door

a motor-bus left for the mountain village, enabling me to see
the procession proceeding along the crest of the mountain
towards the church. Another band of pilgrims had taken
over the task of carrying the Madonna, who was in transit
for over four hours. Her gold crown scintillated in the morning sun, and on approaching her chapel a great concourse
greeted her, lining the rocky platform of the church, gay
with fluttering green, white, and red flags. The world and
his wife, together with children and grandchildren, were
there. They had trekked in from all the surrounding villages,
some of them having started at four o'clock on the steep
mountain paths.

When the Madonna was carried to her place by the altar,
the church was packed. Outside a still larger crowd had
congregated and the hubbub was so great that a priest went
to the loud-speaker and begged them to make less noise as it
interfered with the service that had begun within. After
some persistence, I succeeded in getting into the church, to
be amazed by the beauty of the interior decoration of a
building that had been stark and ruinous. In that packed
assembly of Italians I realized how short in stature the race is,
for I towered head and shoulders over them, uncomfortably
self-conscious. Curiosity satisfied, I struggled out. The service and Mass would continue for an hour yet.

Outside on the shady north side a great crowd, vividly
dressed and in the highest of spirits, made a Breughel-like
picture. The background of this scene was magnificent. On
the south-east side one looked down a great amphitheatre of
hills, with Alassio diminutive on the curving shore of the
Mediterranean. On the opposite side there was a steeper
declivity. Beyond the deep valley partly occupied by Albenga's aerodrome, a hundred forested terraces with their
scattered villages and tall campanili rose towards the grey-
blue barrier of the Alps. Their summits, still snow-laden,
sparkled in the morning sun, a majestic and beautiful
spectacle.

I began my descent eastward along the ridge, but instead
of turning off towards Vegliasco, I followed an old peasant
and his wife. They told me they were returning to their

village in the Albenga plain. They had risen at 4 a.m. and had been present at a six o'clock Mass in the Madonna della Guardia. I decided to follow and make my way down to Albenga, returning home along the sea coast. For a time we kept to the mountain crest, treeless at this altitude, and were rewarded with a magnificent view of the crescent bay, and the great headland of Capo Mele under which Alassio nestled, microscopic in relation to the mountains enfolding it. Over a ridge, the coast towards Genoa lay mistily blue below me. Then we began to descend through pine woods that opened on to meadows ablaze with spring flowers. In half an hour I picked mauve and yellow cistus, mountain anemones, blue gentians, the gold and crimson ranunculus, white butterfly orchids (so well named Santo Spirito, for their white sepals are like angels' wings), dog-toothed violets, purple milkwort, and the heliotrope wild iris. The growing heat was marked by a rising chorus of cicadas singing in the branches of the aromatic pine trees. Presently I bade farewell to my peasant friends. They chose a precipitous descent into a ravine that led to their invisible village. They were both over sixty, and I marvelled at their toughness in attempting such a descent.

Half an hour farther on, in the deep leafy shade of chestnut trees, I heard a welcome sound. It was the delicious tinkle of water. I do not know through how many centuries it has made its music in that umbrageous nook. Part of a tree trunk had been fashioned to conduct it to a pool into which it fell. Evidently it was a spring known by wayfarers. I cupped my hands for the cold water and drank. It was then that I remembered when last I had drunk in this fashion—but at how immortal a source! For only a month earlier, at sacred Delphi in Greece, I had drunk of that pure Castalian spring, descended from the snows of Parnassus, haunt of the Muses; there at the fountain under a great precipice, chestnut-tree shaded, in the most awesome scene of classic Greece, I had slaked my thirst. No other fount could match the wonder of that moment. Yet, here, in a mountain cleft, under the leafy shade, the crystal cold spring might have been the haunt of nymph or naiad.

When at length I emerged from the wood I beheld the sea, and, far below, Albenga with its long delta running out into the azure bay. A little shrine of the Madonna, with its tribute of flowers, marked a faint diverging track. Adventurously, I ignored the path down to the Albenga plain, and turned in the opposite direction, towards Alassio. As I hoped, the track led through some olive terraces, past a peasant's hut, entered a pine forest, faintly emerged, and suddenly gave me an entrancing view of the island of Gallinaria swimming far below in the jade-green and topaz sea. I knew then the name of this track. My heart gave a leap in excitement, for I was on none other than the nigh two-thousand-year-old route, later the Via Aurelia, leading from Albenga to Alassio. The next four miles were sheer excitement; the blue Mediterranean far below, the faint coast road like a purple ribbon; the steep olive-grove terraces, Cyclopean furrows on the earth's brow; the sweet odour of sun-baked pinewoods; and, a crowning glory of this May-day paradise, the luminous gold petals of clumps of genista whose perfume filled the air. Presently Alassio's old gateway of defence stood silhouetted on Santa Croce high above the sea. In half an hour I was home at the close of a glorious pilgrimage.

There was another Madonna who made a journey that day. In the town there is a boys' municipal college of excellent reputation. It is one of the remarkable scholastic institutions founded by Dom Bosco, a priest, born in 1815, who created at Turin the Society of the Salesian Fathers. Its missions have spread all over the world, but it is as an educator of youth that his name is best known and perpetuated in over a hundred schools of high scholastic standing. He was proclaimed a Saint by Pius XI in 1935, forty-seven years after his death. In Alassio Dom Bosco bought the former monastery of St Mary of the Angels, founded by the Franciscans in 1458. Though changes have been made, its church and cloisters remain. Dom Bosco put the church, then in a ruinous state, into repair. The place now abounds with young life. There are classrooms, a large dormitory for boarders, two cloisters, a playing-field, and an old orchard, green with orange and lemon trees, a vine pergola, and a great cypress tree. There is a singular modern fresco at the end of the second cloister, painted in 1949. It depicts a young peasant lad walking a tightrope tied to two trees, while below he is observed with astonishment by twelve companions and a dog. This commemorates the legend of young Bosco who, at the age of twelve, gave tightrope performances for the boys of the village in order to raise funds for foreign missions.

This second cloister is ornamented with the painted flags of twenty-eight countries, representing the seats of Salesian Missions. The college has a red-brick campanile converted into an observatory. This tower is one of the features of Alassio, and shares the skyline with the campanile and dome of the adjacent parish church. On festive occasions it is gaily outlined with electric lights.

It is not likely that Dom Bosco's college would allow the Madonna della Guardia to take all the limelight in the celebrations of Ascension Day. It has a reputation for putting on a good show. So that same evening the college brought out their Madonna, and with a brass band and candles, preceded by a long procession including the priests, mayor, choir, nuns, and scholars, she circulated the town. The most striking feature was the Madonna's escort of pages. The Italians have a genius for this sort of pageantry, as the Palio at Siena witnesses. Twenty boys carrying shining metal wands preceded the Virgin's carriage. They were attired in white silk hose, embroidered doublets of satin, with capes of crimson, blue, and gold. Their silk bonnets were adorned with plumes. In the carriage itself sat four cherubs in white silk doublets, with large cream feathers crowning their caps. As if not to be outdone by this splendour of the male, there was a bevy of girls dressed as angels with gauze wings. They wore crowns of gold in which shone a star illuminated by an electric bulb! Down The Drain, to martial music drowning the chanting of the priests and pilgrims, they slowly paraded towards the piazza. In the narrow market streets the windows were decorated with candles, chinese lanterns, carpets, and banners.

II

The piazza below my terrace is a source of continuous entertainment and surprise. In the centre there is an ornamental fountain that crowns a flight of steps leading down an avenue ending in a vista of the blue sea. The fountain never founts, but continuously trickles into a shimmering basin. Last winter there was a crisis in the life of the town. All Europe was locked in a cold spell. Old folks in Paris, sparrows in London, lions in the Brussels Zoo, died of exposure. It has never been admitted that ice could exist at Alassio. A fall of snow, lasting not more than twenty-four hours, is a rare possibility, so rare that it has been photographed by the authorities and published on postcards with the comment "Look, you've never seen this. In 1908 there was snow on the streets!" As for ice, that would be a ruinous miracle for the town's reputation. Alas, in the long hard winter of 1953–4 there were two terrible days when Alassio's reputation was in jeopardy. The fountain was frozen. Not so the authorities in the Municipio who looked down in horror on this tell-tale fountain. They immediately appointed a watcher with a hammer who was instructed to break up any ice that formed a blemish on the town's reputation.

The gardens in the piazza are my continuous delight. There is one corner that has a special fascination for me, since it has suffered a singular transformation. In the shade of a giant palm, and discreetly embedded in bushy pink oleanders, stood a 'public convenience'. The entrance to it was something of a maze to those unfamiliar with its contours. From our terrace above we had an aerial view of this conundrum, but sometimes our guests, puzzled by patrons coming and going in and out of the oleander bushes, would ask, "What are they looking for?" Then, one autumn, returning from our holiday, we had a shock. The oleanders and the shrouded lavatory had gone. There was a blank space. Not altogether blank, for there had been planted on the former site, in proximity to a palm tree, three inhospitable giant cacti as a warning that the place had gone out of business.

Ingenuity is never absent from the piazza. On the opposite corner below us, bordering the highway, the company that runs the autobus services along the Italian Riviera has been permitted to convert a corner of the garden into a ticket office and waiting-room. One wonders why a private enterprise was allowed to take over part of the public gardens. But what might have been an eyesore has been avoided by architectural ingenuity. Two splendid palms were menaced by the new building, but they were spared. Holes were made for them in the flat roof of the new bus station, and now the great green fronds seem to be rising out of two enormous flower-pots.

The main entrance to the Municipio is on the garden side and looks over an open gravelled space. There is no predicting what may be enacted there. One morning a cavalcade of automobiles drew up. For half an hour youths and maidens, with banners of a strange device, entered the building. Then we detected the chief of police and the mayor, with other local notables, waiting on the steps, flanked by the two carabinieri allotted to Alassio. Alas, although these wear trousers striped with red, white gloves and bandoliers, they no longer sport the dark swallow-tails ornamented with brass grenades, and the Napoleonic hat with red-and-white cockades. They are now more businesslike but less ornamental in service tunics and peaked caps.

Obviously something was afoot in the bright December morning. A large limousine leading the cavalcade, preceded by two policemen on motor-cycles, drew up to the Municipio steps. Then there was a brief splash of colour, crimson and purple as the carabinieri saluted, and a Cardinal, accompanied by the Bishop of Albenga and a bevy of fluttering black clericals, stepped forth.

The Cardinal offered his ring to be kissed, there were low bows to him and the Bishop, and then the Prince of the Church vanished into the building. We had seen one more note of vivid colour in the town's life.

When our second annual carnival came along in February, the four sides of the piazza formed the processional route. Formerly the procession had gone down the Via Aurelia, turned east just below us, and proceeded to a piazza facing the sea, site of a demolished church. This piazza is a kind of dumping ground. Here briefly rest itinerant caravans with roundabouts, flying-boats, shooting alleys, and sometimes a tent theatre. At election times it becomes a public rostrum. Here one evening a female Communist speaker held forth for two hours without once pausing for breath, a Niagara of vituperation. Her impassioned oratory faintly echoed on my terrace. The continuous vocal bombardment while I laboured at my desk sent me down to the street to look at this remarkable young woman. Such a feat of unbroken ejaculation did not seem possible. "She's on fire, signore," said my concierge, borrowing a term from his sea-going days. I could conceive of no broadside that would sink that vessel of oratory.

The first carnival I witnessed from my terrace ended, as customary, in the burning of King Carnival. He went up in a sheet of flame, and for several days his sad skeleton of blackened wire bore witness to the nemesis of a gay life. The second carnival ended in no holocaust. It was a sad carnival. Stands for spectators were erected round the public piazza. The highway was cleared. All traffic through Alassio was blocked. For four hours no one could proceed on the road to Rome no matter how urgent his mission. King Carnival ruled. Alas, he could not rule the weather of this atrocious winter. *Carnevale al Sole*, 'Carnival in the Sun', proclaimed the hoardings. Bunting hung from post to post, flags fluttered, the giant floats were vivid with their great grotesques of enormous white swans, pirouetting ballerinas, walking clocks, a Sultan's harem, luminous fishes, whirling dervishes, and prancing Red Indians, these and the floral carriages revolved five times round the piazza.

The day before there had been a preliminary procession of tiny tots in fancy costume, entrants in the competition for the *più simpatici bambini*, 'the most attractive children'. But the elements defeated the spirit of the carnival. The icy winds tore at the decorations, a deluge of rain drenched the spectators and performers. *Carnevale al Sole* mocked the posters. King Carnival richly deserved to be burnt if only to warm the crowd, but this year he was spared for some reason. We were fortunate to be able to witness this dismal carnival from behind our rain-lashed windows. Two mornings later in the station piazza small boys joyously demolished the papier-mâché elephants, tigers, giants, swans, and fish. There is something sadistic in this lusty destruction each year of the cleverly modelled figures of the carnival.

The rain could not damp the enthusiasm of the crowd for one feature of the procession. This was the band that played vivaciously and marched with military precision. Its members were dressed in blue sailors' trousers and jerseys, with berets with red-and-white pompons. It was a curious band with violins painted white, trombones, conch-shells, rattles, and what appeared to be tridents covered with nets, a Neptune's Band, putting all the others into the shade with its smart turn-out and marine air. Our guess was not far wrong. It transpired that it was a fishermen's band from the village of Finale along the coast. Some bright spirit there had organized the intermittently employed local fishermen, drilled them, rehearsed them, and dressed them. The result had won for them a widespread fame along the Riviera, where they took all the prizes and commanded a fee for carnival appearances that substantially supplemented their scanty earnings from the sea.

At the civic centre, the piazza thus provides a continuous change of scene. My terrace commands a splendid view of all the town's activities, and we have acquired what I call a 'balustrade bend', for we spend much of our time leaning over the marble parapet to note the diversions of Alassio. The Italians are extremely wasteful with electric current, since it is somewhat cheap. Many of the mountain villages never trouble to turn off the street lights. Here in Alassio, the cafés, often with no customers in them through the winter months, keep up a blaze of light long after midnight. From my bedroom window overlooking the piazza I discovered that its arclights are not turned off until dawn. The result is that in the silence of midnight the town is ablaze with lights, lights marking a starry path up to the foothills with their scattered villas, lights along the avenues threading

the town, lights along the promenade bordering the bay for
more than a mile, lights in the distant fishing village of
Laigueglia, lights of automobiles high up on the cliff road
rounding Capo Mele, coloured neon lights of the hotels, and
winking suspended lights at the traffic points below us—all
these illuminations in white, silver, green, yellow, and
crimson give a carnival air to the town by night. In the
winter months, despite this nocturnal illumination, all
Alassio goes to bed early and the place is silent. In the summer months Alassio never goes to bed, and the Italian passion for noise is fulfilled.

There was an occasion in the month of March when the
piazza provided an astonishing sight. In the dim light of the
wintry dawn I awoke imagining that, in a nightmare, I had
heard the roar of lions. In the semi-consciousness of waking
I tried to recapture the details of a nightmare that had lions
in it. The previous evening, as customary, had been a sober
one. I had retired early, read awhile, and fallen into an easy
slumber. It happened that in a few days I was embarking at
Venice on a cruise of the Greek islands. My tour included
once again a visit to the ruins of Mycenæ. I had been reading, before I had lapsed into sleep, an account of Agamem-
non's stronghold, approached through the famous lion gate,
four thousand years old. There was some kind of basis, therefore, for my lion nightmare. Then, as I lay tracing this
dream labyrinth, there came to my ears the unmistakable
sound of the roaring of lions. This was no nightmare in my
darkened room but an absolute reality from the outside
world. I got out of bed and opened my shuttered windows.
What I saw there in the breaking dawn told me that the
lions belonged to the living day and were not phantoms of a
dream. In the piazza below there were fourteen long coaches.
They looked exactly like the sleeping coaches of the Compagnie Internationale des Wagons-Lits that passed regularly
along the Marseilles–Rome line visible from my windows,
except that these long coaches were made of shining alu-
minium, with bright blue shuttered windows. Apart from
the roaring of the lions I was left in no doubt of their nature
by the inscription in large blue lettering on the curving roofs

—Zoo Manucci. The fourteen wagons were accompanied by six others which I later discovered were living-quarters, box-office with portable music, and hospital-dispensary for the animals. There were also four large tractors and a small tractor. The latter was now busily manœuvring the wagons into a circular position round a central kraal. The plan was ingenious. The wagons had concertina-like connecting-links, as on railway coaches. The spectators, entering at one end of the looped wagons, proceeded along the circuit of exhibits. Four of the wagons had no corridors. Their fronts opened on to the inner kraal into which the spectators passed. In these wagons were the larger animals, lions, leopards, tigers, bears, baboons, etc. There was no elephant. He was not transportable.

The nimble little tractor was now busily shunting the great camions into position. It was a very difficult and long manœuvre. I have never discovered why the zoo took up its position in the restricted space of the piazza, with its Municipal building, its palm trees and flower-beds, when, a few yards distant, there was the open piazza by the sea, used by the travelling amusement shows. But there is no accounting for the vagaries of the official mind.

It took a considerable time for these long vans to be pulled into the required circle. Their entrance faced the highway, where a neon sign was erected above a box-office. I was left in no wonder as to the contents of these shining vans. The roaring of the lions was audible information. It was break-fast-time and hunger as well as the shunting made them restive—also on the vans were painted the names of their contents. *Reparto Rettili* ('Reptile House'), *Reparto Sauril* (apparently containing Shetland Ponies), and *Villaggio Scimmie* ('Monkey Village'), etc.

The cavalcade had arrived at dawn. By eleven o'clock it had occupied the piazza with military precision. An entrance arch, illuminated, a broadcast system with siren, a water supply, an electric-light circuit for night-time, were all achieved without confusion or noise. At two o'clock the zoo opened for business.

Curiosity impelled me to make it a visit, a little against my will. I have a dislike of all caged things. But curiosity is a powerful force, and to it was added my reluctant admiration of the owner's enterprise in touring the countryside with this large team of animals, a zoo noteworthy for its shining neatness and mechanical ingenuity. However, a cold kept me in bed all the next day, and it poured in torrents. But if I did not then go to the zoo, the zoo came to me in a singular fashion. About three in the afternoon, while I was sunk deep in my post-lunch siesta, there was an urgent ringing at the door. It was answered by my housekeeper, also roused from her siesta. Then from the hall I heard sounds of deep Italian male voices, joined with the excited treble of my housekeeper. This was too much for me. I rose, put on a dressing-gown and went into the hall. I found there three dark young Adonises, all flashing eyes and teeth, rain-drenched, attendants from the zoo. It transpired that a small monkey had escaped. He had been seen sitting on the balustrade of my terrace! I was incredulous. I knew that monkeys could climb, but how was it possible for a monkey to climb the façade of a five-storied building?

"But, signore, it is true—he's on your terrazzo," declared one gypsy-like Adonis.

"Now?"

"Only a few minutes ago."

I led the way into the salon where a French window opens on to the terrace. I opened the window and peered out, for it was raining heavily. There on the edge of the marble parapet sat a monkey. The men rushed out, but he was too quick for them. With a great leap he was on the balcony of the adjoining apartment. There followed a hair-raising episode. My terrace is one hundred feet above the piazza. When on one occasion I put up a ladder to reach the pergola that I wished to repair, my housekeeper almost had hysterics, foretelling a terrible death from what she picturesquely called a *giro di testa*, a 'roundabout of the head' or attack of dizziness. I was obliged to desist, and when workmen were called in they made an elaborate platform, built out on ingenious scaffolding, and railed in protectively. But now, at the sight of the monkey, one of these young men did not hesitate to mount the wet, slippery parapet and, like his quarry, take an acrobatic leap on to the next balcony. The monkey again leapt and scaled a rain-spout up to the flat roof of the palazzo. Defeated, we all went back into the salon.

The roof above me has an area large enough to accommodate six tennis courts. From there we have magnificent views of the town, sea, and mountains. All it contains are countless chimney-pots of an entrancing variety—Norman, Ligurian, and Venetian—and the motor-house of the palazzo's lift. Since there are curious people who have a passion for hurling themselves from great heights, no one is allowed on the roof. The key is kept by our concierge, Giovanni. He was now brought into the chase. For the next twenty minutes there were thudding sounds of four pairs of feet scampering on the roof over our heads. Again the monkey was elusive. He leapt down to a balcony on the north side. It happened that a window was open. By this time he was a very wet and possibly frightened monkey. Liberty was not all that it had been cracked up to be in monkey village. He took refuge in a room, to the surprise of a maid. She approached the poor little fellow and in his terror he bit her. Wisely fastening the window and door, she brought news of the capture. The chase was at an end. The men returned, with profuse apologies for the disturbance. Rough lads, they had the manners of Venetian ambassadors. We replied that it had been a great entertainment. Then I went back to bed.

There remained the mystery of how the monkey had got on to my skyey terrace. Giovanni supplied the explanation. The young monkey, escaping during the cleaning of the communal cage, had run across the avenue of palms separating us from the piazza into the entrance porch of our palazzo. Here, disturbed by someone entering, he had leapt on to the roof of the lift, to find himself transported to the fourth floor by an incoming tenant! As soon as the lift stopped he scampered up the remaining flight of stairs, and then, with agile climbing, went by the outside staircase to the great open roof. From there he had leapt down on to my open terrace, where he was seen by his hunters below.

The next day, fine, and the last of the zoo's three days' sojourn, I visited the zoo and asked after the escapee's health. I was shown him in a corner of the animated monkey village, happily munching a piece of apple, surrounded by the faces of delighted small boys. He was none the worse for his adventure.

The zoo went as quickly and quietly as it had come. Not even a lion roared in the dead of night when it began to move out. The long wagons were skilfully manœuvred between the palms and flower-beds out into the Via Aurelia, and headed in the direction of Albenga, from which they began their climb in the mountains to their new destination, Pieve di Teco, a hamlet of the Ligurian Alps at 2,000 feet. The next morning when I opened my shutters there was not a sign of the zoo that had lodged in the piazza. It was cleanly swept, the flower-beds were intact.

The zoo story produced another which had filled the Italian newspapers a few months earlier. It had a tragic ending. One day, during a performance with a lion and tiger in a travelling zoo, the tiger attacked the trainer. He was immediately rescued by the lion, who had an affection for him and who beat off the assailant. But the tiger was a mean beast and had a long memory. Some weeks later while the travelling zoo was approaching Noli, a fishing village on the coast, some fifteen miles from Alassio, the drivers heard a tremendous uproar in one of the wagons. They stopped the cavalcade and approached the cage with the lion and tiger, whence the noise came. When they lowered the shutters they discovered that the van was swimming with blood and the lion was dead. He had been attacked by the tiger, which had taken its revenge.

On the March morning after the departure of the zoo, when I looked down on the piazza, I knew that spring had come although the air was still cold. It was not the new green fronds sprouting from the centre of the palms below me that told me, but a young couple walking through the gardens. Unknowing that from above them there was an observer, as they approached some oleander bushes the youth stopped and caught up the girl in an impassioned embrace, sustained for some time in the heady delirium of young love. I remembered with a pang that I had been young and in love, and out of Ægean-borne Lesbos, that I was to see in a few more days, came Sappho's choriambic timeless lament—

᾿Ηράμαν μέν ἐγώ σέθεν, ῎Ατθι, πάλαι πότα.
("*I loved thee once, Atthis, long ago.*")

And I had been not only a lover but also a lion, I reflected. For any zoo now evoked memories touched with a tender grief for one who had died young. Near my Pilgrim Cottage, in the Oxfordshire countryside, there had lived a merry freckle-faced lad of fifteen. I encountered him one day at our rose-embowered cottage post-office, a sprite in corduroy shorts, with springy coltish legs and wild hair. He reminded me of an unbroken foal, for he was prick-eared and his treble laugh was almost a whinny. He moved jauntily, intermittently shy and impish. I was then, on the very eve of the outbreak of World War II, haunting the Bath road in the last throes of writing *And So To Bath*. He became my eager companion on those car trips in quest of data, until the day of his return to boarding-school. I never saw him again. The war broke out and I was away in America. Then one day I had a letter that took the sun out of the sky. It was from his mother informing me that he had been killed in action in North Africa, a boy subaltern. It was hard to credit that my winsome companion had been caught up and butchered in an evil war. She added, "He had a deep affection for you—did you ever know that he always called you 'The Local Lion', because of 'fans' who called on you from all over the world?" The Local Lion. I can see now the ripple of slightly derisive amusement that would play over his impish, freckled face as he said it.

As he came to mind and the embracing lovers left the cover of the palms and oleanders, I had yet another reminder that spring was upon us. There was a swift flash of wings from the overhanging eaves above me, and I saw that the house-martins who were with us last summer had returned. They were building another mud nest up against the projecting cornice. It seemed odd to me that these birds should leave us to winter in the south. Evidently they had not the estimate that humans have of our Riviera winter climate. Mr and Mrs Smith come out from England and halt here to escape the winter. Mr and Mrs Martin, who summer here, have different ideas, and after autumn wing their way to somewhere in Africa, taking no chances. But here they were again, and I could apply to them the verses I had written to their English companions, lined up one October day on the telegraph wires outside my Chiltern cottage:

Winter approaches, the Martins are going South.
Strange! though they know quite well where they're going to stay,
They can't give me any addresses by word of mouth,
Nor leave them in writing, nor cable them on their way.

I didn't know where they had been but they had missed the severe winter in Europe this year, and now here they were, flashing and twittering as they prepared a new nest for a new family.

With spring, young love and birth came in the air, but there were reminders of our mortality. One afternoon as I was writing I heard a murmuring down in the Piazza. My curiosity aroused, I went out on to the terrace and looked down. On the east side I saw the beginnings of a long procession. No carnival this, but the last journey to that cypress-haunted cemetery on the opposite mountain. This last tribute was made on foot, a long trail of mourners, the Cross borne before, the chanting priest and choir, the veiled nuns, the women and men, separated, in pairs. The procession wound slowly down one side of the Piazza, then turned in towards The Drain, up which it passed before crossing the town to ascend the hill to the cemetery. It was a long solemn tribute of friends and neighbours, very moving in its almost stealthy simplicity.

CHAPTER EIGHT

THE VIA AURELIA

I

IT is impossible to travel, least of all to dwell for any time, on the French and Italian Rivieras without coming across traces of the Romans. They slowly pushed their way westwards along this sea coast for some three hundred years. To do this in any considerable force, and to found permanent settlements, they had to create a road for easy communication. They had also to subdue hostile tribes spread along the Rivieras and up in the Alps behind. By 191 B.C., with the extermination of the rebellious Boii, they hoped they had made themselves masters of Cisalpine Gaul and the province of Liguria situated in it. The Ligurians were a formidable race, powerful before Rome was founded. They had been in possession of their territory for upwards of three thousand years. They might claim to be of the purest blood and the oldest race in Western Europe. Few books have been written about them, the best, possibly, is Bullock Hall's *The Romans on the Riviera and the Rhône*, but they merit a study to themselves. Physically there were two classes, the product of their geographical situation, highlanders and lowlanders. The Ligurians bred in the Alps were called by the Romans the *capillati*, the long-haired; the lowlanders they called the *tonsi*, the short-haired. Both classes were tough and inured to hardship. The highlanders were the fiercer. They preyed upon the lowlanders, being driven by winter hunger like wolves to raid their neighbours on the coast. They stole the cattle and the farm produce. They were untameable brigands. They clung to their mountain strongholds and were the last to be subdued by the Romans. They stopped even Julius Cæsar in his tracks in the Alps behind Monaco and Nice.

The lowlanders, the *tonsi*, were more civilized. They lived in the rich alluvial valleys. They built ships, and fished and had a coastwise traffic. They were fierce warriors. Physically they were short, nervous and inexhaustible. They maintain these characteristics to this day. These Ligurians were of an entirely different character from their fellow Italians. They were in demand as mercenary soldiers, being tough campaigners. The Gauls, their neighbours, were no match for them. One Ligurian was considered the equal of any two Gauls in campaigning in Italy. The women were Amazons, bearers of lion-cubs, tillers of the soil.

The first mention of the Ligurians in history is in 600 B.C., when they ceded territory to the Phocæan Greeks who founded Massilia (Marseilles), emigrating from the coast of Asia Minor when Cyrus the Great overran the Greek coastal cities. They turn up in history again fighting as hired mercenaries at Himera in Sicily in 480 B.C., when Gelon the Tyrant of Syracuse won a resounding victory over the Carthaginian invaders. It is possible they went there as comrades-in-arms with a contingent of Greeks from Massilia, whose shipping interests were constantly menaced by the Carthaginians. Later the Ligurians resented the Greek colonies being established on their territory and besieged Massilia, which they would have wiped out but for the assistance of the Romans. Much as Massilia built up a prosperous port under the ægis of the Romans, so the Ligurians later built up Genoa, in temporary alliance with Rome. It was because of this affiliation that Mago fell upon the port, sacked and burnt it.

After the Boii were suppressed the Ligurians had other means of checking the Romans. They closed the coastal roads so vital for the holding of Spain. The Romans battled for eighty years before they succeeded in forcing a road through, some eight feet wide. It was a continuation of the Via Aurelia. To open this road and keep it open was the task to which Rome arduously applied herself. It was a long and costly work. As a territory Liguria had no assets for the colonizing Romans. It was mostly arid and mountainous. The Roman recruits disliked service in Liguria. Livy described the reasons:

"In Liguria there was everything to put soldiers on their mettle; positions to scale, in themselves difficult enough without having to oust a foe already in possession; hard marching through defiles lending themselves to constant surprise; an enemy dashing but light-footed, rendering every spot and nook insecure; wearisome and perilous blockadings of fortified strongholds, in a country barren of resources and yielding no plunder worth mentioning, with no camp-followers and no long line of beasts of burden; no hope but in cold steel and individual pluck."

In 181 B.C. the Ingauni Ligurians staged one more revolt. The Romans made a camp in the plain of Albenga. They were besieged there in such numbers, 40,000 to a garrison of 8,000, that at nightfall messengers were dispatched to the Roman general at Pisæ beseeching reinforcements. But the Legions there had gone to Sardinia. The Senate, on receipt of this grave news, conscripted every man under fifty and ordered the fleet in the Gulf of Lyons to sail for Albenga. The besieged Romans sat tight, and allowed nothing to tempt them to make a sortie. Their camp proved impregnable. The Ligurians becoming slack, took to drink. The Roman commander chose his moment, made a sortie from his four gates and worked havoc on the half-drunk enemy—15,000 were slain, 2,500 made prisoners. They also suffered a crushing defeat at sea, losing thirty-two of their ships. The Ingauni Ligurians surrendered unconditionally, and were treated liberally. Many of them took service with the Romans, and, Gurkha-like, became a famous fighting force in arduous hill campaigns.

Towards the western end of the Riviera dwelt another tribe of Ligurians, the Intemelli, in their stronghold of Intemelium, known by every traveller in Italy as the frontier town of Ventimiglia, the Customs station between France and Italy. In Roman days Intemelium marked the beginning of the most formidable barrier of all, the Maritime Alps. Later the Romans so civilized the place that they built villas there, thus establishing the Riviera season. It was at her villa near Ventimiglia that Julia, the mother of Agricola, was murdered in A.D. 69 by the soldiers of Otho, in revenge for the help she gave to his rival, Vitellius.[1]

The high ranges between Ventimiglia and Nice were for long the most serious obstacles in the Roman coastal communications with Gaul and Spain. They were avoided by a long detour up through the Pass of St Genèvre, the alpine route used by Pompey, who opened it up on his march to Spain, and by Julius Cæsar. In the conquest of Liguria on both sides of this range of the Maritime Alps, the Romans conveyed their armies by sea, and maintained communications with bases at Pisæ, Forum Julii and Massilia. For a long time they made no effort to create a road running through the whole of Liguria. Their allies the Greeks at Massilia, with their colony at Nicæa (Nice), looked after this western section for them. In 155 B.C. the Massilians were in trouble. They sent an envoy to Rome begging assistance against their Ligurian foes. Nicæa and Antipolis (Antibes),[2] so-called from being the 'polis' opposite Nicæa, were besieged. The Romans sent three Commissioners to try to bring the invading Ligurians to reason. They landed at Ægytna (Cannes) near the camp of the tribesmen. They were attacked in the act of discharging their baggage. Two of the Commissioners' retinue were killed and one of the Commissioners, Flaminius, was seriously injured.

On the news of this outrage the Senate at once fitted out an expedition. The Roman general landed at Cannes, levelled it to the ground, and sent his prisoners to the slave markets of Rome. Antibes fell next. The Romans handed over the conquered territory to the Massilians, stipulating

[1] Her son, Julius Agricola, was the real conqueror of Britain, to which he proceeded as Governor in A.D. 78. He established the Roman dominion in Britain beyond the Forth, built a chain of forts between the Forth and the Clyde, and navigated the coast, discovering that Britain was an island. Tacitus, his son-in-law, wrote his Life, regarded as a model of biography.

[2] A touching memorial of the Roman occupation was found. It was first set up in a wall of the Town Hall and is now in the Antibes Museum. It is a memorial stone inscribed:

D.M. PVERI SEPTENTRIONIS QVI ANNORUM XII ANTIPOLI IN THEATRO BIDVO SALTAVIT ET PLACVIT.

"To the memory of the boy Septentrion who, aged twelve years, twice danced and was applauded in the theatre of Antipolis."

that they made a coastal road from Nice to Marseilles. There followed the years in which the Romans conquered Provence (Provincia), settling a large colony at Narbonne. There was still no continuous road from Italy into Gaul, where the Romans were always fighting. Cæsar's famous conquests lay ahead.

The death of Cæsar brought a division among the Consuls. Marc Antony opposed the assassins. To his dismay the young Octavius, the dead dictator's grand-nephew, presented himself in Rome as the heir and asked Antony what he had done with the 4,000 talents, about one million sterling, due to him under Cæsar's will. It had gone in bribery. A quarrel followed. In 44 B.C. Marc Antony sought to establish himself in Cisalpine Gaul. Octavius marched upon him at Modena. There was a Roman coast road, in addition to the Via Aurelia, created by Emilius Scaurus in 109 B.C., extending from near Volterra, through Pisa and Luna to Vado (Savona). This was called the Via Æmilia Scaurus. Down to Vado came Marc Antony from Modena, where he had suffered a resounding defeat at the hands of Octavius, aged twenty. The pass over the Alps behind Savona was used in preference to the arduous way by Genoa. Outstripping his pursuers, Marc Antony arrived at Vado with three Legions and five thousand cavalry led by his brother, all that had escaped from the battle. Vado lies west of modern Savona, and the tradition of the Roman camp survives.

Marc Antony had a considerable force, but it was not strong enough to meet the Legions pursuing him. He had no alternative but flight along the Riviera, across the Maritime Alps and the formidable Esterel into Roman Provence, where he could recruit for his army. It was a desperate undertaking to march 20,000 infantry and 5,000 cavalry for a hundred miles along an arid coast, over two ranges of mountains, with scarce supplies of provisions and water. Pompey and Cæsar, marching into Gaul, had avoided the route by the coast; they knew its ardours. But Antony was a singular mixture of virility and decadence. Plutarch gives us a portrait of him in this crisis:

"In his flight he was overtaken by distresses of every kind and the worst of them was famine. But it was his character in calamities to be better than at any other time. Antony in misfortune was most nearly a virtuous man. On this occasion he was a most wonderful example to his soldiers. He, who had just quitted so much luxury and sumptuous living, made no difficulty now of drinking foul water and feeding on wild fruits and roots. Nay, it is related they ate the very bark of trees, and, in passing over the Alps, lived upon creatures that no one before had even been willing to touch."

From Vado, Antony's desperate Legions marched in April, 43 B.C., along the Ligurian mule-tracks through Albenga and Alassio, Ventimiglia and Nice, through the gorges of the massive Esterel, where many perished in the thickets, until they arrived, starving scarecrows, at the gates of the Roman colony of Forum Julii (Fréjus). Here Marc Antony rested for two weeks and refreshed his exhausted army. Then he marched forth to challenge the pursuing Lepidus. He succeeded in winning over his adversary, who committed an act of treachery that shocked the Senate. Its representative with Lepidus committed suicide rather than survive such a shameful transaction. Octavius became reconciled to Antony, and together with Lepidus, in November, 43 B.C., they were appointed triumvirs for five years. Near Bologna, on an island in the River Reno, the three men met and proscribed their political and personal enemies. Shakespeare in *Julius Cæsar* has made us familiar with the scene where they agree upon a list of victims, each colleague treacherously obliging the other with the life of a friend. Antony could not forgive Cicero for his Philippics pronounced against him, and Octavius sacrificed the man to whom he was so deeply indebted. Cicero's right hand and head were nailed up on the Rostrum in the Roman Forum. It is said that the wife of Antony, Fulvia, stuck a gold pin through the orator's tongue.

At this conference of the three triumvirs Antony received Gaul as one of his provinces. It saw little or nothing of him.

Cleopatra lured him to his ruin, and at Actium, three years later, Octavius won the naval battle that led to the utter defeat of Antony and Cleopatra. Four years later Octavius, as Cæsar Augustus, was created Roman Emperor.

In 12 B.C. Augustus turned his attention to the construction of a coastal road through Liguria from Savona to the valley of the Var at Nice. It joined up with the existing roads, the Via Aurelia and Via Emilia Scaurus, and was named the Via Julia Augusta, after the only child of Augustus, wife to Agrippa and Tiberius. Augustus carried his road over the Alps above Monte Carlo. Visitors there are familiar with the monument on the pass, at La Turbie, 1,500 feet high. It celebrates his final victory over the Alpine tribes. This Tower of Augustus, crowning the Grande Corniche, is a much repaired ruin, vivid against the sky. It is a relic of the trophy erected by the Senate to commemorate the Emperor's victory over the forty-five tribes of Liguria and Southern Gaul. It originally consisted of a colonnade of pillars surmounted by a colossal statue of the Emperor. It marked the frontier of Cisalpine and Transalpine Gaul. An inscription read:

HUCUSQUE ITALIA ABHINC GALLIA
('Hitherto Italy, Henceforth Gaul'.)

This monument is even today, in its half-ruinous state, still imposing. It originally stood one hundred and fifty feet high, and was mounted on a base one hundred and twenty feet square. Napoleon took away part of the inscription and sent it to the museum of St Germain-en-Laye, giving La Turbie in exchange a copy of Raphael's 'St Michael and the Dragon'.

It is a singular fact that the Via Aurelia, which runs from Rome to Arles in Provence, is the name of a combination of Roman roads, part of it following very ancient native tracks. It does not owe its name to the Emperor Marcus Aurelius or the Emperor Aurelianus of the second and third centuries. It was probably derived from a much earlier Aurelius, a Roman censor of 241 B.C., who was in charge of road construction. The highway, which started out of the Porta Aurelia at Rome went to the harbour below Volterra, the

ancient Etruscan fortress, and on to Pisa, a distance of about
175 miles. After that it took the name of the Via Emilia
Scaurus from the censor who constructed a further section
of it. There is a Roman milestone in the Campo Santo at
Pisa which bears the inscription VIA ÆMILIA A ROMA
M.P. CLXXXVIII—to Rome 188 miles. The M.P. indi-
cated *Mille Passuum*, the Roman mile, which consisted of
1,000 paces. A pace was about five feet, calculated from the
distance between the lifting up and the putting down of the
right foot. A Roman mile thus calculated was about one
hundred and forty yards shorter than the English mile.

There are few records of this ancient highway other than
these surviving milestones and two books, one the *Itinerary of
Antonine*, the other the *Table of Peutinger*. The former is a
small volume with the names of the roads and the posting-
stations. Its title runs: "Via Aurelia. The road to Rome via
Tuscany and the Maritime Alps as far as Arles. 797 miles."
The other record, the *Table of Peutinger*, is in the form of a
map with an extended East to West Section.[1]

These records do not go back earlier than the third century A.D., and were compiled, probably, in the reign of
Theodosius the Great, but the general picture is fairly clear
concerning the Via Aurelia. The first part from Rome to
Volterra was the work of Aurelius, 241 B.C.; the second of
Æmilius Scaurus to Savona, 109 B.C.; the third, of Augustus,
to Nice (Var), 12 B.C.; the fourth, made by the Massilians to
Fréjus, 154 B.C.; the fifth by Domitius, to Arles, 121 B.C. It
is an astonishing fact that by the time of Augustus it was
possible to travel, for a large part over the Via Aurelia, from
Rome to Britain and not require a passport or to pass a
customs barrier, a journey that today involves both passport
and three customs inspections.

The Via Aurelia that now runs through Alassio may not
be over the old route, for there is a theory that it avoided the
swampy plain and passed at some height along the amphitheatre of mountains, from Santa Croce to Laigueglia. This

---

[1] This was a world-map of the third or fourth century A.D. It was taken from
a lost original by a Colmar monk in A.D. 1265, whose copy came into the
possession of a sixteenth-century scholar named Peutinger.

old Roman road between Albenga and Alassio, some five hundred feet above the new coast highway, offers the most enchanting views of the island of Gallinaria and the Mediterranean Sea towards Genoa. It makes its way, now clear, now faint, through olive groves, around the shoulder of the mountain for about four miles. At Albenga it went over a bridge, still intact, as also in the Andora valley beyond Alassio. Walking on that narrow track, often cool and shady above the highway hideous with advertisements and perilous with motor-buses, lorries, and automobiles, it is thrilling to know that here came Marc Antony and his Legions, pursued by Lepidus. But innumerable are the ghosts of this road traversing two thousand years of history, since those far-off days when the fierce Ligurians peered through the woods at the passing of the Roman eagles.

II

It is a beautiful day. Let us go into Albenga, not by train or by bus along the low road, but by foot on the high Roman road. Before the coastal road was made, this was the only means of communication between Albenga and Alassio. In the eyes of the former, Alassio is an upstart. It has no Roman records, there is no mention of it before A.D. 940, whereas Albenga was an important Roman camp, and, as we have seen, Mago landed his troops there in 205 B.C.

A fairly steep road brings us high up on the headland of Santa Croce which ends the Bay of Alassio. On the cobalt sea below us lies the island of Gallinaria. In front of us, steep against the sky, above a crumbling watch-tower, one of the many lookouts to guard against raiding Saracens, stands the old chapel of Santa Croce, almost a complete ruin, built in A.D. 998. Why this historic landmark should be allowed to go derelict is a mystery. Near by a belvedere has been built that looks seawards and down the coast beyond Albenga and Genoa, as far, on a clear day, as the mountains of Carrara. At the side of the old chapel there is an arched gateway. It is part of the fortifications built by the Alassians to protect themselves against the Albengans with whom they were always quarrelling. For Albenga was once rich, renowned, and ruled over by a powerful bishop. Alassio was poor but refused to be reduced to serfdom. The contest went on with varying fortunes for each side for some five hundred years. When Alassio was not menaced by Albenga she was afraid of losing her freedom to Genoa, whose aid she sometimes sought.

The little chapel on the promontory of Santa Croce was built by the monks of Gallinaria Island. Its apse merges into a fortification, with loopholes commanding the road from Albenga. When you stand in the open arch that commands the steep road on either side, you see two views of this superb coast. Northwards lies Albenga and its delta running out to sea; southwards the arch frames an enchanting vista of the great bay of Alassio, with its golden sands, and the roofs and villas of the town far below.

In view of Albenga's patronizing airs, how old is Alassio, how did it get its name and what is its history? One has to fall back on a legend, which well contents Alassio, for it is a romantic one.

In the year A.D. 936, Otho, the son of the Emperor Henry I of Germany, succeeded to the throne. His reign was a successful one, in peace and war. He brought many turbulent tribes under subjection, he extended his kingdom and achieved almost supreme power in Italy, being strong enough to impose his edicts upon the King of Lombardy and the Pope at Rome. He consolidated the power of various German kings, and his influence was wide enough to be able to establish Christianity in Scandinavian and Slavonic lands. He became known as Otho the Great.

Naturally he had many enemies. He had conquered Bavaria, Bohemia, and Poland. Then he found his power contested by the King of Denmark and the King of Hungary. Hard-pressed from the north and south, he entrusted the command of his army to a gallant young soldier named Aleramo, a member of a noble family of Acqui in Piedmont. Aleramo proved himself a skilful soldier. He induced the Hungarians to follow him over a bridge of the River Lech, and then attacked and defeated them. He next marched north and, taking the King of Denmark a prisoner, forced him to surrender and to accept baptism. Otho rewarded Aleramo with many honours, but he became frantically jealous of the young warrior's fame and popularity. He called him to court, and thereby was able to separate him from the army that adored him. A complication ensued. Aleramo fell in love with the Princess Adelasia, or Alassia. Beautiful and young, she returned Aleramo's passion. For some time they succeeded in hiding their love from the jealous Emperor, but the courtiers began to observe the state of affairs. At any moment they might open Otho's eyes. The lovers decided to flee. One night they fled the court by horseback. Adelasia was disguised in male costume. They hid all the next day and journeyed again by night. At one village they heard a proclamation read by the public herald for their arrest, to be rewarded by a large sum of money. They went on again, seeking the country Aleramo had known through boyhood. The Emperor, furious that the lovers had succeeded in evading him, disowned his daughter, put a price on Aleramo's head, and under pain of death forbade anyone to give them food or shelter.

At last, after many adventures, the runaways reached the Mediterranean coast, hiding in the woods above the bay where Alassio now stands. The only people that they dare make contact with were the humble charcoal-burners. Aleramo, faced with the problem of earning a living, went into Albenga and sold his horses, buying a strong ass. He had resolved to make himself a charcoal-burner. For years they contrived to exist, disguised as peasants, among the early settlers around Alassio, who had no idea that an Emperor's daughter was in their midst.

There was one thing troubling the mind of the young couple even more than their fear of discovery; their union had not been legalized, which was only possible by first obtaining absolution and having a church ceremony. Greatly daring, the young man went into Albenga and, through an intermediary, obtained an interview with the Bishop. Aleramo arrived at the palace and threw himself on his knees, confessing his sins, asking for absolution and the blessing of the Church on his union. The first part of the confession made, Aleramo, with the greatest fear, but trusting to the pledge of absolute secrecy given by the Bishop, divulged the identity of Adelasia and himself. The Bishop was alarmed, for the Emperor was a violent man, powerful throughout Italy, but he resolved to befriend the lovers. The marriage was solemnized. The couple returned to their charcoal-burner's hut.

After a few years, the peace of Lombardy was imperilled by Berengario II, who had seized Brescia. The Emperor Otho called up reinforcements. Albenga contributed a detachment, being one of his vassal cities. The Bishop, a temporal as well as a spiritual power, put himself at the head of the Albenga force. Among it was the young charcoal-burner, serving in the ranks. In the assault on Brescia's walls the courage and resource of this young soldier excited so much talk and admiration that the fame of his deeds came to the Emperor's ears. He sent for the Bishop and questioned him about the young soldier. The Bishop was so hesitant and confused that the Emperor commanded him to be frank. The young soldier, said the Bishop, was not an ordinary ranker. He was of noble birth, but had been compelled by events to disguise himself and seek shelter in his diocese. Beyond this the Bishop would not satisfy the Emperor's curiosity. Aleramo, distressed to see the ill-favour in which the Bishop stood through his reticence, gave him permission to reveal his secret, and prepared himself for the worst.

So the Emperor was told the whole story. After a time his wrath abated, particularly when the Bishop assured him that the fugitives were a perfectly happy couple, despite all they had suffered, and the parents of beautiful children. Otho, filled with emotion, sent for Aleramo. Providing the young soldier with an escort of men-at-arms, he bade him bring the Princess back to her home. So the lovers were restored to their high estate, and lived happily ever after.

It was in the woods above Alassio, claim the Alassians, that Adelasia or Alassia lived, and from her the town derives its name.

How much of it can one accept as true, if any? We know

that Otho the Great existed, that there was a war with Berengario, that there was a militant Bishop of Albenga. Like all old traditions, it varies. There is a more highly romantic one to the effect that the Princess fled with a nobleman, who later accused her of infidelity and walled her up in a tower from which a knight-errant, Aleramo, rescued her. The poetical version of this variation very ungallantly narrates that the poor lady had such large hips that when the knight tried to rescue her she stuck in the window, half in and half out! A third version had her imprisoned in a tower on Lake Garda by Berengario II because she refused to marry his son, Adelbert; but this seems confused with the story that Aleramo, after Adelasia's death, married Berengario's daughter, who brought up his children by his first wife. Behind all this there are indisputable records that give a foundation to the legend. By a deed signed at Ravenna on March 23rd, 967, the Emperor Otho created Aleramo Marquis of Montferrat, Saluzzo, Ceva, Savona, and Finale. He was also given estates, with the title of Marquis of Corrati Alamio. He was confirmed in his possessions by a deed conferring on him estates in Piedmont, Lombardy, and 'land conquered from the Saracens'. The Saracens descended on Liguria in 849. They swept over the mountains, carrying fire and sword into Piedmont as far as Asti. It took some time for the Princes of the House of Savoy to evict them. It is therefore quite probable that Aleramo received some of this retrieved land.

In the deed confirming the gift from the Emperor, Aleramo is described as the son of Guglielmo, and there are documents proving that Aleramo was the son of a rich Ligurian noble, Count Guglielmo. There are chronicles which state that he married a daughter of the Emperor Otho. Lastly, there is the record of the burial of Aleramo in the Abbey of Grassano in 993.

That Aleramo existed there is no doubt.[1] One of the

[1] The House of Aleramo descended through Boniface III, head of the Fourth Crusade, who died fighting the Saracens in 1207; William, who was made a prisoner at Alessandria and condemned to die of hunger in an iron cage, 1291; and John, his son, last of the Aleramidi, who died 1305. The Aleramidi were succeeded by a branch of the Palæologi of Constantinople, who ruled Montferrat from 1306–1533.

versions makes the young couple hide in a cavern in 'the rugged Ardennes', which carries the scene wholly away from Alassio, but the people of Garessio, beyond the San Bernardo Pass, point to a cave called Pietra Ardena as their refuge; and that brings the story back from France to Liguria. The Alassians go still further in their claim. They adopt the tower story, and point out the tower above the town at Vegliasco as the scene of her rescue, big hips or no big hips. The civic authorities seem to have endorsed this. Over the main doorway of the Palazzo Municipale hangs the coat-of-arms of the city. It shows Adelasia coming out of the top of the tower. She is wearing a cuirass or corsage embossed with the imperial eagles, which shows that she was the daughter of a German Emperor. No wonder the German tourists flocking to Alassio feel at home. *Deutschland über alles*—including the tower!

Now the grievous thing about all this, a shattering blow to the legend, is that there is no record that the Emperor ever had a daughter named Adelasia or Alassia! Yet somehow the legend got a start and somehow Alassio got its name, and it will stand for no nonsense about the authenticity of the lady.

However it be, there is no doubt concerning Alassio's existence. Its history is inextricably involved with that of Albenga, which is believed to be the parent city. Alassio, it is thought, was founded by Ligurian Ingauni fleeing from Albenga before the Roman Legions. They settled, it would seem, on the hillside above the bay, for the sea came more inland then, at a place called Castello, another reason for the tower or castle in the coat-of-arms.

As we go down through the archway at Santa Croce, the Roman road takes us past the ruins of the church of Sant' Anna dei Monti. It was founded by the Bishop of Albenga in A.D. 940, and is therefore Alassio's first place of worship, the second being the Madonna della Guardia, founded a little later.

Two hours' walk along the beautiful terrace formed by the old Via Aurelia brings us down into the valley of Albenga. Its towers, reminiscent of San Gimignano, rise above the

wide plain, the source of her horticultural wealth. The
plain is watered by the alluvial River Centa, which in the
course of time has divorced old Albenga from the sea by a
delta half a mile long.

Let us go into the old town named by the Romans as
Albium Ingaunum, then a post much favoured by them and
the Carthaginians. One can imagine Mago's galleys moored
offshore, and the town thronged with his dark Numidian
troops, the earth-shaking elephants, the twelve thousand
African troops, the cavalry, and the wiry inquisitive Ligurians, allies in this attempt by Mago to assist Hannibal. Here
the wounded Mago was brought, defeated, sick unto death,
and carried on board his galley. There was also the day
when Marc Antony's harassed Legions appeared at its
gates, pursued down the Alpine gorges. But who had not
appeared at its gates in the course of the centuries? The city
dates from about A.D. 420, when it was founded by Constantius III, the half-brother of the Emperor Honorius and
husband of Galla Placidia, the Byzantine lady who gives her
name to that exquisite tomb in Ravenna. It was this Constantius who built the stone bridge, five hundred feet long,
that is still one of the show-pieces of Albenga. It stands a
little outside the town, half-buried and without any water
under it, for the river has shifted its bed to half a mile away.
It is a sad relic of late Roman days, for now the main road
to Genoa runs on one side, and on the other are buildings
and orchards. No motorist slows up or looks at this bridge
that once linked Rome with her western empire, that was
once as crowded with traffic on its ten-foot span as the
macadam road of today. Constantius kept to the quadri-
lateral building plan of the Romans. He walled and gated
the city. It is still walled and gated. Through the gates
Albenga is a little grim with its secretive palaces, dark houses,
and overshadowing towers.

What retinues of the great thronged these narrow streets!
Francesco Sforza, Duke of Milan, was received by the
authorities in 1464, that illegitimate son of a peasant who,
with his sword, carved out a dukedom, took Ancona from
the Pope, and married the beautiful Bianca Visconti. In

1489 came Queen Isabella of Aragon, on her way to Genoa, whence had come the man she sent to discover the new world, Columbus. And from that great seaport came, in 1524, the man who made Genoa great on the sea and commanded her ships at the battle of Lepanto, Andrea Doria, who refused the crown of the Genoese Republic, and died, the idol of his people, at ninety-five. He landed in Albenga with 8,000 soldiers and spent eight days there. In the same year the little city saw the resplendent Francis I, King of France. He spent almost a month there with his army, one year before his crushing defeat at Pavia by the Emperor Charles V, who came to Albenga in 1536, with much pomp and a large retinue. Fourteen years later Albenga welcomed the Duke of Savoy and his wife, Margaret of Austria. The greatest soldier of them all, Napoleon, marched into Albenga from Alassio.

Things had not gone well in 1795 with the French army invading Italy. The fall of Robespierre in the previous year had resulted in no activity on that front. In an offensive Austria had pushed back the French in Piedmont, and the blockading British fleet had seized the port of Vado. Napoleon wrote a *Note sur l'armée d'Italie*, outlining a forward move on Vado and Savona. The plan was so bold that General Schérer, in command of the army, resigned rather than support it. But the young general of twenty-six got his way. He was gazetted to the command of the army in Italy on March 2nd, 1796. On the 8th he married Josephine Beauharnais, on the 26th he reached his headquarters at Nice, where he held his first review and changed his name from Napoleone Buonaparte to the French Napoléon Bonaparte, thus wiping out his family's Corsican-Italian origin. He was young, eager, of poor physique, and so much in love that he showed his wife's portrait to everyone. But when he put on his general's hat and issued orders, he not only seemed a foot taller but his voice told his staff that the army had a leader. On April 2nd, 1796, he slept at Alassio. On the 3rd he was in Albenga, his headquarters for the move against the Austrians at Ceva, thirty miles north. He was planning the battle of Millesimo and Mondovi. In the pressure of

planning, he wrote to the Directors: "I can't tell you the life
I lead. I come in tired out, then have to be up all night hard
at work, hurrying here, there, and everywhere to restore
order." Even so, he found time to write one letter, the love-
letter of a newly married man, to Josephine in Paris. It is
dated 'Albenga April 5th, 1796', a week before the battle of
Montenotte opened the way to the conquest of Italy.

"It is one hour after midnight. Someone has brought me
a letter. It is sad, my soul is affected, it tells me of Chauvet's
death. He was chief commissionaire of the army, you met
him at Barras's home. Sometimes, my love, I feel the need
of being consoled; it is in writing to you *alone*, whose
thought influences my moral reflections, that I find it
necessary to express all my troubles. What will happen in
the future, what does the past mean, what are we, that
magic fluid that surrounds us and hides from us the
things it is most important for us to know? We are born,
we live, we die in the midst of miracles. Is it astonishing
that the priests, the astrologers, the charlatans should have
profited by this singular circumstance to use and direct
our ideas to their own purposes?

"Chauvet is dead. He was very attached to me. He
served his country nobly. His last words to me were that
we should be united one day. Yes, I see his shade now, he
is all around, his voice sounds in the air, his soul floats in
the clouds, he will be propitious for my destiny. But,
absurdly, I am bathed in tears for our friendship though
I know I should not be mourning for what is irreparable.

"Soul of my very existence, write me all the news, I cannot live otherwise! I am very busy, Beaulieu moves his
army, we are now in the middle of things. I am a little
tired, I am every evening on horseback. Adieu, adieu! I
am going to sleep with you; dreams console me. You will
be at my side, I shall hold you in my arms! But, alas, on
waking I shall find you are three hundred leagues away
from me!

"Greetings to Barras, to Tallien and his wife,

"Napoleon."

There are few memorials of all these distinguished visitors to Albenga. There was once a monument to Constantius, but all that remains of it is three stone lions behind the Cathedral. It was there, complete in 1288. Albenga has its legend also. In the third century there was a Bishop called Verano. A dragon was the terror of the countryside, and was only appeased by the tribute of a maiden once a year. Then its appetite grew, and it wanted its morsel every month, then every week, and finally every day. This was too much for the Albengans, so they went to their Bishop, suggesting he should call in heavenly powers to deal with the dragon. Dressed in full vestments, he walked to the monster's cave. The dragon came out "belching forth flame and smoke and bitumen", so the record runs, but the good Bishop raised the Cross three times, called on the Almighty, and so scared the dragon that it turned tail and drowned itself in a lake. The question of where was the lake is easily disposed of. The Albengans say the monster made the water boil until it evaporated and no trace was left.

The remarkable Baptistry, fifth-century, was probably a Roman bath or temple converted to Christian use, and its eight pillars of Corsican marble may have belonged to the pagan temple. How much the town has risen can be seen from the original level of this building, quite thirty feet lower. The Baptistry was the only place in the whole diocese where baptism could take place and the sacrament be administered. Converts and children had to be brought great distances on the eve of Easter and Pentecost.

The Bishops of Albenga wielded immense power, more than the overlords, the Marquises of Clavesana. There were bloody feuds between the civic and ecclesiastical factions. The citizens were wealthy. They built and owned ships. On the appeal of Peter the Hermit they sent galleys to the First Crusade, 1096–9. The overlord in 1158 was Frederick Barbarossa. Albenga suffered later, having Genoa as an ally when that city warred with Pisa for the mastery of the Mediterranean. A Pisan fleet descended on Albenga in 1165, sacked it and burnt it, causing the inhabitants to flee into the mountains before the Genoese fleet arrived on the scene. Weakened, the town gradually fell into the hands of Genoa and was reduced to a fief in 1199. Then began a long struggle, associated with other towns of the coast, to throw off the yoke of Genoa. They all rose in 1226, and Albenga marked the event by slitting the throats of all the Genoese in the city. A year later Genoa reduced the town and took away one hundred and sixty hostages. She also captured Savona, and from that time on dominated all the towns along the coast.

But two other feuds continued. The Bishop was always at war with the sturdy Albengans. He would excommunicate the city, and then the Pope would make peace for a time. The great feud between Guelphs and Ghibellines raged throughout Liguria, for the two factions were represented locally by the great Spinola and Doria families. This feud engulfed Albenga up to the close of the fourteenth century, but her stormy passage was not at an end. In 1625 the Duke of Savoy sent his son, the Prince of Piedmont, into western Liguria. Albenga, powerless, opened its gates to him, as also neighbouring Villanova. The Prince marched in, established himself in the Bishop's palace, and left behind a garrison of three hundred soldiers in possession of the city. Their conduct was so outrageous, with rape, pillage, and drunkenness, that after a month the Albengans insisted on their withdrawal, with the help of the Genoese, who took the troops off by sea. But they left behind them an outbreak of plague that devastated nobles and commoners alike. Eleven years later this tough, unfortunate city, just raising its head again, was threatened by the ferocious Barbary pirates, who seized the people on the coast and either slaughtered them or carried them off into slavery. The legend runs that on this occasion Albenga was saved by the Madonna of the Roman Bridge, who caused such a brilliant flame to burn over her church that the pirates were frightened away.

What a record of disasters, with the help of miracles or otherwise, this little city has survived! In 1745 she was invested with Spanish and French troops. Carlo Emanuele of Savoy marched in after the Peace of Aix-la-Chapelle and levied heavy tribute. In 1795 its plain saw the battle of

Loano. In the next year Napoleon made the city his head-
quarters, planning there the victories of Montenotte, Ceva,
and Mondovi that broke the Austrians' line of defence. No
wonder Napoleon was fatigued. He wrote from Albenga, in
a period of ten days, fifty-four letters to his generals in the
field, seventeen on one day, mostly written late at night. In
addition to planning the victory of Mondovi, he had to com-
bat the appalling morale of his troops. "When I got there,"
he wrote to the Directors, "it was under the influence of
disaffected agitators, without bread, without discipline, and
without order. I made some examples, I took every step I
could to organize the commissariat, and victory did the rest.
All the same, our lack of wagons, the badness of our horses,
the greed of contractors, reduced us to absolute penury.
Men without bread indulge in outrages that makes one
blush for human nature . . . either I restore order or give up
my command over these brigands."

Liguria was converted into a Republic under the Consu-
late, and knew French rule until Elba received its prisoner.
Then it fell under the dominion of Sardinia, until in 1861 it
became part of the Kingdom of Italy. Albenga experienced
this change of fortunes also. Today it is a quiet, industrious
little place, its towers are crumbling, its palaces are falling
into ruin. Has it come to the end of its history? In 1943 it
seemed probable at one moment that history might be repeated at Albenga, where Mago had brought his elephants.
The Allies contemplated a landing there, the seizure of the
large plain and aerodrome, and of the two roads that lead
over the mountains to the plains of Piedmont.

Albenga has had a strange fate. Its rival, Alassio, which
for so long it oppressed, has outstripped it in size and fame.
Visitors in Alassio now take a bus ride to Albenga to look at
the quaint old city with a great silence in the dark narrow
streets. The sea is now half a mile away. The Alassians no
longer keep a wall and a frontier gate to protect them from
the hated Albengans.

The early growth of Alassio was partly due to the misfortunes suffered by her rival. When the Pisans descended
on Albenga with a force of thirty galleys and sacked and

burnt the city, the homeless Albengans fled to Alassio. They
fled again when Boniface, Marquis of Clavesana, in the
Guelph and Ghibelline feud, put the city to sword and fire.
The Republic of Genoa was behind most of these feuds between the towns on the Ligurian coast. They aided now one
and now the other, with the purpose of dividing and ruling.
They feared any town that prospered as a seaport, and
seized or destroyed it. As with all these places, local greed
and ambition led to wars and seizures. Albenga swallowed
up Villanova and Calizzano; then she obtained Gallinaria,
through a deed that was always declared to be fraudulent by
the Alassians. This started a long and bitter feud between
the two towns. In the sixteenth century the Albengans discovered that by a deed of 1303 they had the right to collect
feudal dues from their neighbours. They applied for two
centuries of arrears. These were indignantly repudiated,
whereupon Albenga put a fine of five thousand gold ducats
on Alassio and levied new taxes. The Alassians threatened to
take up arms, but were persuaded to lay their case before the
King of France in Genoa, asking for their independence to
be maintained. They failed. The Albengans succeeded in
getting the Doge of Genoa to order the Alassians to lay down
their arms. They refused, and in 1513 marched along the old
Roman road on the town of Albenga. There was a clash outside the city walls, but the battle was a stalemate. Bowing to
their fate, the Alassians sent a deputation to the Podestà and
the Council of Albenga. The terms imposed were generous,
and in the parish church of Sant' Ambrogio they swore on
their knees an oath of fealty to Albenga. But in September
1516, the Albengans were at their old tricks, demanding
back taxes. The indignant Alassians manhandled their envoy and threw him out of the town, for which violence they
were rebuked by the Doge of Genoa.

The Alassians now decided to build a wall round the town
as a defence against their two chief enemies, the marauding
Corsairs from Africa and the Albengans. Everyone worked
on the wall, including women who had memories of their
sisters being carried off to Moorish harems. They contributed
their jewels towards the expense. One noble lady, Bettina

Fignone, gave a massive gold necklet and prevailed upon her husband, Captain Stefano, to advance five thousand ducats. By a queer twist of fate the Bishop of Albenga came in 1521 and blessed the foundation stone of the first bastion by the south gate. It is still there, with an hotel built over it. The town was enclosed by a thirty-foot-high wall. By a happy little reversal of fortune, Captain Giuliano Berno captured a Turkish ship off Laigueglia, liberated some of the Laigueglians who had been seized by the raiders, and set eighteen of the pirates to work on the walls. I like to think that my palazzo is founded on some of the stones of the walls these cut-throat Saracens were made to lay. Over each gate the pious citizens put a statue of the Madonna. These have been saved. One stands in a niche at the north end of The Drain, almost under my terrace, the other at the south end.

The Albengans, now feeling less secure themselves, went to work on their defences in 1534, but by ill-luck the flood of the River Centa swamped the valley and washed part of them away. In contrast, Alassio became alarmingly prosperous. She built ships, she had a thriving coral-fishing industry, she manufactured ropes and spun silk. The wars between Charles V and Francis I had assisted her, for the two rivals sent transports of soldiers through Alassio and lodged them on the rich Albengans' soil. The very richness of the territory invited disaster. It ruined the Albengans. The Alassians were delighted. The latter now swore fealty to Genoa and gained her assistance. The Republic built towers of refuge along the coast, and watch-towers on the hills to give warning of the approach of the corsairs. These towers are a feature of the coast today.

Relations between the two towns did not improve, and Genoa had to issue safe-conducts for the Alassians visiting Albenga on market-days. A quiet war went steadily on between the neighbours. When today you walk through the old gate at Santa Croce and along the Roman road towards the ruined church of Sant' Anna, you are on a track once haunted by two forms of robbers—highwaymen and Albengan customs officials. The Doge of Genoa was compelled

to address a strong note to the Podestà of Albenga. This has
a familiar ring today.

Magnificent Podestà!

These differences and disagreements between Albengans and Alassians have given and continue to give us
annoyance. So much so that one day it will be necessary
for us to take steps which will be displeasing to both
parties, because an equitable decision as to the rights of
the case cannot apparently be arrived at. But no more of
this for the present. What has caused us fresh annoyance
and displeasure is that the roads are not free for travellers.
There has arrived with the galleys from Spain a gentleman
of the Duke of Savoy's household. On account of sea-
sickness or other causes, he landed at Alassio, intending to
travel thence by land. He and his retinue had great
difficulty in finding posting accommodation from fear of
not being able to pass through Albenga in safety. According to a letter written by you to Stefano de Franchi, you
gave the gentleman a safe-conduct valid, we take it, for
one journey only, implying that future attacks will not be
lacking. By this it would seem that safe-conducts from you
are necessary to enable travellers to pass through our
dominions in safety. It is your business to give such
guarantees freely, and to make the roads secure. On this
account we are lost, not in admiration but in amazement,
and therefore we make it known to you that we desire the
highway to be free and safe to all, and we must request
that no further news of this kind shall reach our ears.

From Genoa, the 12th day of January 1569.

Genoa was a heavy overlord for both Alassio and Albenga.
The two places found themselves caught up in the Republic's
quarrels with her rivals. Alassio never knew tranquillity. If
it was not the Albengans, it was the Saracens, the Spaniards,
the French, the English. In 1660 an English trading vessel
lay in the bay when a Neapolitan fleet of thirteen sail
attacked it. The Alassians went to the aid of their customer.
The piracy of the corsairs provided some racy stories of

such daring feats as would satisfy any schoolboy. There was Eligio Miralta of Alassio. In 1688 he owned and commanded a brigantine, armed as a fighting ship. He was given letters of marque by the Genoese Republic. He loaded grain at Girgenti in Sicily, and set sail for home. One morning at daybreak he saw a caravel, a Turkish ship-of-war, with a single-masted vessel, a tartan, in tow. As soon as the Turkish ship spotted Miralta's she threw off the tartan and started in pursuit. Rather than be captured and be taken with his crew into slavery, Miralta decided to fight the Turkish vessels though he was badly outgunned. He hoisted the Genoese pennant and opened fire on the Algerian pirate. By skilful seamanship he avoided the caravel's return fire, prevented her from boarding him, and putting his bow athwart the pirate ship cut away her foremast. Then, lying alongside, he cleared a space on her deck with hand-grenades, grappled and boarded her, pistol and cutlass in hand. He captured the ship, took command of her and sent a boat to take over the tartan. This accomplished, he hoisted sail with the crew of the tartan and forty liberated slaves on the caravel, and took his three ships into Genoa, where he had a tremendous ovation.

Two years later another Alassian demonstrated of what bold stuff her seamen were made. Erasmo Simone, cruising off the Sicilian coast, was captured with his shipmates by a Turkish vessel. In due course they used his skill as a navigator and gave him authority over his fellow captives. One day, anchoring in the Dardanelles, the Turks incautiously went ashore to celebrate a Mohammedan festival. This gave Simone his chance. He assembled his fellow slaves and persuaded them to mutiny. They overcame the Turkish guard and made a break for the open sea. The Turks on shore manned a boat and went in pursuit, but Simone trained such a hot fire on them that they gave up the chase. Simone then put into Valetta harbour. He had a great reception, and was invested with the Order of the Knights of Malta.

Alassio's fleet when not fighting went coral fishing off Sardinia. In 1720 it suffered a frightful disaster. In a storm the entire fleet foundered, and only one Alassian seaman survived out of five hundred and six. It was a mortal blow to the profitable coral industry and Alassio turned to tunny fishing.

By the eighteenth century Albenga, falling on evil days, had little power to injure Alassio, though she kept up her pin-pricking policy. The pirates were still a thorn in the flesh, and when at last they were disposed of the French battened on the Ligurians. In 1795 the army of the French Republic marched into Liguria. This drew upon Alassio a blockade by the British men-of-war. The French ordered the Alassians to fire on the British. They protested, saying they were under the Genoese flag, a neutral. The French Commissary insisted that the guns of the city's bastions should fire at the British vessels. The return fire would destroy the town, it was pointed out. In this crisis the foremost Alassian, the Marquis Onorato Ferrero, approached the French commandant, with whom he was on terms of friendship, and begged his intervention. Thus Alassio was saved from drawing the fire of the British fleet, which drew off.

The period under the French occupation brought ruin and stagnation to the two old rivals. Then, in the latter part of the nineteenth century, Alassio was discovered as a health resort. It attracted a large British colony that brought it back to prosperity. Alas, World War II wiped out the moneyed and pensioned British. Exchange control and devaluation of the pound reduced a resident colony of five hundred to fifty.

Albenga, too, has had a resurrection. The Albengans, with a prodigious rise in profits on garden produce, have left the old town to crumble into decay and have built a new one on the delta of the Centa. They have also built an aerodrome and fly their fruit and vegetables all over Europe.

One lovely spring day I walked out of the old gateway at Santa Croce, along the partly vanished Roman road high above the sea, down to the plain of Albenga. I wandered through the gloomy old town with its decayed palaces and empty piazza, past the Palazzo Fieschi-Ricci, the twelfth- to fourteenth-century home of the Fieschi, bishops of Albenga in 1460 and 1588, with its original windows and black

171

marble door. I went on past the grim tower of the Palazzo Lengueglia-Doria, and the Loggetta of the Four Corners, both thirteenth-century, to the piazza with the stone lions of Constantius. Seeing a door open at the top of a flight of ancient brick steps, I went up and found myself trespassing in a room embedded in the high tower, that dates back seven hundred years, now housing the *comune* and the civic museum. Long tables covered with glasses and confectionery told me that I had trespassed upon a civic reception, but kind Albengans invited me in, although I was not a delegate of the conference being entertained. There were some old engravings on the walls. One of these particularly drew my attention, a 'Vue de La Ville d'Albenga'. It was a French engraving, commissioned by the Quartier-Général de l'Armée. A line of fine type informed me that it was a drawing made on the spot by Capitaine-Ingénieur Géographe Bagetti; the date followed his name. It was April 5, 1796. So he had drawn it on the very day when the lovesick Napoleon Bonaparte had written from Albenga to his bride Josephine!

Napoleon wrote his letter from a large palazzo at the far end of the Piazza Michele, the large square facing the cathedral. It is one of the several palaces in the town that are truly astonishing in size when one enters them. A Roman naval museum is established in the former palace of the Aste family. The last of the Astes died a few years ago. One ascends a wide marble staircase with ancestral busts over the doors of the salons to the third floor where a suite of rooms of astonishing loftiness speaks of the past wealth and glory of Albenga's aristocracy.

CHAPTER NINE

IN THE FAMILY TREE

I

AT the far end of the piazza I can just discern from my terrace the trees in the garden of the Palazzo Ferrero. It might be termed the manor-house of Alassio. It is a large colour-washed mansion, venetian-red, with green shutters, and with two storeys terraced on the garden side. A balustrade round the roof carries ornamental urns silhouetted against the sky. The other side of the palazzo shows a long high façade to The Drain, and overlooks the small square that takes its name from the family. There is a massive studded door with a pair of fine bronze knockers. The portal is crowned by an armorial shield carrying the Ferrero coronet and arms.

The garden in front of the palazzo originally extended across the town, over the present railway-line and up to a belvedere on the opposite mountain. It was in this palace that Napoleon slept one night during his march into Italy in April 1796. He seems to have made little impression on Alassio. Unlike his customary practice, he went off without taking any loot. He was, of course, welcomed as a liberator freeing Italy from the Austrian yoke. Ten years later, Alassio was made a canton in the annexation of Liguria to the French Empire. On the abdication of the Emperor, Liguria, following the Congress of Vienna, was given to the Kingdom of Sardinia. Back came the King of Sardinia to reign in Piedmont in his ancient state until the Austrians threw him out.

One day soon after my arrival in Alassio I met a member of the Ferrero family, Donna Anna, daughter of the Marchese Ferrero de Gubernatis di Ventimiglia. This is a long name for a visiting-card, but it is the Italian custom to display all the ancestral connections. It makes family-tree climbing easier.

Donna Anna invited me to the Palazzo Ferrero, and

inquired if I was at work on a new book. ("The Signor Inglese who has just gone by writes books," said the barber to a customer. "I hear he is writing a book on Alassio.") I informed Donna Anna that I was working on *And So To Rome*. I mentioned that I had just finished a chapter dealing with the great Italian poet, Count Alfieri, who ran off with the wife of Bonnie Prince Charlie and lived with her until his death. Prior to that he had had a singular adventure as a young man of twenty-two, visiting London. There he had a liaison with the wife of Viscount Ligonier, a lady with a wandering fancy. Her husband eventually divorced her after an affair with a private in his Guards regiment. Ligonier, encountering Alfieri sitting in the Spanish Ambassador's box at the Opera, called him out. The youth and the officer adjourned at once to the Green Park, where they fought a duel. Ligonier, an experienced swordsman, could easily have killed Alfieri, but he satisfied his honour by pricking the young Italian in the arm. Half an hour later, with his arm bound up, Alfieri reappeared in the Ambassador's box, apologizing for his absence.

"How very singular!" exclaimed Donna Anna. "My great-great-grandmother was the niece of Alfieri. Come into the library and I will show you something that will interest you." I followed my hostess, and there, displayed in cases, were the poet's manuscripts, a lock of his reddish hair, and the sword with which he had fought the duel in London in 1771! "And look at this," said my hostess, producing what looked like a stick. "My great-grandfather went with Napoleon on his campaign in Russia, and lost his leg there. Here's his wooden one, all that was left to him of the glory."

It occurred to me that in a family established in Alassio since the beginning of the sixteenth century there must be much interesting history. One day I asked Donna Anna's father, the octogenarian Marchese Ferrero, if he had any data concerning his ancestors in Alassio. A gentleman of exquisite courtesy and modesty, he replied that he could show me a few papers that might interest me. Excusing himself, he left the sitting-room whose windows looked out on to a pleasant terrace, and returned with a book which he presented to me. "This might give you a few facts, if you will accept it," he said. He put into my hand a book of six hundred and fifty pages, in small type, with microscopic notes, together with three four-fold genealogical tables! I looked at the title of this massive volume of two hundred and fifty thousand words. *The Ferreros of Alassio* it ran, by Vittorio del Corno. I know nothing of the author who wrote this work in 1890, but he must have been a man of prodigious industry. What mountains of documents covering more than six centuries he traversed! Nothing escaped him. To three hundred pages of narrative he added another three hundred of notes. I spent a month digesting this massive tome, fascinated by a thousand facets of life in Spain, Liguria, and Piedmont through six hundred years.

I was astonished by discovering that the Ferrero family probably had its origin in England, and is therefore of an English-Spanish-Italian descent. Its history portrays a vivid pageantry of European history since feudal times. Early in the thirteenth century Bernard, a younger son of Earl Ferrers, of a family which was seated at Higham Ferrers in Northamptonshire, became a soldier of fortune. Like many other young Englishmen, he took service in Spain, then in a state of continual unrest in its contending kingdoms. Bernard Ferrers served with such distinction and bravery in the army of James I, King of Aragon, particularly in the war that resulted in the conquest of the Kingdom of Valencia, that he was rewarded with castles and estates. The great advancement of the Englishman in the King's service resulted in bitter resentment among the Spaniards at court. They succeeded in a conspiracy by which Ferrers was charged with treason. He was disgraced, deprived of his estates, and banished. The falsity of this charge being revealed after the King's death, his successor restored Ferrers to his property and dignities. In token of his innocence, the King ordered that there should be added to the helm of the Ferrers crest an infant holding in its right hand a palm and in its left a scroll displaying the word *Innocentia*.[1] He also

[1] The Ferrero arms today carry three coroneted helmets, the centre one being the crest of Bernard Ferrers of Valencia, a cherub holding a palm with the motto *Innocentia* beneath.

accorded to the Ferrers family and its heirs in perpetuity, the office of Viceroy of the Kingdom of Valencia. The Ferrers line added to their own the name of Proxida, derived from one of their estates. The family bred a number of famous men through the centuries, among them two soldiers, Don Bartolomeo and Don Francesco Ferreri, who served the Emperor Charles V. Finding themselves with the Spanish forces under the Constable of Bourbon in the famous sack of Rome in 1527, they succeeded in saving the treasure in the Lateran Basilica from the terrible fury of the victorious invaders. For this act Pope Clement VII ordered that the great door of the Basilica should carry the coat-of-arms of Don Bartolomeo and Don Francesco. It was visible until the alterations made by Pope Innocent X. Prior to these events, two members of the Spanish Ferrers line settled in Italy at Mondovi and Asti; from this line descended the Ferreros of Alassio.

Mondovi is a little town in the Piedmont plain some thirty miles over the Alps from Alassio. Giacomo Ferrero appears to have been settled in Mondovi in the middle of the fourteenth century. He lived in a house with a portico on the piazza, and swore fealty to the Archbishop of Asti. Giacomo's great-grandson in 1441 was a member of the town council. He kept a bank, and was a cavalry captain in the service of the Duke of Savoy. The Ferreros were mayors of Mondovi. Giorgio Ferrero in the late fourteenth century allied the family with the cause of the Marquis of Montferrat against the powerful Galeazzo Visconti, 'The Viper of Milan'. Along with members of the Guelph nobility he favoured the rising House of Savoy and was present when the Council welcomed the Prince Amedeo of Archaia[1] and his barons, inviting him to accept the suzerainty of the town. Now well established,

[1] The Prince Amedeo of Archaia took his title from a principality created by the Crusaders in 1205 after the fall of the Greek Empire. The title came to the House of Savoy by the marriage of Filippo of Savoia with Isabella, daughter of Guillaume II de Villehardouin, whose father, Géoffroi, took part in the barbarous conquest and sack of Constantinople in 1204, and wrote the famous description of the Fourth Crusade, later founding the line of Princes of Archaia in the Morea. The principality was ceded by Isabella to the sovereign Angevins of Naples, who dominated meridional Greece, but the title was retained in the House of Savoy until 1418.

Rising from the seamen's chapel, the modern road, the watch-tower.

(Photo: Omniafoto—Torino.)

The ancient gate on the Roman road at Santa Croce.
(*Photo: Alterocca—Terni.*)

with honours descending upon them, they saw service in many fields; a gentleman-of-the-chamber to the King of France and field-marshal of the Italian troops in his service in 1568; a Knight of Rhodes who fought in its siege by the Turks in 1520; a governor of Barcelona; a President of the Senate of Nice and Grand Chancellor under the regent, Christina of France, in 1641; a Bishop of Alessandria, made Cardinal in 1729; governors of towns and castles, doctors, lawyers, priests, ambassadors, captains of Spanish galleys. So it runs.

Alas, it must be recorded that Gerolamo Ferrero was one of the fifteen hundred citizens of Mondovi who, at the call of the Duke Vittorio Amedeo II, went to massacre the Waldenses and drive more than four thousand of this martyred sect into exile. A son of the President of the Nice Senate, a mayor of Mondovi, and created Marquis of Ceva, he was condemned to death in 1681, along with his son. The reason is obscure, but they were declared innocent a year later.

There were, as in every family history, quarrels and scandals. The portrait gallery of historic houses never tells the whole story—the ancestors are mostly grouped in a pageant shouting Glory! Glory! Glory! The embezzlers, mistresses, bastards, roués, and lunatics are usually quietly dropped.[1] Domenico, a shipowner of Alassio, was disinherited for having accepted a too-large legacy left him by his mother. The Mondovi branch in the seventeenth century was shaken by Livia's conduct. She married, in 1619, Borno Tapparello. Twelve years later the Senate arrested Sergeant Meyrile for having abducted the lady from her husband's house on the pretext of conducting her to her mother's house in Mondovi. They had lived together for six months. When he was arrested, Livia hid in a barrel. The family chronicler stigmatized the lady as 'lacking in dis-

---

[1] I once visited an historic house whose eccentric owner had a habit, when conducting guests through the Long Gallery, of exercising an embarrassing candour. "That's the first Earl, he got his earldom by loaning his wife to King Charles. That's Philip, he was Secretary of War and embezzled a quarter of a million pounds through contracts. That's Countess Ann, a prostitute at heart. She accounts for our looseness. That's James, seventh Earl, a half-wit. He ended with a keeper. We've never recovered from him!" The late Duke of Berwick and Alba, an endearing host, showing the family portraits in his gallery at Madrid, on coming to that of the first duke, a natural son of James II and Arabella Churchill, Marlborough's sister, remarked, "We are all bastards!"

tinction'. She was divorced that same year. Obviously Livia got bored with Borno. But it was a grievous blow to the family, particularly to her distinguished nephews. One of them, Leandaro, was Governor of Barcelona; one Claudio, a Knight of Malta; one Gerolamo, the mayor of Mondovi; and one, Battista, in the service of the King of France, rose to be a Lieutenant-General in his army in Flanders and was created Marquis de St Laurent.

II

Let us follow the fortunes of the Alassian branch. Emanuele Ferrero, who had seen service in Spain, bought land in Alassio in 1548. He made a good marriage with Paola Doria of Oneglia, of the family that gave the great line of Dorias to Genoa. It was their son, Luca, who commanded a squadron of Charles V's navy. His son, Scipione, was captured by the Corsairs of Tripoli and died a slave there in 1645, leaving a widow in Alassio. No wonder his sister-in-law founded in Alassio the Company of the Trinity for the redemption of poor slaves. His brother, Domenico, died a very rich man, owner of many boats. His great-grandson, Emanuele, was created a marquis and married, in 1712, the daughter of Giovanni de Gubernatis, a Grand Chancellor, and of Paola di Ventimiglia, descended from the Counts of that ancient line. Little wonder that Emanuele's son, Luca Marcello, the second Marquis, incorporated the names de Gubernatis and Ventimiglia with Ferrero, whence the long inscription on the family's visiting-cards.

It was Luca's son, Onorato, who by marriage acquired, as mother-in-law, Countess Alfieri, a niece of the poet.[1] When the Ligurian Republic was created by Napoleon, Onorato was sent to Paris as its ambassador, where he opened an embassy in the Rue de Lille. He had already many friends there, among them General Berthier, later Maréchal Berthier, Prince of Neuchatel and Wagram, the Emperor's

---

[1] Onorato's brother, Emanuele, became a Franciscan monk. His thesis was publicly examined in 1773 in the monastery of San Francisco at Fiesole, known to many tourists for the magnificent view of Florence seen from its steps.

favourite. Onorato had met him at Nice in 1800. Like many
Italians, Onorato was buoyed up with hope by promises of
liberty for Italy made by Napoleon. The Emperor, Talleyrand assured him, liked him. He gave him the Legion of
Honour. We hear of Onorato having audiences with the
Emperor, Talleyrand, and Murat, and dining with the
Duke of Plaisance, an upstart financier named Lebrun,
who was promoted Treasurer of the Empire and Governor
of Liguria.

Onorato took his two sons, Luca Marcello and Emanuele,
with him to Paris on December 5th, 1802. He had an audience with the First Consul at the Tuileries. A fortnight later
he was received in private audience at St Cloud, when he
presented his elder son not yet seventeen. Out of this arose a
nomination for the boy to the Military School at Fontainebleau. Three years later, having completed his course,
Luca's father sought the influence of Berthier. This resulted
in Marcello being commissioned to the Regiment of 7th
Hussars and sent to join it at Maastricht.

Onorato himself was in favour, and cut a good figure in
the capital. It is interesting to learn what his establishment
cost him in Paris in 1807. He paid his valet 500 frs. (£20) a
year, a housemaid 600 frs., a maid 400 frs., a cook 500 frs.,
a house porter 600 frs. The family doctor had a flat rate of
600 frs. (£24) a year, with extras for long illnesses! Among
Onorato's ambassadorial tasks was that of seeking help from
the First Consul against the Barbary Corsairs who were
ravaging the Ligurian coast.[1] When he died in his house in
Paris in 1809, aged fifty-three, he had had the satisfaction of
seeing his sons launched on their military careers.

Onorato had been accompanied to Paris by his bachelor
brother Pietro. Let us glance in passing at this *bon viveur*. He
was bright-eyed, energetic, and intelligent. He was con-
versant with Paris and its life since he had first gone there,
tall, slim, youthful, and amorous in 1788. In September of
that year there is a clue to one little 'affair' in an account

---

[1] It would appear even then that the Swiss had a flourishing watch industry.
One pirate had gone off from Nice with a ship containing thirty-eight boxes of
Swiss watches. The cargo was recovered off Antibes.

from a Paris jeweller for the setting of fourteen diamonds, 240 carats, that he had provided for making a pair of bracelets. From Paris he crossed over to England to pay visits and hunt, a dashing young Italian, who ravished the ladies with his dark eyes and exquisite manners. He had had a forerunner there in his sister-in-law's uncle, Count Alfieri, the poet. Unlike him, he kept out of liaisons and duels.

We find Pietro a guest of Lord Pembroke's at Wilton, on November 19th, 1789, "among horses, guns, dogs, books". He returned from London with souvenirs, to be seen in the Palazzo Ferrero today—Chippendale furniture, walking-sticks, pistols, and gold-plated door fittings; these last he placed on the doors of his own suite in the family home. Here he lived, lively, kind, dabbling a little in politics, a member of the Council, a Senator, and head of the Province of Albenga. He came back from Paris after the fall of Napoleon, and divided his time between Alassio, Genoa, and Turin, where he was a popular man about town. But, above all, he was the bachelor-uncle in a growing family, and often as such he put his hand deep in his pocket for the education of nephews and nieces, and for an impecunious married sister.

Onorato's two sons, dashing youths of twenty-two and twenty-three, were avid for glory. The world may never again see the like of Napoleon's young officers. Elegant, perfumed dandies, beloved in the boudoirs, they died gallantly on the battlefields, maintaining the tradition of *beau sabreur*. In Italy, Austria, Germany, Spain, Poland, Lithuania, Russia, they fell in a welter of blood, or, luckier, became marshals and princes of the Empire.

Marcello at once distinguished himself by his valour, and at twenty-four received the Legion of Honour. He rose in fortune, as did many of those who followed Napoleon's star. In 1810, after the annexation of Oldenburg, a large part of the Kingdom of Westphalia, the Grand Duchy of Berg, East Friedland, and the Hanseatic cities, he shared in the general distribution of estates made by the Emperor to his officers. Marcello received an estate near Hanover, from which he was to draw an annuity of four thousand lire (about £200). It was to return to the crown in the event of his having no heirs. He became aide-de-camp to His Imperial Highness the Prince of Neuchatel and Wagram, otherwise Field-Marshal Berthier. One of his favourites and confidants, Berthier sent him into Warsaw to be fitted for a new uniform. "The pelisse is black, the dolman white, the trousers red. I have dined with Talleyrand who spoke of father," he recorded jubilantly.

Marcello was created Baron of the Empire and promoted captain at twenty-five. In that year Napoleon divorced Josephine, and with the birth of the little King of Rome the following year, he was at the summit of his power. His followers, created kings, princes, and dukes, and enriched with the loot of conquered kingdoms, basked in the Emperor's glory. Disaster came with the year 1812. Wellington checked the French at Salamanca, and Napoleon embarked on war with Russia. In May that year the French Court was magnificently established at Dresden with a multitude of ministers, diplomats, and courtiers. The Emperor and Empress of Austria, and Frederick of Prussia, made visits, almost by compulsion. In the summer months of 1812 the march towards Moscow began.

At the end of May, four days before the Emperor left Dresden, the two young officers joined their regiments. Baron Marcello Ferrero, now a captain of the 7th Hussar Regiment, took charge of the 6th Company. His brother Emanuele joined his regiment as a captain of the Dragoons. On May 26th Marcello was at Grathen. He kept a brief diary. "The misery among the inhabitants is extreme," he wrote on June 1st. "With my company I have visited several villages and found the peasants cutting grass, their only food for a month." On June 9th Ferrero was in Friedland, where he saw the battlefield of 1807. On the 24th, with the Grand Army, he crossed the Niemen, in a great storm, at Kaunas. On the 26th, with 20,000 cavalry under Murat, 70,000 infantry under Davout, and 36,000 of his Guards, Napoleon decided to march on Vilno. All seemed to be going well, according to Ferrero's diary. "We are marching on Vilno and we have seen the Emperor." On the 28th he records, "I have mounted my first Grand Guard, six leagues from Vilno.

It has rained all the night, but we had a good dinner thanks to some neighbours." The note is not so cheerful on July 1st. "It is always the same story, march, march, march, always bad and never a battle. It is frightful to go on through such an awful country, pillaged by the Russians, who have committed horrors. There are no inhabitants visible. We arrived at a beautiful château with neither doors nor windows left. Everything had been destroyed. The misery is frightful and terrible to witness."

The Russians in retreat had left a ruin behind them. As Barclay de Tolly withdrew, Napoleon's army marched into a desert. The soldiers became desperate. Thirty thousand men, Bavarians, Württembergers, Italians, Hanseats, Spaniards, French, deserting the ranks, pillaged the abandoned carriages and châteaux of the Lithuanian gentry. What had been missed in the passage of the Cossacks was destroyed by the enraged deserters. The ruin was total. But the great cry of generals, officers, and men alike was, "Where are the Russians—have we to chase them into the deserts of Siberia?"

On July 9th, a new disaster threatened the young captain and his fellow officers. "I am ill with fever and dysentery, due, the doctor tells me, to ten days of fatigue and bad living." Diarrhœa came from a surfeit of pork, the only meat available. At last, on July 16th, they encountered the Cossacks on the banks of the Dvina. Polotsk was memorable for "a good Pole who has given us wine and white bread". On the 21st they marched all night and found the enemy across the Dvina. It was in force. "*Notre situation n'était pas des plus gaies.*" On the 25th Ferrero recorded, "We have fought all day and thank God I am safe. It is the second time I have seen the enemy."

Napoleon was wholly frustrated. He could not bring the Russians to battle. On July 26th, Murat and Ney moved in force on Ostrowno and succeeded in encountering the flank of the Russian army. It was here, in battle, that Marcello Ferrero was struck down by a cannon-ball that carried away his left leg at nine in the morning of July 26th. The campaign in Russia was at an end for him. He was carried to a château, where Murat's surgeon amputated the injured limb. Four days later he was taken to Vitebsk, where his comrades came to bid him farewell. Napoleon sent his surgeon Ivan to inquire after him, and Berthier called on him and brought him sheets for his bed. He remained at Vitebsk seven weeks in the care of Murat's doctor. Marshal Berthier paid a second visit, displaying much affection for this charming young captain. Here the younger brother, Emanuele, the Dragoon captain, came to see him. It was the last time the brothers saw each other. Emanuele went on in to Russia, and was killed in the crossing of the Berezina in the terrible retreat of the Emperor's army.

During his convalescence Marcello was most hospitably entertained at the château of the Polish Countess Sevrinska. "She never forgot anything, she was wonderful to me. How kindly this good family has treated me! I shall keep them in eternal remembrance," he recorded on departure. The long homeward journey to Paris began. He suffered constant pain for seven weeks, with all the jolting and inconvenience of the journey by road in a hired carriage. By the middle of October he was out of pain, his leg was healed, he was in good health. Someone awaited him.

There is a glimpse of him at this time, and of the arenas of war and love, in the *Journal* of Maréchal de Castellane:

Paris, June 10, 1813:
"I have seen Ferrero with his wooden leg. Last winter he took care of Madame L. Berthier, to save the honour of General L., sent Ferrero as captain to the 7th Huzzars— where he lost his leg! Madame L. still has the good spirit to always treat Ferrero well when she meets him, despite his accident. M. de Septeuil, another A.D.C. of Berthier's, was sent to Spain for two years—for not having paid attention to Princess Pauline Borghese (Bonaparte) and for remaining faithful to his mistress, Madame de B.—where he had his thigh carried away! M. de Canouville was sent to the 2nd Chasseurs, following his liaison with Princess Pauline—and was killed at Moscow. Truly, the affairs of the Aides-de-Camp of Berthier turn out badly!"

So thus ended the great adventure, with a brother and a leg lost in the wilds of Russia, but honour retained. With the fall of Napoleon and his abdication, Italy was in the melting-pot again. The estate and annuity in Hanover went the way of all the puppet kingdoms, titles, and wealth with which Napoleon had rewarded his officers. In December 1813, Marcello wrote from Alassio to Berthier, asking for the continuation of his pay and referring to "*mon pénible état, après neuf années de service*".

For the young soldier much remained. No longer a Baron of the vanished empire, he came home to his patrimony, the large palazzo in the heart of tranquil Alassio, where his forefathers had dwelt. He had inherited, along with the family property, the title of *Marchese*. He received the Cross of the military Order of Savoy, and he married the daughter of Count Panissera. One imagines him sitting under the great mulberry tree in the garden of the palazzo, telling the story of his days with Napoleon to his six children, of whom two boys saw service in the Crimea. Then, aged sixty-one, he was buried, fittingly in the church of San Vincenzo Ferreri just outside the city gate, within a few yards of his home. Over a century has passed since he died, and yet how near he was, how much alive he seemed as I sat in the Palazzo Ferrero, while my host showed me the faded little campaign diary his grandfather had kept.

The light had faded before I left, and, as I wished to see the family portraits, the Marchese lit a candelabra and we toured the salons. The walls of the great hall were covered with ancestors, the cardinals, priests, cavaliers, Grand Chancellors, with Paola Doria and Marcello the one-legged, who loomed in the wavering candlelight that glinted on men in armour carrying pikes. In the great salon a fresco on the ceiling, of Phæton falling from his chariot, gave me the date of this part of the palazzo, 1648.[1] In another salon, green and gilt with crystal panels and a massive Venetian glass

---

[1] Phæton, son of Helios, borrowed his father's chariot of the Sun. Unable to control the horses he set the world on fire by going off the sun's course, whereupon Zeus killed him with a thunderbolt. He fell into the Eridanus (the Po River), and his mourning sisters were turned into poplar trees. This Piedmont locale probably accounts for the fresco on the Grimaldi and Ferrero ceilings.

chandelier, we found the young Marcello's three brothers, Emanuele, the captain of Dragoons lost in Russia, Giacchino, a major-general in the King of Sardinia's army, who lived to be eighty, and Pietro, a bachelor who lived in Turin and London. Here they were, all young, bright-eyed lads. The eighteenth-century artist had cleverly graduated their oval portraits to indicate the senior, younger, and youngest brothers. On the walls were portraits by Renaud. Six panels over the door were of delicate ladies who had married into the family, including Grimaldi,[1] Pallavicini, de Gubernatis. There was a smaller salon whose four walls were hung with Gobelin tapestries of pastoral scenes. Ancestor on ancestor on ancestor, in perukes, sashed, starred with orders, they looked at us in the flickering candlelight.

And then, in a bedroom, the most alluring of all the paintings, a large canvas dated 1764, with a stylish lady, aloof, with powdered white hair à la Pompadour, and white satin corsage in the fashion of the eighteenth century. In her delicate left hand she held a small red flower. By her knee stood a little boy of about five, with alert face, bright eyes, and small hands that ceremoniously pointed to his mother's flower. He was dressed in a cerise frock coat with deep buttoned cuffs; he might have been a little girl but for his young masculine head and hair. This was the infant Count

---

[1] On March 5th, 1740, Luca Marcello Ferrero married Maria Grimaldi at Nice. There would seem to have been an earlier connection between the two families. The Ferrero ceiling is a copy of that in the castle of the Grimaldi at Cagnes, near Nice, painted in 1624 by Giovanni Carlone (1592–1677). The castle was built in 1309 by Rainier Grimaldi, Prince of Monaco and Admiral of France.

The Grimaldi, an illustrious Genoese family, were Seigneurs, then Princes of Monaco from A.D. 980 until the middle of the fourteenth century. They held high office in the Genoese Republic, and with the Fieschi were leaders of the Guelph faction. The Monaco line died out in 1731, when the principality passed to the House of Matignon which took the name of Grimaldi. As Dukes of Valentinois, a title once held by Cæsar Borgia, they were peers of France. In 1815 Monaco fell under the protection of the King of Sardinia, and in 1848 Charles Albert detached Mentone and Roquebrune from the principality. The Genoese line of the Grimaldi ended in England on the death at St Albans, February 16th, 1944, of Mr Ernest George Grimaldi, automobile salesman, aged 67. Known as plain Mr Grimaldi, he was twelfth Marquis Grimaldi, the last of his line. The family had fled to England after the French captured Genoa in 1685, and had sustained life there in very humble rôles. The eighth marquis was an ostler, the ninth a cabinet-maker, the tenth an upholsterer, the eleventh a butcher.

Vittorio Alfieri, the dueller in the Green Park, the lover of
the Young Pretender's abused wife, the Countess of Albany,
the poet-dramatist who was the glory of Italian eighteenth-
century literature. It was a composition, gay, tender, and
wholly enchanting. The Grand Chancellor of Savoy, in all
his imposing robes, orders, and full-bottomed wig, did not
command the eye as this festive portrait of mother and son.

The gallery of ancestors still grows. There had arrived that
day from London a portrait of Luca, the heir of the house of
Ferrero, painted by James Gunn, R.A. I imagined a hundred
eyes looking down from their old gilt frames, examining
critically this new-comer with the years in hand and the story
unfinished.

We came at last to another portrait of the campaigner with
Napoleon, to Marcello Luca.

"What was the end of his legend?" I asked the Marchese.

"Marriage, children, the management of affairs, no
disturbing ambitions after the first great adventure."

"A happy life?"

"Yes, a beautiful wife he was deeply in love with—but
once almost a tragedy, which I've only just stumbled upon,"
said the Marchese, with twinkling eyes that have looked on
life for eighty-four years. "During the last war, to occupy myself in that trying time, I started to tidy up the family
papers—boxes and boxes of them! One day I was surprised
to come upon a note that unfolded a singular incident in
Marcello's life. I said he had a beautiful wife, Maria Teresa.
She was the daughter of Count Panissera, who had married
the lovely Amelia di Wurmbrand, a Viennese beauty, so
looks ran in her family. Naturally she attracted much
attention. One evening at a party in Turin, where the company became very gay following games and a liberal helping
of champagne, Marcello, sitting on a sofa at the side of his
wife, beckoned a friend, Signor Pollen, to come over and
keep the Marchesa company. Pollen eagerly crossed the
floor, but Marcello not rising in time to vacate his place,
Pollen stumbled over his legs and tried to save himself by
holding on to the back of the sofa. In attempting this he seems
inadvertently to have touched the Marchesa. She jumped

up with a little scream. Marcello at once took the rôle of an offended husband, pushed Pollen roughly aside, and then strode away from him across the room. Pollen rose, pale with anger, and went over to Marcello, demanding in a lively voice what he was so angry about. "Haven't I every reason to be, considering your conduct?" said Marcello. "I am at your service!" said Pollen shortly, and walked away. This incident, observed by all, created an icy silence for a few moments. Then the party appeared to go on as usual. But poor Signora Pollen, affrighted by the thought of the impending duel, burst into tears and had to be taken out of the room by her brother-in-law. Pollen remained behind, still belligerent, but Marcello avoided him. Thereupon, Cavour, who was present, appealed to by Pollen, who vowed he had intended no affront in accidentally touching the Marchesa, volunteered to try to make peace. Cavour went at once to Marcello's house, convinced him that the whole thing had been an accident, and that Pollen was sorry for his hasty challenge. To Marcello he pointed out that any duel would create a scandal that could in no way benefit either of the parties. Marcello expressed his satisfaction with the explanation and considered the incident closed. "I suppose," said the Marchese, smiling, "my grandfather, 'touchy' about his beautiful wife, would have fought the duel, one-legged as he was, if Cavour hadn't shown a little of his famous gift for diplomacy. Anyway, we know Marcello and his lovely Teresa had six children and lived happily together all their lives."

My host insisted on escorting me down the long flight of black marble steps from the *piano nobile* to the ground floor. In my hand I carried the seven-pound volume of the history of the Ferreros. Outside the palazzo gates the hundred lights of Alassio's summer cafés shone in the warm evening. Two wild youths in a murderous racing-car deafened my ears. It seemed a swift transition from the past to the present.

CHAPTER TEN

THEY CAME TO A CASTLE

I

EVERY morning when I get up and throw back my shutters I see beyond the town, in the far corner of the bay, shining twin belfries and a cluster of roofs. It is Laigueglia, the fishing village that nestles by Capo Mele. The place is as old as Alassio, and being less than two miles distant along the sands, its history has always been closely connected and interwoven with that of its big brother. Laigueglia is still today what Alassio was fifty years ago. It will not retain its primitive charm much longer. Already it has thrown out a lamplit promenade, and on its outskirts the concrete apartment houses are rapidly rising. The little village itself is intact, with its ancient narrow highway, its low arches spanning the streets. Old sailors stand around on the jetty. The fishing-boats, whose flares during the sardine fishing at night jewel the bay and provide such an enchanting vista from my terrace, are drawn high up on the beach during the day. One has to step carefully over the long brown nets spread out for repairs along the quay. It is a place of fantastic houses with springing arches, alcoves, outside staircases, odd windows at odd angles, a conglomeration of roofs, thick walls, porticoes, galleries, terraces, and small piazzas, all colour-washed in green, ochre, venetian red, blue, and pink. The long main street blazes with fish- and fruit-stalls. Off the street there are blinding vistas of the sea at the end of little arched tunnels formed by massive masonry carrying tall, shuttered houses.

There is a quietude in Laigueglia unknown to Alassio. One enters it through the old arched gateway. The motor-buses, the motor-cycles, and the trains, representing the twentieth century, follow a new road behind the town. Across the adjacent railway stands the church. One reaches this amazing baroque edifice by diving through an arch under the line. The size of the church is staggering. It would seem as if the whole of Laigueglia could assemble in one of the aisles. Whence came all the money to build these glorious twin belfries with majolica-tiled domes? The answer is that Laigueglia was once highly prosperous with coral fishing, then, like Alassio and Cervo along the coast, ruin fell upon it on that disastrous day in 1720 when a tempest off the Sardinian coast sank thirty boats and drowned five hundred mariners. Laigueglia had always been the breeding-ground of brave sailors, who were recruited for the Genoese navy and saw many sea fights. Steam struck a blow at its sailing vessels; and as late as 1807 there were thirty oil presses all doing a good export trade, which has vanished.

Napoleon was annoyed with many of the low arches spanning the main street. They interfered with his transport. A man on horseback was in danger of being decapitated. Napoleon peremptorily ordered some of the arches to be demolished, despite the risk of the houses collapsing. But neither Napoleon nor earthquakes, nor modern pensions and apartment houses, have destroyed the ancient charm of this old place. It cannot have altered much—electric light, railway, and motor-buses apart—since 1191, when the fief of this place was granted by the Republic of Genoa to three of her vassals, one Gandolfo di Tirasso from Alassio and two from Albenga, in equal shares.

Behind Laigueglia rises the long promontory that ends at Capo Mele, surmounted by a signal station at a height of 750 feet. From my windows at night I look on this great black wall, with Laigueglia sparkling at its base and the stars gemlike above the rim. The road from Ventimiglia and France comes around the bend where the cliff face has been notched to make this highway. There is a brief flash from the headlights of cars rounding this point before they go down the slope to Laigueglia and the bay of Alassio. For over a year, at breakfast-time on my terrace and at dinner in the last evening light as the sky glows rosily above this black promontory, I felt impelled to make an ascent from Laigueglia and walk along the great ridge. I was told that on the other side I should see the valley of Andorra and find there an ancient castle and a Roman bridge.

There was a spring morning of such brilliant clarity that, with the sun already risen from the sea at seven o'clock, I decided to make the excursion. I set forth to Laigueglia. At nine o'clock I was well up the steep hill behind it, following an ancient mule-track out of the town. It proved to be yet another section of the old Roman road. Before the steep cliff face had been notched to carry the new highway, all travellers from the time of Marc Antony had crossed the promontory at a point called Colla Micheri, crowned by a village of that name.

All the way up the track I kept pausing to look down over the great bay, with Alassio diminutive below and an ever-extending vista that embraced the far promontory in whose sweep lay Genoa, and, fainter on the horizon, the Carrara mountains. Looking straight out seawards, I became aware of something on the dark blue horizon that was more than a cloud. It held its shape too long to be of such a transient substance. I asked a man coming down the track with a heavily burdened donkey whether what I saw on the sea's horizon was a cloud or an island. "It's Corsica," he said.

In three-quarters of an hour, having passed the ruinous gateway of an old princely villa, flanked with cypresses, I stepped into the small piazza of a silent village. The road continued under a low arch built over with houses, going down towards the valley shining through this keyhole vista. The place was utterly dead. Around me the old houses were windowless. Some of the roofs had collapsed. In the walls there were decaying doors that had not swung on their hinges for a century. I stood still in the middle of the little piazza. Its high rectangular houses gave it a fortress-like air. Then, high up in the dark face of the wall rising above the arch, I saw an open window. In it sat an old crone. She was so old and gnarled that she looked as if she had forgotten to die. Was she the last inhabitant? She watched me warily from her eyrie.

"Childe Roland to the dark tower came," I murmured, and then shouted up to that effigy of embodied time.

"*Per favore*, where is this?"

"Colla Micheri."

"Does anyone live here now?"

"Five families, *signore*."

"How many houses?"

"Thirty."

"How many in ruins?"

"Twenty-five."

"What do you all do here?" I asked.

The old crone gave me a gummy smile over a geranium-pot.

"We wait, *signore*," she croaked, and crossed herself. I had no need to ask her for whom she waited.

"How long has it been deserted?" I called.

"Since the earthquake destroyed it."

"The earthquake! The earthquake in 1887?"

"*Si, signore*. I saw it. I was married the day before—there, and we had nowhere to sleep."

"May I ask how old you are?"

"Eighty-seven."

"Have you lived here all your life?"

"*Si, signore*; except for one year. I went to Genoa in service when I was thirteen. I cried so much they sent me home."

"Thank you. Do you live alone?"

"No, with a granddaughter."

On what and how do they live, I wondered, but I refrained from further questioning. I wished the old lady *Buon giorno*. I looked around the square and saw for the first time a little church. It was so small and plain, a blank wall with a door, under a single gable surmounted by a small arch in which hung a bell, that it had been easy to miss it. It was shut up. I wondered when last a priest had crossed the threshold. And then I saw something that made me catch my breath. Over the door was a tablet with an inscription. I read it, and then I carefully copied it, my hand shaking with excitement. Italy is like that. You turn a corner by some decaying building and suddenly four or five hundred years of history are unrolled before you, like a carpet in a store. I stood quite still and let the inscription sink into my consciousness.

"Here came on February 14th, 1814, on his way to Rome, His Holiness Pope Pius VII, and blessed the people," I read.

The old woman high up in the window watched me. Then she broke the silence.

"My grandmother was blessed by the Holy Father when he came here," she said.

It was a simple inscription, but what an astounding story lay behind it of the Corsican adventurer who raised himself to a throne and made a sick Pope journey from Rome in order to officiate at his coronation in Notre-Dame. Pius VII could have had few illusions about Napoleon, despite the fact that, in 1801, he had restored the banished Church in France by a Concordat made with the Papacy. The Pope's predecessor, Pius VI, had had his provinces, Ancona, Bologna, and Ferrara, seized by Napoleon in the Treaty of Tolentino. He had also been made to pay an indemnity of one million and a quarter sterling. Later, Berthier had marched on Rome, seized the Castel Sant' Angelo, and called upon the Pope, by Napoleon's orders, to renounce his temporal sovereignty. On his refusal the Pope was seized, hustled to Siena, then to Florence, and afterwards to Valence on the Rhône, where he died worn out by age and grief at eighty-two.

Pius VII, a saintly man, had few illusions, therefore, about Napoleon, although he had restored the states filched from Pius VI. He obeyed the summons to Paris to perform the Emperor's coronation service. The departure of a cavalcade of six cardinals, ten bishops, five abbots, a surgeon, five secretaries, two valets, some hundred and eight persons in all, in three convoys of thirty coaches and one hundred and thirty horses, created consternation among the people of Rome. They had seen the former Pope taken into exile and go to his death.

The journey was long and arduous in the November days. Through Florence, Parma, and Turin rattled the coaches and wagons. Over the Mont Cenis they just missed the winter snows, for the weather was bitter. Napoleon contrived

The dead piazza at Colla Micheri; the chapel on the right where Pius VII, home from exile, blessed the people.

The Municipal Palace, the campanile and baptistry of Albenga,
13th-15th century.

(Photo: Instituto di Studi Liguri.)

an insult to His Holiness when the convoy neared Fontainebleau. Instead of meeting it ceremonially, Napoleon chose
to come upon it casually while out hunting. He meant to
show thus the hand of the master. When, finally, the Pope
was housed in a wing of the Tuileries, the Emperor was
somewhat dismayed by the warmth of the welcome accorded
to the Holy Father in Paris.

To appease his colossal vanity and impress the world,
Napoleon's first idea was to claim the succession of Charlemagne who, a thousand years earlier, had been crowned
'Emperor of the Romans'. He went so far as to put up a
column modelled on Trajan's in the Place Vendôme, and
order a statue of Charlemagne to crown it. When the statue
was disclosed it proved to be not Charlemagne but Napoleon,
attired in classical dress à la Roman Emperor! The next idea
was a crowning and anointing by the Pope, a slap in the face
for the arrogant Bourbons, and for the Comte de Provence,
who claimed the throne as Louis XVIII and stubbornly
refused Napoleon's invitation to abdicate. Napoleon claimed
that he held his throne by the will of the people, and now he
would hold it also by the blessing of the Church, which he
had in his hand.

Pius VII, in fear, tact, and the hope of gaining some ad-
vantage for the disestablished Church in France, made the
journey to Paris. A difficulty arose there. To his horror it was
disclosed that Napoleon's wedding to a divorcée had never
been blessed by the Church. Napoleon had hoped to keep
this fact dark, but Josephine had blurted out the truth to
Cardinal Caprara, who informed the Pope. Horrified to
learn that the Emperor was living in sin with Josephine, he
refused to perform the coronation ceremony unless a Church
marriage removed their sinful state. So, on the afternoon
before the great ceremony in Notre-Dame, uncle Cardinal
Fesch privately performed the marriage rite for the royal pair.

Pius VII had come to Paris to anoint and crown the
Emperor. This seemed like giving too much power into the
hands of the Church. Napoleon declared he would himself
place the crown on his head. The Pope agreed to this re-
vision. There were more objections. Napoleon informed the

Pope that he would not repeat the second part of the coronation oath, acknowledging the dependence of the Emperor on the Pope; neither would he be publicly made a good Catholic by taking part in the Mass which concluded the coronation ceremony. The Pope, for his part, refused to be present during the pronouncement of the civil oath which recognized the State's tolerance of Protestantism. With these reservations on either side, the ornate ceremony took place in Notre-Dame.

David, commissioned to commemorate the event on a huge canvas thirty feet by nineteen, made a false picture. It was a masterpiece with over two hundred portraits in it. Pius VII was placed a little behind the Emperor. A shaft of sunlight was imported to fall upon the scene at the august moment of the coronation, thereby implying heavenly endorsement. Napoleon was increased in height from his diminutive five feet two inches, and Josephine was given a girlish figure to disguise the spread of forty-one years. With all this faking, it was the Pope who captured the canvas. David was deeply impressed by the sacred majesty of the Holy Father and reflected this in his canvas. He caught the simplicity and piety of this humble man amidst all the pomp and pretentious opportuning of a crowd of adventurers. The Emperor insisted on an alteration. Pius had been depicted with his hand on his knee. Napoleon instructed David to raise the Pope's hand as if in the act of blessing Josephine. "The Pope didn't come all the way to Paris to do nothing," he commented. So Josephine goes down through history as being blessed by the Pope. It is not unfitting. She was probably the best character among the riff-raff, uniformed and decorated, on this first Sunday in December 1804.

Pius VII stayed on in Paris for three months. He was astonished by his reception in the bloody capital of the Revolution, formally vowed to atheism. He was received everywhere with deference and enthusiasm. His graciousness and simple piety captivated the French. Crowds thronged the churches and came to Mass. Rings and rosaries were offered for blessing. He made a wonderful riposte to one young man who showed open hostility. "Monsieur, you have nothing to fear. No one was ever the worse for an old man's blessing." And when on the eve of his departure Fouché asked him in what state he found France, he replied that he had everywhere observed a people on its knees.

He could not foresee that within six months of his return to Rome Napoleon's troops would again seize Ancona, and, within four years, the whole of the Papal States, and make him a prisoner, arrested in the dead of night. With scaling ladders French troops forced their way into the Quirinal, and in half an hour the Pope was being hustled into a carriage and through the silent streets of Rome on his way to exile. He had no change of clothes, one companion, and only twenty-two *sous* in his pocket. A delicate old man of seventy, he was rattled over shocking roads, slept in wayside inns, suffered from dysentery, bad food, and the heat. He must have thought of his predecessor Pius VI, carried by force over the Alps into France, ten years earlier, where he had perished from the arduous journey. He must have recalled the cardinal who accompanied him on his journey to Paris and had died exhausted in Lyons. Now he, in turn, was hustled over the Alps to Grenoble, then to Avignon, then along the Riviera to Savona. Here, living in austerity, he was deprived of secretaries, of writing-paper, and ink. He revealed a stout dignity. He refused to drive out, or to receive money. He washed his own clothes and sewed on his own buttons, living like a monk in seclusion and prayer. He flatly refused all the overtures of Napoleon by which he sought to deprive the Church of its sovereignty. The whole world, horrified, watched the old saint's sufferings. At last Napoleon seemed defeated by his benign adversary. He had him brought to Fontainebleau. Pius started out from Savona at midnight on June 9th, 1812, in a carriage with hooded lights, muffled wheels, and with the white mules of the papal cortège blackened and unshod. They went over Mont Cenis, where the Pope became so ill that the doctor called a halt. He was given the *viaticum*, recovered somewhat, and was carried, prostrate, overland to Fontainebleau. He was back in his old quarters, no longer an honoured guest for a coronation but a prisoner.

Meanwhile the finger of doom drew towards the Emperor. At Moscow he suffered a reverse. The Russian snows engulfed his army. He came back to Paris, as he had never before come, a defeated man. He now tackled his prisoner and a long, wearying duel ensued. Finally, lonely, exhausted, worked upon by a combination of charm, cajolery, and threats, the Pope conceded and recognized the annexation of the Papal States to the Empire. Twenty-four hours later he recanted, but Napoleon suppressed the recantation, increased the ardours of imprisonment, and hurried off to retrieve his fortunes at Leipzig. But defeat engulfed him again. The game was up. He gave orders on January 21st, 1814, for the Pope to be released and sent back to Rome. It was ironical that while Napoleon, a prisoner, sat huddled in the carriage conveying him through Provence to exile in Elba, not daring to wear his uniform, thereby earning his sister Pauline's bitter reproaches, the Pope was travelling south by the same route, fêted everywhere by enthusiastic crowds. And thus on the morning of February 14th, 1814, the papal cortège wound up from the valley of Andorra to the village of Colla Micheri at the head of the pass to Laigueglia, on the route to Rome, where the benign old Pope paused on the threshold of the village church, and blessed the people on their knees in the little piazza.

II

After I had copied the inscription on the church a shaft of sunlight fell upon an old sundial painted on the end of a house. It looked like early seventeenth-century work. Above it I could just discern a faint hand-painted motto—

> *Vuoi saper l'ora ch'è? Te'l dirò subito—*
> *È l'ora d'operar da uomo onesto.*

> You wish to know what time it is? I'll tell you—
> It's the hour of work for an honest man.

It was a half-dial that ingeniously marked the hours from 6 a.m. to 6 p.m. It would seem, therefore, following the admonitory motto, that a good working day for an honest man ran from 6 a.m. to 6 p.m.! The sundial still records the hours. It pointed to 11 a.m. when I observed it, and checking the time by my watch it was absolutely accurate. While I was doing this a native observed me, thinking that I was struggling to read the time on the dial. "It's no good, signore," he said with a disparaging wave of his hand towards the sundial, and, proudly tapping a clumsy wrist-watch he wore, added—"This is a good watch! It's eleven o'clock." He would have thought me mad had I told him that I would exchange a hundred such watches for that lovely old sundial. How strange to surmise that it was there, counting the hours, when Pius VII may have looked up at it.

The old woman in the tower observed me wonderingly. I wished her 'Good morning' and went down under the arch that forms the gateway of the village. Everywhere the need of defence had dictated the shape of this place. Through the arch the cobbled road fell sharply, amid neglected olive groves, to the valley of Andorra. The view was enchanting, a wide valley with a river, gay with oleanders in bloom, a background of mountains, and a well-cultivated plain. In the near distance there was a hill crowned by an ancient castle, one of those romantic settings familiar in the Italian hills. What was its name, what was its history, I wondered? I set off down the steep track towards the battlemented stronghold. As I drew nearer I saw it was a vast ruin, with a church, a strong high tower, with Ghibelline battlements crowning it, and a village at all levels enclosed within a strong wall. As I went down the steep track I was suddenly confronted by a church of a beauty and age that crowned with perfection this ravishing scene. There was an old man sitting by the tower guarding a herd of kids. Until I saw him the place seemed utterly deserted, so deserted and silent with its great gaunt walls and its lovely romanesque church that I had the feeling that, after a lapse of six hundred years, I had stumbled on a village where life had ceased, following some swift catastrophe. There were houses, piled high up on each other, but not a door or window was open, not a face seen nor a voice heard.

The old goat-herd was very deaf. I caught him in the act of reading a battered paper-covered book, *The Life of Pius IX*. I bellowed at him, making an outrageous noise in that deathlike silence. "What is the name of the place?" I asked. "Castello d'Andora," he said. I pointed to the church and asked him about it. It was in such excellent preservation that it seemed almost new. It was a fine example of late romanesque architecture. The rounded arch of the beautiful main doorway had four recessed pillars supporting it. There was a circular window above, with the glass broken, the work obviously of stone-throwing boys. At the east end there were three apses. The whole of the exterior was made lively with flat arcading of fourteenth-century workmanship. I had observed, when descending from the hill, that a new roof had been made. The church had signs of recent care. What was this magnificent building, the size of a small abbey, all shut up, doing here on this deserted hill? There must have been, in ages past, a large community living in this silent village to support such a spectacular church.

The old goat-herd, Niccolò, told me it was the Church of St James and St Philip. I asked him if it was used. "On the Saints' Day," he replied. I asked him when that was. "On the first of May—then there is a Mass and the Madonna makes a *giro* of the *città*."

I was entranced by the idea that the Madonna came out and made a tour of the 'city'. I thanked him and proceeded to inspect the *città*. It was a fairy-tale place with everything requisite to the stronghold of a bold bad baron, a beautiful princess, and a valorous knight. There was a cavern suitable for the abode of a fire-breathing dragon.

I inspected the tower first. It was of massive strength, a guard tower with a Ghibelline fish-tail parapet. There was an arched gateway under it, the obvious entrance to the castle. On one of the walls there were faint remains of a fourteenth-century fresco of the Sienese school. The castle was a ruin, massive, a polygon in shape. It had once been a formidable stronghold. Now the grass grew in its courtyards and unroofed chambers. Behind it, clustered on the steep hill, lay the *città*. It was built within the sturdy walls. A fortified gatehouse commanded the road that came up out of the valley. There was one large villa that had established itself on part of the massive ramparts. Its terraced garden suggested that it was inhabited. By an old sunburnt door in the high wall I came upon a human being, an old woman carrying a brass urn of water on her head. In reply to my questions she told me that about forty persons lived in Castello d'Andora.

"But where are they?" I asked.

"*La siesta, signore,*" she replied.

Of course! It was two o'clock. Full of spaghetti and wine, the village was fast asleep, including the dragon. Only mad Englishmen clambered about in the midday sun.

"It is a very old place?" I observed.

"Euh—euh—euh!" she exclaimed, flapping a hand in the manner in which Italians express the inexpressible. "Julius Cæsar and Dante once lived in the castle."

I loved the juxtaposition. I had a vision of Julius Cæsar and Dante, with possibly Cleopatra and Beatrice for companions, watching the sunset from the ramparts. It was quite possible that they had both been here in Castello d'Andora. It stood by the ancient Roman way, but this castle had never echoed to Cæsar's footsteps; to Dante's possibly, it was of his time.

I got home that evening, going back over the Colla, down to Laigueglia and along the beach, in a state of excitement. In the next three days I unearthed a little of the history of this ancient place. It had belonged to one of the powerful Marquises of Clavesana whose name marches with the medieval history of this coast. One of them sold the castle in 1252 to Genoa for 8,000 lire. It became another of a hundred strongholds by which Genoa held Liguria in subjection, but only by fierce warfare among the contending factions. It was in the age when northern Italy was riven by the fanatical feud between the Guelphs and the Ghibellines, the feud that ruined Florence and sent Dante into exile. Genoa belonged to the Guelph faction, temporarily dominant, which exiled the Ghibellines. Some of these took refuge in Albenga. In one of the onslaughts on the castle, held by the Genoese Guelphs, the powerful Bishop of Albenga,

Emanuele, of the great Spinola house of Genoa, came with reinforcements to join his fellow Ghibellines who were besieging the castle. He came by sea, but on landing and marching from the shore he ran into a Guelph ambush and fell with his horse in the conflict. What feuds, what fury, what bloodshed and anarchy had possessed this quiet valley of olive groves and peaches, where the mountain torrent trickles in summer over its stony bed! One may cross the Merula by the lovely old Roman bridge.

I waited ten days, and then, on the afternoon of May 1st, I set off for Castello d'Andora. I had learned that the church would be open for a service at four o'clock in celebration of the Saints' Day. May 1st is the festival of St James and St Philip in the Christian calendar. There is some doubt about the identity of St James. He was not James the Elder, brother of John, one of the twelve apostles, who after a presumed journey to Compostela returned to Judea and was beheaded by Herod Agrippa. Our Saint of the festival is James the Minor, the legendary brother of Jesus, who became the first Bishop of Jerusalem. His emblem is a club, supposed to have been used in his martyrdom when he was thrown from the Temple. Hegesippus wrote that St James prayed unceasingly for his people "inasmuch that his knees became hard and brawny like those of a camel by reason of his continual kneeling." He died aged sixty-three. His birthday is honoured by the Greek Church on October 9th, but by the Roman Church it is always coupled with that of St Philip on May 1st.

Up to the fall of Jerusalem in A.D. 70 the early Church was dominated by the Church of Jerusalem under James, with St Peter and St John as his chief lieutenants. This Church was a body within the Jewish fold. Paul, with his conception of a Church embracing the Gentiles, represented an heretical body within the Christian fold. When Paul went to Jerusalem to end the quarrel, he was humiliated by St James. With the fall of Jerusalem in A.D. 70, Paul's faction triumphed, and the Gospels were tampered with and the words of Christ were changed to fit the Pauline conception rather than the Jamesian. In a sense Titus, by his conquest of

Jerusalem and the wiping out of the Jamesian Church, established the Petrine Christian Church in Rome. Its rival disappeared for ever.

The history of St Philip is obscure. He appears in the Fourth Gospel, a practical-minded apostle who wants to go into the heart of the matter—"Two hundred pennyworth of bread is not enough." He wondered how they can afford that much. He is of an inquiring nature. "Lord, we know not whither thou goest, and how can we know the way?" he asked, provoking the eternal reply, "I am the way". To Nathanael at the crisis of his life, he said "Come and see". He liked plain evidence. Legend says that after the Ascension he went to Scythia; then to Hieropolis, where he found the people worshipping an enormous serpent. He commanded the serpent to disappear. It did, but left behind such an awful stench that many people died of it. The king's son fell dead in the arms of the Apostle, who restored him to life. The serpent's priests, enraged at being put out of business, stoned St Philip to death, and St Bartholomew, an old friend of Scythian days, buried him. His remains are said to be now with those of St James in the Church of the Twelve Apostles at Rome, which was founded in their honour by Julius I in the fourth century.[1] St Philip's emblem is a staff with a cross on the top, and he often carries a basket of bread and fishes.

I went to Castello d'Andora by way of the coast road, and then walked up the valley. From the road below I could see that the doors in the main façade of the church were wide open. The beautiful front shone in the westering sun as I climbed the hill. When I came through the arch I met a concourse of men in the small piazza before the church, which commanded a view of the wide valley and the mountains beyond it. I found the Mass had begun within. Gradually, in the dim light, I discerned the interior architecture. Its great age was more apparent here than in the

[1] Rebuilt in 1420 by Martin V, it is the burial church of the Colonna family whose palace is near by. Opposite lived James III, the Old Pretender. There he worshipped and there his wife, 'Queen of England', lay in state. He in turn lay in state there for five days, crowned, sceptred, and in royal robes. Until removed to Florence, Michelangelo was buried there, having died in the same parish. In 1873 the traditional grave of St James and St Philip was opened during its restoration. Two bodies were found in a sarcophagus of translucent marble.

restored exterior. It had a noble simplicity of design. Four
massive stone pillars, of rough but imposing workmanship,
supported pointed arches of the late romanesque era. They
had square bases with claw feet and cushion capitals on a
square abacus supporting the arched roof. At the side of the
simple altar stood a blue and white Madonna that was to be
transported round the ancient walls. The floor of the church
was filled with women, a few men, youths, and many
children, all standing. The coloured blouses and wraps of
the young women made rich colour in the soft light. Up at
the altar a very old priest officiated at the Mass. He was
robed in gold vestments with a richly embroidered cope. A
younger priest assisted him to kneel and rise, for he was
feeble. About them there was much movement, with the
service of four little acolytes in crimson and white cottas.
They had the beautiful heads of young angels in a Botticelli
picture. I wondered if they were the urchins who had thrown
stones and destroyed the rose window!

The large west door being wide open, the lowering sun
sent its warm rays directly down the pillared nave on to the
altar. It lit the rich vestments of the old priest and threw a
golden light over the altar ornaments, the flowers, the lit
candles, and on the large blue and white Madonna that
stood at one side. The collars of the acolytes burned crimson.
The warm light played over the congregation, heightening
all its colours. Every object seemed lit within that sombre
stone church as though the limes of a theatre were projected
over the scene. Children, beautiful as flowers, tawny and
lustrous-eyed, created a fringe of innocence around the great
stone pillars. After the Mass there was a pause. Two acolytes
came forward and gently led the old priest, who leaned on
them, to a chair placed on one side of the altar. The assistant
priest came forward. There was a movement of choristers
with tall candles and of maidens with banners. Four stalwart
youths took up the stand with the Madonna on it. They had
beautiful features, their heads crowned with black curls. For
a moment they had a pagan air, with their brown throats
and classical features. They might have been the participants
in an epiphany of Apollo here in the sunlit temple on the hill.

How the branch trembles of Apollo's boy!
How the whole shrine! Hence, sinners all, away!
Now Phœbus with his beautiful feet assails
The threshold. Look! On a sudden gently vails
The Delian palm her crest; while heavenwards soars
The swan singing. Lift up your bolts, ye doors,
And be ye turned, ye keys! The God is near,
Prepare you, lads, for song and dance, prepare!

Thus Callimachus three centuries before the conquering Galilean.[1] The syrinx of Pan might even now sound in the olive groves. But the Madonna, raised high, is moving. For a moment she is silhouetted against the level sun in the great doorway. Then out into the light she passes, escorted by chanting priest and acolytes, leading the bannered train of women and maidens. She sways gently, delicate and light blue. She rounds the church, mounting the grassy path towards the ramparts, then she is gone out of sight on her tour of the village.

The church is almost empty, but by the altar the old priest, too old to climb that steep track, rests on a chair, alone. He has a beautiful time-worn face, a head of grey curls, and the features of a knight blessed with the grace of God. I estimated his age at eighty. I wondered how many confessions he had heard in this village and what changes he had known, and whether again on the Saints' festival day he will be here to say the Mass, kneeling and rising slowly, assisted by the young priest and the little acolytes. I left him, reclining in the chair, his eyes closed, his hands folded over his surplice, bathed in the golden sunlight slanting down the nave.

Outside in the grassy piazza, pinnacled above the silvery olive groves that terraced the slopes, a crowd of sombrely clad men awaited the return of the Madonna. I learned then the name of the priest—Don Raffaele, eighty-three, beloved and long of this parish. And a mystery was solved. I had marvelled at the clear dark features and the vibrant black hair of most of those around me. "Sicilians," said

[1] Callimachus (310–240 B.C.), Hymn II, trans. R. A. Furness.

my informant. "Sicilians?" I echoed, surprised, "here in Castello d'Andora—some ancient invasion?" For these things are possible. I had seen how, through the long centuries, a Greek colony had kept its features and costumes in Piano dei Greci, an upland town in Sicily.

"Oh no—not ancient, a very recent invasion. This place was sold some years ago. The new owner imported four Sicilian families to work the land—the village had died out. They are good workers."

I asked why it was that so many of the men stood outside the church and scarcely any went in. My informant hesitated, smiled, and said quietly, "It is the Saints' Day, but it's also Labour Day. Some of them are Communists—but they let their women and children go in to the service. Some of them would carry the Madonna if the others weren't looking! Communisti, Fascisti, it's all the same, *signore*. They don't know what they are! Black, white, blue, or red shirts, they change like bunting on a signal-mast!" He spat contemptuously, and hitched his coat over his shoulders. No, he didn't live in Andorra, he had a shop down by the railway. "This place's been dead three hundred years. No bus, no cinema, no station, no shop, no post office, no inn," he said.

"But there seem plenty of children," I remarked.

"*Si, si, signore.* The only pastime. The Sicilians are heavy breeders. Perhaps they'll repopulate the place. But how can a man live here—on what?"

The question went unanswered. The sound of chanting drew near. Up the steep path to the little piazza, in the shadow of the *città's* strong wall, the swaying Madonna came into sight. She drew nearer, a trail of praying women, fingering rosaries, following behind. The Madonna approached, passed, and was lowered to go into the church. The men in the piazza observed the procession. Silent, motionless, wholly apart. I went into the church. Don Raffaele was assisted up from his chair and went to the altar. The service continued. Then he turned towards the congregation, and very gently came down three steps towards them, assisted by his young priest. An acolyte brought him a rush chair. I thought he was going to sit on it and address his flock, but he stood upright resting his hands on the back of the chair before him. He began his sermon, in a low, gentle voice. The last golden light of the setting sun touched his grey curls. He spoke for fifteen minutes, without a single pause in the homily which flowed softly as a stream over his congregation. Possibly they knew beforehand everything he said, possibly he had said the same thing in the same manner in this church for fifty years. They listened to him patiently, standing, not moving, with the little bare-legged boys and girls huddled against their mothers' skirts, their bright eyes restless over the scene.

Don Raffaele finished at last. He blessed them and smiled gently. Then he left the chair-back, and was assisted up the steps towards the side of the altar. The young priest and a youth took off his vestments. An acolyte snuffed out the tall candles. The Madonna shone faintly above her flowers. We followed Don Raffaele out. The boys, who high up in the watch-tower had tolled the bell for the procession of the Madonna, came clambering down. Don Raffaele, stick in hand, slowly mounted the path out of the piazza, his arm held by the young priest who had come over from a neighbouring village to assist at the festival. The ancient sacristan laboriously closed the great doors of the church. They would not be opened for another year, on the Day of St James and St Philip. The piazza was almost empty. I took the track under the high tower that led me through the vines and olives up towards Colla Micheri in the waning light.

III

I had wondered if I should ever again see the venerable Don Raffaele. Two months later, eager to show an American guest the glories of Castello d'Andora, I went there again. This time I chose another route, going by the sea coast and then up the Andorra valley. Before turning off on a track leading up to the castle and the church on the hill, curiosity prompted me to inspect an old church just off the road. I had noticed on my visit to Castello the beautiful slender campanile, with open belfry, rising from the plain. I now discovered that this

was the church of San Giovanni. What parish it had served
was a mystery. There were not half a dozen houses near it,
and it stood on a knoll in the middle of orchards, surrounded
by a broken wall and some picturesque cypresses. The whole
scene belonged to a forgotten epoch.

The heavy door was locked. The façade had a faded fresco.
We walked round the church, wondering what we might
find inside. A little distance away there was an old one-storey
outhouse, with a discarded stable on the ground floor. On a
door was a notice saying that the key of the church could be
found at a farmhouse up the lane. While we were studying
this and wondering whether we should go for the key, a small
window opened above and an old gentleman, who had
evidently been reading in the warm July afternoon, took off
his spectacles and peered down at us. He was dressed in
black. Almost at once I identified the benign face above us.
It was the *parroco* of Castello d'Andora, Don Raffaele! He told
us that a little boy would bring the key, and, as if by magic,
a blond-headed bare-legged boy, Pierino, a cherub of eleven,
appeared with an enormous key weighing some five pounds.
Don Raffaele had been startled when a strange Englishman
had addressed him by name, but he learned why when told
that on May Day I had attended the Mass conducted by him
in St James' and St Philip's at Castello d'Andora. We had a
brief cordial conversation. I learned he lived here, that this
was his church, and he only went over to deserted Castello
d'Andora on the few occasions that it had a festival.

Then, in charge of the small boy, we entered the church.
As so often, it was a revelation of decaying beauty, notable
for its height and dignity, above all for the beautiful *settecento* frescoes and floral painting on the massive piers and
walls. There was a polychrome wooden statue of the patron
saint, complete with staff and lamb, and a gorgeous carved
group, gloriously coloured, of Tobias and the Angel Raphael.
The little Tobias had a splendid, large fish and a delightful
dog. Raphael's wings were of a truly paradisian hue. I felt
the journey up the valley, rewarded by the discovery of old
Don Raffaele living over a simple stable, and of this statuary
group, had been a lovely side adventure. I found my young

American friend had never heard of the story of Tobias, and later, recounting my discovery to others, I was surprised to learn how few know this delightful story from the Book of Tobit. It is the most wonderful short-story in the world.

Tobit, an Israelite, had been carried into captivity with the ten tribes to Nineveh. As he had lost his eyesight and could not make the journey to Rai in Media, he sent his son Tobias to collect some money he had lent a relative. Tobias was joined on the way by an unknown youth, the angel Raphael in disguise, who guided the boy and his dog. On the journey Tobias halted, to wash his feet in the River Tigris, a refreshing act in all hot and dusty countries. While doing this he was attacked by an enormous fish. The angel Raphael helped him to overcome it, and told him to take from it the gall and the liver. With the first, Tobias cured his father's blindness, with the second he drove away a demon that had slain the seven husbands of a Jewish girl called Sara, his cousin, a virgin, whom he married later.

"Eight husbands? We've quite a lot of girls who achieve four or five in the States, but they don't get eight, even in Hollywood!" commented my guest. "I guess they just don't know a demon."[1]

Little Pierino with the large key locked up the church, after a superhuman effort. He was of the size and beauty of Tobias within. Since he had neither a dog nor a fish, I compensated him with the means of acquiring a large ice-cream, and then we set off up the hill to Castello d'Andora, where again

[1] This story in the Apocrypha is variously attributed to an Hebraic source, originally written probably in Egypt, before the second century B.C. in Greek; or alternatively, to a Persian source, since the dog was a sacred animal with the Persians and an unclean one with the Jews. The great fish caught by Tobias in the River Tigris was probably an Egyptian crocodile. The smoke of its liver was deemed a cure for epilepsy, epileptics being regarded as possessed of a demon, and its gall as a cure for blindness. Tobit, restored to sight, wrote a psalm of thanksgiving which relates how he enjoyed a hundred years of happiness after this event. Tobias lived to be one hundred and twenty-seven years old, and had six sons.

The story of Tobias has been a favourite theme with the great artists of the Renaissance—Rubens, etc. There is an exquisite version by a follower of Ver-rocchio in the National Gallery, London. Tobias carries in his hand the fish, and a scroll on which it says *Ricordo*, possibly the account of the debt to be collected. The winged Raphael delicately carries a little box of the magic gall or liver one assumes, while the little dog with them would appear to be, ana-chronistically, a Skye terrier.

I encountered Niccolò, the deaf Sicilian goat-herd. He told me he had finished *The Life of Pius IX*. He went off to get an equally massive key to open the church door. The church, dismantled, was now very sad. It lacked the bright vestments, candles, and altar cloths. The Madonna, who had made a *giro* round the castle walls, had gone too, but, more sad even, I missed the venerable old Don Raffaele, in his golden cope, with the westering sun lighting his beautiful face.

The poet, Count Vittorio Alfieri, and his mother, 1764.
(Photo: Ferrero Collection.)

The golden beach with sun umbrellas like anemones.

(Photo: Angeli—Terni.)

CHAPTER ELEVEN

THE GHOST OF LUSIGNANO

I

IN the little dead village of Colla Micheri where I saw the old crone in the tower looking down on the deserted piazza in which Pius VII had blessed the people, there is the ghost of an eighteenth-century lady of fashion and letters who played a singular rôle throughout the reigns of Louis XVI, Napoleon, Louis XVIII, Charles X, and Louis Philippe. She lived to be eighty-four, and wrote more than one hundred books, all of them now forgotten. Her title to fame, once literary and international in extent, rests today on her rôle as governess to the princes and princesses of the House of Orleans. She was the most famous of all governesses. One of her pupils ascended the throne as Louis Philippe in the year of her death.

Let us in Colla Micheri and, if report be true, in the village of Lusignano, a few miles up the Albenga valley, evoke the ghost of Stéphanie Felicité Ducrest, later Madame de Genlis. Before she died she wrote her memoirs. In them she described her journey along the Italian Riviera to the court at Naples. Unhappily she is silent about the return journey and the route she took. There is also a mystery concerning her movements which I have failed to solve. I will come to that later, and to the wild-goose chase that I was led, delightful in every detail.

Madame de Genlis was born in 1746 of an impoverished but noble family living near Autun. At the age of seven she was made a canoness in the noble Chapter of Alix, one of those rich religious institutions abounding before the Revolution. They afforded persons of noble birth elegant quarters, a pension, and no duties, under the pretext that they were *religieuse*. In this Chapter the young canonesses received titles, and were addressed as Madame la Comtesse. These benefits were achieved after a close examination of the applicant's proof of noble blood. So at seven, Stéphanie journeyed with her mother to Lyons. It was the duty of the Comte de Lyons to examine the pedigrees of the applicants. The process took fifteen days, whereupon, the pedigree approved, mother and daughter proceeded to the nunnery at Alix. This consisted of a number of charming little houses, each with a garden, around the central palace of the abbess. The new seven-year-old canoness and countess was welcomed by all the aristocratic inmates. She was dressed in white, and with much pomp was conducted to the chapel. All the canonesses were there, fashionably dressed in robes of black silk and ermine mantles. After the recital of the Creed by the grand prior, the candidate knelt on a velvet rug. The prior then cut off one of Stéphanie's curls, but as he was very old and almost blind he also cut off a bit of her ear, "which I supported heroically without complaint", recorded the victim. Next a gold ring which had been blessed was put on her finger; then a black and white strip of cloth called *un mari* (a husband) was placed on her head, and a red cord with a beautiful enamel cross was hung round her neck. A belt of black moiré silk was fastened round her waist. The ceremony ended with a Grand Mass, after which the new canoness was embraced by all her elderly colleagues.

The rest of the day was spent in visiting all the canonesses in their little houses, where they played games. From now on the child canoness was addressed as Madame la Comtesse de Lancy, a name taken from her father's seigniory. "The pleasure of being addressed as Madame la Comtesse surpassed all others," commented the little snob. She used the title until her marriage at seventeen. Can one wonder that the French Revolution, arising from the misery and hunger of the people witnessing these pseudo-religious farces and the privileges of a decadent aristocracy, swept them away in a torrent of blood?

Six months later, a child of talent, Stéphanie had a great success as a dancer, attired as *l'Amour*, in some amateur theatricals at Autun, after which the canoness-countess donned the robes of a boy, which she wore for the next six months. It somewhat surprised her that neither the pious local priest nor anyone else seemed scandalized by her costume. Precocious in every way, she was eleven when she had her first grand passion for a youth of eighteen. It came to an abrupt end. The poor youth, encouraged, wrote her a love-letter. "My first reaction," said the canoness-countess, "was that of being deeply shocked that the son of a doctor, a man who was not a gentleman, should dare speak to me of love." She showed the letter to her governess, who took it to her mother. The youth was severely reprimanded by his father and sent away. Thirteen years later she was pleased to learn from the father, who called on her in Paris, that his son had been in tears for three years (!), had prayed for death, but had made an excellent marriage and was happy and *un très bon sujet*. Meanwhile our young canoness was fluttering the dovecotes. The doves were all elderly and rich. Precocious, with much talent at thirteen, she could dance, act, write verse, and play the harp, clavichord, and guitar. When with her mother she departed after a visit to her aunt, that lady took her in her arms, kissed her and cried, "Poor child, you will never be happy. You are too sensitive!"

Stéphanie was not dismayed. She proceeded from the doctor's son of eighteen to the conquest of her host, Monsieur de La Popelinière, a man of sixty-six. They stayed all the summer in his house at Passy. A farmer-of-taxes under the Crown, he had amassed an immense fortune by this iniquitous system. He was a man of considerable culture and benevolence, who kept open house in a mansion maintained with great pomp, where he entertained men of letters and all those distinguished in the arts. Gifted, he wrote novels, comedies, and songs. One of his songs, '*O ma tendre musette*', is sung to this day in France. Alas, poor man, he was not lucky in love. His first wife had a scandalous liaison with the Duc de Richelieu. She had a revolving fireplace in her bedroom by which the duke entered from the house next door. The outraged husband, discovering this, turned her out, despite the intercession of Maréchal Saxe, back from the victory of Fontenoy. Madame was taken in by the duke until she died. At sixty-eight M. de La Popelinière married the

young daughter of a city magistrate. She made him so un-
happy that he died eighteen months later. The little Comtesse de Lancy, to all the precocious talents that enraptured
the old gentleman, added the gift of second-sight. Asked
what she thought of a guest, an abbé, she replied, "I'm certain he'll be hanged!" It was the Abbé de la Carte, who had
been a marriage-broker for his host. He was accused later of
criminally libelling his customer, as well as others. He was
tried, condemned, had an iron collar fastened round his
neck, and was sent to the galleys. Madame la Comtesse was
a formidable little girl.

It was while staying with M. de La Popelinière that she
took to the harp, an instrument loved by her host. She had
lessons from an old German musician that he kept. She
showed a real gift for the instrument, and was soon enchanting her host by playing his own compositions. A master of
the ballet came and taught her to dance. M. de La Popelinière was enchanted by her grace. "What a pity she is only
thirteen!" sighed the old widower. When they returned to
Paris, two men of talent attended her mother's salon to hear
her play—the famous scientist d'Alembert and the celebrated composer Rameau.

Meanwhile affairs were not going well at home. Her father
had to sell his estate, and departed for America to repair his
fortune. They went to live with Stéphanie's grandmother,
whose second husband was the Marquis de la Haye, known
as Beau Haye. He was killed in the battle of Minden.[1]
Stéphanie's father on returning from St Dominique was
taken prisoner by the English and interned at Launceston.
Here he made the acquaintance of another prisoner, the
young Comte de Genlis. The elder man read to the younger
the letters received from Stéphanie, and showed him his
daughter's portrait. Genlis fell in love with the unseen girl.
As soon as he was liberated he hurried to Paris and called on

---

[1] He changed history. He was Gentleman of the Wardrobe to the twelve-
year-old Duc de Bourgogne, elder son of the Dauphin. One day la Haye placed
the Prince on a rocking-horse, from which he fell heavily. There was no frac-
ture or visible injury. He asked the boy not to mention the accident, which
seemed to be slight. Soon afterwards the Prince was mysteriously ill and died.
It was then discovered that he had an abscess on his spine. Had he lived, the
ill-fated Louis XVI would not have ascended the throne.

Stéphanie's mother. The father returned soon afterwards. True love found no obstacles. Spurning the wealthy heiress produced by his uncle, though poor himself, Genlis married the penniless Comtesse de Lancy, to the uncle's great anger. Charles de Genlis, a grenadier colonel, was handsome, brave, and of excellent character. He was twenty-seven years of age. His bride was sixteen. It was a secret marriage because of his uncle. Soon after their wedding the young husband was ordered to join his regiment. He placed his girl-wife in a convent at Origny, where she had a charming apartment and two servants. Happy there, she played the harp to the abbess and sang in the choir. She also ran along the corridors at midnight dressed as a devil with horns and a blackened face to frighten the young nuns. On the old ones, heavy sleepers, she put rouge and moustaches. When they woke and hurried to early Mass, dressing without looking in the mirror, they made surprising apparitions in the convent chapel.

Stéphanie's mother joined her at Origny for six months, having her own apartment. When Genlis returned they went to live in Paris for a short time, where his wife gave birth to a daughter. Later they went to the Marquis de Sillery, his brother, who had a large château in the country. It rained all day. Madame la Comtesse de Genlis wrote for three-quarters of an hour and played the harp for an hour each day. One evening the Marquis de Lusignan came to the château. He bore a name she was to know well in later days.

The winter over, the young couple went to live at L'Ile Adam. It was here that Rousseau, wishing to hear Madame de Genlis play the harp, called upon the young couple. She played and sang for him. Rousseau was delighted and accepted an invitation to dinner the next evening. He proved humble and amiable. He talked of his *Confessions*, and asked his hostess if she had read his works. With great candour she told the great man she had not. "Why not?" he asked, fixing his little, piercing eyes on her. She said that she had not read them because they were irreligious. "It is true I am not a Catholic, but no one has written about the gospel with more conviction and feeling," he replied. Notwithstanding her answer, he came frequently to dine.

Madame de Genlis attended the marriage of the future Louis XVI to Marie Antoinette. Her aunt, Madame de Montesson, clandestinely married the Duc d'Orléans.

It was by virtue of this connection that the Comte de Genlis obtained the position of Captain of the Guards with the duke's son, the Duc de Chartres. His wife became a lady-in-waiting to the duchess.

She had begun a singular phase of her life. She moved into the Palais-Royal. "I left a most honourable home to go to a dangerous place," she wrote many years later. "I took there an irreproachable character, I began a new career." She was given an apartment with mirrored rooms, a magnificent boudoir, and a staircase opening on to the Rue de Richelieu. It was here that Gluck, then at the height of his fame as the composer of *Iphigénie*, came with a violinist friend to make music with the fair young harpist. Soon to Rousseau and Gluck she had added the great Voltaire, whom she visited at Ferney. He was very amiable at dinner, but his voice was like thunder when he denounced his enemies in a sonorous dining-room. Afterwards he took her out in his carriage to look at the model village he had created. It was the visit of a fellow author, for Madame de Genlis, on the birth of her first child, a daughter, had published *Reflections of a Mother of Twenty*.

She liked the Duchesse de Chartres, and they became great friends. The duke, later to be known as Philippe Egalité for his Revolutionary sympathies, was a roué. The Duc d'Orléans, his father, had given him a mistress at fifteen, and he was surrounded by the fast young men at Court. He had first noticed Madame de Genlis at an opera ball, where he had sent an enormous cat into the ballroom, frightening all the ladies but one, Madame de Genlis, whose cool demeanour was admired by the duke. The giant cat proved to be a little Savoyard boy he had disguised. As companion to his wife it was easy to see much of this young woman, wife of the Captain of his Guard. She was beautiful, amusing, good-tempered, and kind. It was not long before an intimacy sprang up between them. The liaison progressed under the very nose of the unsuspecting duchess. In Paris, in

1775, Madame de Genlis gave birth to a son, who died within a few days. Recovered, she travelled south with her husband, in the court of the duke and duchess. They were all at Toulon when, the duke having departed on a sea voyage, the duchess and her companions took it into their heads to make a trip into Italy. Having departed without the king's permission, the duchess wrote a letter of apology from Cap d'Antibes, saying a desire to visit her grandfather, the old Duke of Modena, had overcome her.

It was in Antibes that the two runaways from the Court found agreeable companions. There they also tasted a singular soup. Their host, M. de Rouffignic, in their honour had his tame bear killed and made a bright red soup from it! The ladies had never tasted anything so good. At Antibes also they collected three agreeable French gentlemen as travelling companions. One was the Marquis de Clermont, appointed French Ambassador to the Court of Naples, a good musician with an excellent tenor voice, and his two young secretaries, M. de Nidisdale and M. de Moustiers, both handsome and amiable. The former attached himself in the rôle of cavalier to the first lady-in-waiting, the latter to the second, Madame de Genlis. With servants they made a party of sixteen. Madame de Genlis took her harp along, on top of the carriage. She had it transported to her bedroom every evening, and always played before going to bed. There were musical parties every evening that lasted two to three hours.

After three days the party embarked on a felucca for Nice. It carried an armed guard as protection against the Algerian corsairs who menaced the coast. In Nice they rested for six days, making excursions in the mountains. Hearing that it was possible to reach Genoa by land instead of by ship, they unwisely took to the perils of the road. When they hired mules and asked the man about the journey, he very honestly told them that he was afraid for his animals as in the past year he had lost two from a fall of rocks, which often came down from the precipices along the Corniche road. But off they started, MM. the French Ambassador, de Moustiers, de Nidisdale, and de Genlis on mules, the ladies in sedan-chairs. They had sent their servants and luggage by sea.

All was well for a time. They found at La Turbie an excellent *al fresco* lunch awaiting them, a compliment to the duchess from the Commandant at Nice. Later they admired the view from Eze. From Monaco to Mentone they were enchanted with the scenery though terrified by the precipices, and often they dismounted from their sedans and walked along the stony track. At Bordighera they were entranced with the flowers and palms. Darkness falling, they halted at Ospedaletti. The very name, 'hospital beds', seemed too much for them. The three ladies shared a room. A bed was extemporized for the duchess from mule blankets and leaves. The other two ladies slept on a great pile of grain, which the innkeeper assured them would be comfortable. A rug was thrown over the grain and the delicate court ladies mounted their singular bed. All night they were in a state of constant agitation caused by the sliding down of the grain. They were happy to see the daylight.

The next day's journey was frightful, they made seven miles. Often they had to walk along a precipitous narrow track. They were in even more discomfort in their sedans. The porters, who spoke no known languages, quarrelled among themselves villainously. They took their hands off the staves and, with the sedans supported only by their shoulder straps, gesticulated and menaced each other. At Porto Maurizio they were well lodged. Out came the harp after dinner. The road from Porto Maurizio to Albenga seemed the most frightful of all, but arriving at Colla Micheri they were enchanted by the view of Laigueglia below and Alassio in the half-moon curve of its bay.

Today one likes to recall the royal party in its sedans and on mules passing under the arch, with the houses built above it, after they had come up from the Andorra valley. The scene can have changed little. There was the long window in the towered façade from which the old woman peered at me one hundred and eighty years later. All that time ago doubtless some old peasant had looked down from the same window on the Duchesse de Chartres and her attendant ladies and gentlemen. There was the church as now, but with no plaque commemorating the Pope, who, liberated from his

confinement at Fontainebleau by Napoleon, had halted and
blessed the people forty years later. Colla Micheri was not
then a deserted ruin, the olive groves and vines were in full
cultivation. The little piazza must have been animated that
early morning with these great ladies and gentlemen, mule-
teers and sedan chairmen. The superb view of the Mediterranean bay below, seen through a veil of olive branches,
cannot have changed in any degree. It was as paradisian a
vista as it is today. One wonders if they took the time from
the old sundial on the house.

The party made the descent to Laigueglia, stony and steep
then as now. So rough that they walked almost barefooted,
recorded Madame de Genlis, the soles of their shoes worn
out by the tracks they had traversed. At ten o'clock, from a
point on the old Roman road, they looked down on towered
Albenga in its valley. The aridity of the snow-crowned
mountains was in great contrast to the smiling luxuriance of
the plain at their feet. The weary travellers thought it was
paradise, with the flowers, the vines, the fruit and the tall
pampas grass waving in the soft breeze. Madame de Genlis
could not know how, when her world had collapsed in blood
and ruin, that here, in the little village of Lusignano at her
feet, she would one day take refuge. All this was unseen in the
future. Today she found the Albenga valley ravishing. She
noted the handsome peasants, all the young girls with their
luxuriant hair coiled over their heads, and crowned on the
left side with a small bouquet of flowers. They were all jolly,
with elegance in their movements.

They continued their journey. In four days they reached
Genoa, with feet all swollen and blistered, but they were in
good health, and felt, despite their ardours and endurances,
that the journey had been a wonderful experience. The rest
of the route through the states of the Duke of Modena was
without incident. The old duke greeted them warmly. He
was a singular figure, eighty-four, blind, with rouged and
powdered cheeks and pencilled eyebrows. He had two old
spinster sisters living with him. After some days the duchess
and her attendants left for Mantua, where they were
splendidly entertained in the great castle of the archduke. In

Rome, Cardinal Bernis, among the richest of the cardinals, entertained them with the greatest magnificence. The cardinal paid Madame de Genlis a singular compliment. Every evening when she was in her bath he would come with his 'nephew' and converse with her for three-quarters of an hour. It was a habit not so surprising in one who thirty years earlier had been present at the *toilette* of Madame de Pompadour. He informed Madame de Genlis among many things that the men of Rome were not given to seduction but to murder. The largest number occurred in August when the heat was greatest. But the streets were safe at night. When Madame de Genlis inquired the reason for this singularity, he explained, smiling delicately, that the cardinals, proceeding to their amours, went out disguised in mufti. The desperadoes, aware that the murder of a priest was the greatest crime of all, in fear of killing a disguised cardinal attacked no one. Cardinal Bernis gave *conversazioni* in honour of the duchess that were attended by three thousand people.[1]

The royal party arrived at Naples to visit the King and Queen there. In driving down the Via Toledo the baggage of the ladies was stolen. It contained their court costumes. The ambassador said he could recover it. He would speak to the chief of the bandits, saying the King would be greatly displeased. The baggage was returned intact. The thieves were tolerated by the government, who received part of their spoils.

The duchess's party was most graciously received at the royal Court. Madame de Genlis played the harp. M. Clermont sang a duet with the Queen; the King in compliment sang one old French song. He was very affable, but his education had been so poor that he could only speak a Neapolitan dialect, in which all the comic operas, for which he had a passion, were written. Two customs surprised the

---

[1] Cardinal Bernis (1715–1794). A pretty little hand-kissing abbé at Versailles, he was sent by Louis XV to train Madame de Pompadour in Court etiquette before installing her as his mistress. He was a poodle-dog around the Court, wrote flowery verses, and was dubbed by Voltaire 'Babet la Bouquetière'. Promoted Ambassador to Venice in 1752, to Madrid in 1755, he became Minister of Foreign Affairs, was dismissed in 1758, exiled, consoled with a cardinal's hat, and made Archbishop of Albi. Later he was sent as Ambassador to Rome, where he amassed a great fortune.

guests. The King gave his hand for all the ladies to kiss, and they preceded him in to dinner, things unknown at the French Court.

Soon after their return to France the Duchesse de Chartres gave birth to twin daughters, greatly to her delight. It had been arranged that if such an event occurred, Madame de Genlis should be appointed governess. She had a genius for teaching. She professed to be disgusted with Society, and formed plans for entering a convent with her two charges. This was agreed. A special pavilion was built at the convent of Belle Chasse. Here Madame de Genlis lived in state, receiving all the world each Saturday. She was then, in 1777, thirty-two years of age. "I have retained the figure of a much younger woman," she observed complacently. She gave up rouging herself despite the protests of the Duc de Chartres.

The new pavilion was connected with the convent by a long pergola of roses. There was a private garden. Everyone who came to visit her was enchanted. There is no word about the Comte de Genlis's feelings on this curious establishment. She retained her official apartment in the Palais-Royal, with its gold panels, mirrors, and tapestries.

All seemed perfect. Her German gardener married her milkmaid. They were established in a small dairy to provide milk, cream, and butter for the twin princesses. Madame du Deffand, Horace Walpole's friend, joined her circle of acquaintances. The little princesses flourished. They were pretty and talented. Madame de Genlis's little daughter, Pulchérie, took lessons with her charges. One chambermaid spoke English, another Italian, the gardener German. The children learned three languages.

There was now a very singular event that caused tongues to wag. In order to improve his children's English, the duke wrote to a friend in England commissioning him to send over a little girl of five or six, after she had been inoculated! This took some time. The child had to be examined by the doctors and pronounced free from scrofula, etc. Then the duke sent over his ostler to collect a new horse and the child. The friend in London who had transacted the business wrote to the duke: "I have the honour to send to your Royal Highness the prettiest mare and maid in England."

She arrived, delighted Madame de Genlis with her beauty and grace, and had her name changed from Nancy to Pamela. The little princesses had a new playmate to improve their English. All the world said the child was the duke's and Madame de Genlis's, smuggled out of France at birth.

In 1782 the duke, having now three sons, proposed that Madame de Genlis should add them to her educational establishment. They were the Duc de Valois, later Louis Philippe I, the Duc de Montpensier, and the Comte de Beaujolais. A new house, St Leu, was bought and fitted up. The system of education was unique. The royal children talked German in the garden and also on their walks with the valet. On the evening walks, before dinner, they spoke only English; at dinner, only Italian. The chaplain, an eighty-year-old abbé, taught them French literature and philosophy. A botanist and chemist accompanied the children on their country walks. A young Polish artist was put on the establishment to teach them painting in gouache, and also design. Madame de Genlis had a magic-lantern for which the Pole made slides illustrating Roman, Chinese, Japanese, and Indian history. The pupils thus toured the world once a week.

Another pupil, the little orphaned niece of Madame, Henriette de Sercey, joined the establishment. She was aged nine. Later the celebrated artist David visited St Leu and helped to design scenery for the plays acted by the children in their private theatre. Madame de Genlis wrote special text-books with great success. These firmly established her reputation as *première gouvernante du monde*. "I was the first instructor of princes who had the idea of having children learn living languages by daily usage," she wrote. Theatricals were of great assistance, for they learned by pleasure. The Duc de Valois surpassed all the others. When Chartres succeeded as Duc d'Orléans in 1785, Louis Philippe became Duc de Chartres. Then, at long last, the Duchesse d'Orléans' eyes were opened as to the true relations between her husband and her former lady-in-waiting. The scandal became

so great that Marie Antoinette refused to receive Madame
de Genlis at Court.

Comte de Genlis, having inherited a large fortune, wished
to retire from court circles. His wife refused. She later bitterly regretted her action, for she believed she could have
induced him to go to England with her on the outbreak of
the Revolution. He separated from her. Amiable, intelligent,
now Marquis de Sillery, he had been a Girondist and was
guillotined in 1793. The Duc d'Orléans, with ambitions for
the throne, was sympathetic to the revolutionary party and
became known as Egalité. Madame de Genlis shared his
sympathies, being estranged from the King's party. She
even went as far as to encourage her charges to dance with
the people in the gardens of the Palais-Royal after the fall
of the Bastille. The duchess was outraged at this corruption
of her children. It was thought wise for Madame de Genlis
to make a journey to England. The education of the young
Duc de Chartres was completed. He was eighteen and set up
in his own establishment. Madame de Genlis departed, taking with her the young princess, Mademoiselle d'Orléans,
her niece Henriette, and the adopted Pamela. She was received by everyone, partly for herself, as the authoress of
Adèle et Théodore and a dozen other popular works, and as
governess of royal princes. It was October 1791. They attended a sitting of the House of Commons, a rare favour.
They met Fox, Sheridan, Burke, Wilkes, the Duchess of
Devonshire, and Miss Fanny Burney. The Prince of Wales
gave them a fête at Brighton. Burke showed them Oxford.
Madame de Genlis was invited to Windsor, where she had
an hour's audience with the Queen, met the princesses, and
stayed to dinner. They called incognito at Blenheim. The
Duchess of Marlborough, discovering this too late, was
chagrined, and sent a valet with flowers after their coach.
Horace Walpole gave them a garden party at Strawberry
Hill. They stayed with that odd pair Lady Butler and Miss
Ponsonby, the Ladies of Llangollen, who had bought a
mountain and transformed a farm on top of it into a mansion. Despite the entreaties of their parents, these ladies had
quitted their homes in Ireland at twenty and twenty-one

and had never returned. They lived together for sixty years. The visitors found the old ladies full of charm, good musicians, well-read, and serene in their ivory tower.

Madame de Genlis visited Samuel Richardson's home, The Grange, Fulham, a guest of the novelist's son-in-law. She was thrilled to see the manuscript of *Pamela*, and to sit in the garden and in the author's chair, the right arm of which opened to form a writing-desk.[1] Then they returned to Paris. On the eve of a theatrical party at St Leu, July 1791, the Revolution began. The King had fled to Varennes, and had been brought back. There was a massacre in the Champ de Mars.

The menaced Court made charges against the Duc d'Orléans, who was in touch with the revolutionary party. It assailed the duchess for permitting her children to be brought up in that atmosphere. Most particularly it execrated Madame de Genlis. The duchess, indignant with this woman who had corrupted her children and had been the mistress of her husband, threatened a separation. It was decided that Madame de Genlis should go to England. She obtained permission to make a second journey there as soon as the constitution accepted by Louis XVI was established. On the eve of her departure she learned that the Duc d'Orléans had gone at five in the morning to London and awaited her there. The pretext for Madame de Genlis's journey was that the health of Mademoiselle d'Orléans, a girl of fifteen who would not leave her, demanded a cure at Bath.

They left on October 11th, 1792. They went first to a house that the duke had bought in London, then on to Bath, where they stayed two months. They were living in Bury St Edmunds when the news came that the King was to be tried. Madame de Genlis wrote a letter of protest against this violence, which she showed first to Fox and Sheridan for

[1] In 1952 the Fulham Borough Council threatened to demolish this historic old house. Following an organized protest, the Ministry of Housing made an order suspending the demolition. The Council, determined in its vandalism, opposed the order, but after a public inquiry the Council was defeated. Thus a house in which the father of the English novel lived and wrote, where Burne-Jones had his studio, and Rudyard Kipling and Stanley Baldwin spent some of their boyhood, was saved. See *And So To Bath*, Chapter I.

their approval. This letter only served to increase the hatred of Madame de Genlis in both royalist and revolutionary circles. Immediately after the September, 1792, massacres the Duc d'Orléans, who had returned to Paris, demanded that Madame de Genlis send home his daughter, in danger of being proscribed as an *émigrée*. Madame de Genlis protested. It was too dangerous, but in the end she had to give way. The party arrived back in Paris. Before they left, Sheridan, a widower of forty-six, bankrupt and a confirmed spend-thrift, proposed to her adopted daughter Pamela, aged eighteen. He advanced the peculiar reason that she re-sembled his deceased wife, who had been a close friend of Lord Edward Fitzgerald, son of the Duke of Leinster. Pamela accepted him. They were to be married in Paris, it was alleged by Madame de Genlis who, dubbed Josephine Surface by her English critics, was said to have contrived the match. They stayed a month at Sheridan's house at Isle-worth, where he utilized the bailiffs in it, as in his play, to serve ices to his guests. Then in November Madame de Genlis and her charges left. Sheridan saw them off. At Calais the royal princess was warmly welcomed. As they went inland the crowds became hostile. They reached Belle Chasse to find there the duke, the Comte de Genlis, and others, all deeply depressed by events. There Madame de Genlis learned that the princess was placed on the list of *émigrées* for being abroad. It was decided that they should go to Tournai in Belgium until the list had been revoked. Comte de Genlis refused to go. He said a Frenchman's duty was to face things out in his own country, a decision that took him to the scaffold. Of the duke's three sons, the Comte de Beaujolais was a confirmed Bourbon, and stood devotedly by the imprisoned royal family. He sent privately a note of loyalty to Marie An-toinette. "This amiable boy feels a tender sympathy for my misfortunes," she wrote. He died young. "The death of this young prince deprived me of the happiness of opening the gates of France to him and rewarding his noble sentiments," wrote Louis XVIII twenty years later. The other two sons of Egalité had imbibed the republican sympathies of their father and governess. The Duc de Montpensier found refuge in Italy; the Duc de Chartres, his eyes opened to reality, fled with Madame de Genlis and his sister.

On the eve of their departure for Tournai Madame de Genlis, her husband and party went to the theatre to cheer up their spirits. In the audience was Lord Edward Fitzgerald, who, struck by Pamela's resemblance to his loved friend, Sheridan's late wife, fell in love with Sheridan's fiancée! The next day the duke and Madame de Genlis's husband bade them farewell. It was all too clear that the harassed duke's infatuation was at an end. He escorted his daughter and Madame de Genlis to their carriage, and gloomily said good-bye to them. They never saw Egalité again. Generally execrated for the rôle he had played, he went to the scaffold later, on the fall of the Girondists and the advent to full power of Robespierre. The fleeing party had no sooner arrived at Tournai than up turned Lord Edward Fitzgerald, infatuated. The fickle Pamela changed fiancés and the couple were married and left for England.[1] In Tournai came the news of the King's execution. The young Duc de Chartres was horror-stricken. He developed a violent repugnance to the infamous part played by his father and to the past influence of his governess. He left the party for Switzerland. His brother, the Duc de Montpensier, had been to visit them, and had written to his father saying that he never wished to return to France.

Whatever Madame de Genlis's faults, she had courage. She bore up under the news of the execution of her husband and the duke. Denuded of everything, she supported herself and the ailing princess by her pen. A weary pilgrimage of exile followed from one haven of refuge to another. She was shunned and denounced for nine years. In turn they went from Tournai, to St Amand, Mons, Schaffhausen, Zurich, and Zug. In this last place someone, learning that the son and daughter of the infamous Egalité were in the inn, broke its windows. They found refuge in a convent in Bremgarten.

---

[1] Some years later Lord Edward, hiding in a house near his home in Ireland, was arrested for organizing an invasion by the French. He fought so fiercely that he killed one of the officers and was himself mortally wounded. He died in gaol, attended by his wife. Cobbett, who served under him in Canada, said he was the only truly honest officer he had known.

Madonna in procession at Castello d'Andora.

Tobias and the Angel, by Verrocchio (follower of).

The Duc de Chartres departed to Coire in the Engadine. There, under an assumed name, he became the master of mathematics in a college. The Duke of Modena being afraid to receive his niece, the young princess found a home with her aunt, Princess Conti, near Fribourg. The parting so deeply affected Madame de Genlis that she shut herself up in her room on the last morning and sent the princess a note saying that she had gone out for the day to avoid the scene of separation.

She was alone now except for her niece Henriette. They left for Berlin, whence they were expelled by order of King Frederick William, and went to Altona and Hamburg. Madame de Genlis was worried about the fate of her surviving daughter. The elder, Caroline, had married the aged Baron Löwenstein, a rich Belgian. It was a happy marriage lasting five years, when she died at twenty-one of a confinement. The baron seemed inconsolable. He had the candour to show his wife's diary to his mother-in-law. It contained two tables. One, headed "Calculation of the infidelities of my husband during five years," gave a list of twenty-two. The other, headed "Let us see mine", ended with the comment "ooo. Total satisfaction".

The other daughter living, Pulchérie, had married the Vicomte de Valence, one of the most dissipated men in France. Handsome, brave, he emigrated, refused to fight against his own country, and was restored to favour by Napoleon. In Hamburg, to the great joy of Madame de Genlis, they were united. Here she laboured, her pen busy, her conscience uneasy at the part she had played, but outwardly she was always gay. She played the harp, was vivacious in conversation, and hospitable within her means. She entertained Talleyrand when passing through Hamburg. He expressed his admiration of her spirit. She fulfilled her passion for teaching by adopting a little boy and girl. Then, in 1801, with France under Napoleon, she had permission to return. She found everything changed, her old places of abode in ruin. She was given quarters in the Arsenal and a pension of six thousand francs, but she never went to the Imperial Court. Most of the Imperial family called on her.

She was delighted at the compliment of being made inspector of primary schools in her district. She lived for nine years at the Arsenal, wrote incessantly and saw her friends. On the fall of the Empire she lost her pension. At the Restoration she was out of favour. The daughter of Marie Antoinette would naturally not receive her. The Comte de Beaujolais had died in exile, as also the Duc de Montpensier. The Duc de Chartres, now the Duc d'Orléans, returned to France. "Monsieur, you have much to do to repair the crimes of your father . . . but that is all ended. From today we will begin to know one another," said Louis XVIII to the man who would ascend the throne as Louis Philippe I.

At first the Duc d'Orléans was cold towards his governess, but one day when she called he brought in his young wife, who greeted her graciously, saying, "Madame, I have always longed to know you, for there are two things I love passionately, your pupils and your books." She was allowed a small pension. In old age she wrote more and more, with less and less accuracy. As is often the failing with elderly authors, her reminiscences grew more imaginative. It became impossible to separate fable from fact. A particularly scandalous book of society gossip, *Dîners du Baron d'Holbach*, brought her into disrepute and Sainte Beuve made a scathing comment on her work. In old age she retained her industry and vivacity. She held a little salon in the Place Royale, she saw her pupil the Duc d'Orléans ascend the throne, was surrounded by her grandchildren, and lived to see her adopted son make an excellent marriage and keep a home she often visited and called saintly. She outlived her vogue, but after many disasters and scandals she ended her days, aged eighty, in an aura of aristocratic respectability and affection.

II

And now for a little detective work, and the story of a wild-goose chase amid the vines and peaches of the valley of Albenga. Edward and Margaret Berry wrote an excellent book about the Italian Riviera which they knew intimately. They called it *At the Western Gate*. It is the fullest and most authoritative book on this area. They lived long on the coast, they were serious scholars and meticulous in their facts. One cannot believe that they wrote anything lightly or without substantial basis for their statements. They tell us, "At Lusignano Madame de Genlis lived for some years, and dated many of her letters from this remote house, a large villa with a walled garden at the left side of the road as one goes up the valley."

Two and a half miles from Albenga, up the valley of the Centa, before one reaches the medieval walled town of Villanova, lies the small village of Lusignano. It is a cluster of houses on the north slope of the mountain range that shuts off Alassio from the plain of Albenga. When I came upon Lusignano on the local map, it at once invited speculation. The name is written large in the history of Cyprus and Jerusalem. The founders of the Lusignan line, kings of these two places, originally migrated from Lusignan, a small French town near Vienne. How came this name, slightly Italianized, to be attached to a small village in the Albenga valley? Names are valuable clues. They are not usually given to places without reason. There seemed a probability that some member of the royal house had been connected with this Italian village bearing his name. My speculation was not unreasonable. Two of the Lusignan kings had been held in exile as hostages of the Genoese Republic. When the boy king, Pierre II, came to the throne in 1369, there was a dispute between the Genoese and Venetian consuls at the coronation. It was traditional for these two consuls to lead on either hand the king's horse in the coronation procession. A dispute arose on a matter of precedence between them, and flared into a bloody affray. The King sided with the Venetians. The Genoese, touchy in the matter of their sworn enemy and incensed by the slaughter of some of their countrymen, sent a fleet to avenge their deaths. Famagusta was taken, Cyprus was sacked, and the island was held by the Genoese Republic. Following the Genoese investment, Jacques I, uncle of Pierre II, was carried off to Genoa, and held there as hostage. While a prisoner he married Helen de Brunswick. In that city his son Janus, King of Cyprus

1398–1432, was born. The successive Lusignan kings were allowed to reign by the Genoese up to the time when Jacques II threw off the Genoese yoke, in 1464, in exchange for that of the Venetian. Jacques' posthumous son lived for only a year and the line expired in 1474.

But to my quest. There dawned a heavenly June day when the atmosphere, cooled by rain overnight, was crystal clear. The sea was a blue mirror on which glided the white sails of little boats. The pine-tree-fringed mountains stood vividly against the sky. On the far horizon lay Corsica like a faint cloud, rosy and white. I decided that it was a day on which to go and look for the villa in which Madame de Genlis had lived at Lusignano, that name reminiscent of the medieval kings of Cyprus and Jerusalem. So with a young American guest, I set out early, carrying a picnic lunch, and took the old Roman road high on the cliff's face, beyond the portal at Santa Croce, past broom-scented ravines opening on blue vistas of the sea until we came to the almost obliterated path that descended towards the valley of Albenga. We saw below us, stretched along the spur of a wooded foothill, an old village. We judged, from its position in the Centa valley, that it must be near Lusignano. Twice we almost lost our way, so faint was the track, but wherever we turned an earthly paradise of mountains and pinnacled villages shone about us. Presently, having rapidly descended, we came to a long line of roofless and windowless houses. It seemed as if some disaster had smitten them. Wild briers and vines encircled the broken walls and rubble encumbered the courtyards. There were outside staircases that ended purposeless in the air, and flying arches that no longer carried superstructures. A heavy silence brooded over this narrow cobbled lane which they shut in. At a corner we found a fountain. The water in it still ran cool and musical in the sunny morning. There was a tablet over it with an inscription, "From a grateful population that applauded the inauguration, June 1895." It was erected in the time of Mayor d'Aste. I wondered if this was the Marchese d'Aste whose palace in Albenga is now the Naval Museum.

We turned the corner. A long narrow street went down the

hill to the valley. Half-way down a very pretty girl was carrying a bucket of water. What beauty comes out of these little
village hovels, so primitive, poverty-stricken and with no
sanitation! Here was a head worthy of Raphael tumbled over
with black curls above lustrous eyes. She had a wonderfully
lithe figure, walking barefoot with a bucket on her head.
What a haul to bring up water! I asked her the name of the
street. It was the Via Costa in the village of San Fedele, in
the Albenga plain. Lusignano was only a mile farther up the
road. So we had chosen well. All the way down the steep
street there were deserted houses, almost medieval in their
rough strength, with broken doors opening on to ruinous
courtyards, and outside staircases romantically rising to
upper floors, all windowless. The sadness of departed generations was over the place. It looked as if the houses were semi-
fortresses built to defy the Saracen raiders from the coast or
the marauding bands that devastated the countryside. And,
as always, I played with the idea of buying for a song one of
these feudal strongholds, with courtyard and open staircase
and terrace, grown over with vines, and offering from glass-
less windows superb views of mountains and valley. But
with no roads, no sanitation, no water, no easy communications, such deserted places, however romantic, are impractical
for daily life.[1]

We sought the little osteria in which to eat our lunch. The
scene was Hogarthian or, more correctly, Goldonian—plain
wooden chairs and tables, colour-washed walls, a primitive
bar, a door opening on to a littered courtyard shady under

[1] Looking back, the places I almost bought! But the time has gone. There
was a Renaissance fortress overlooking the sea at Levanto, on the Riviera, for
the sum of two hundred pounds, in 1922; a small palazzo just off the Grand
Canal, Venice, for one thousand pounds, in 1924; a schloss with fifty acres of
pinewoods on a precipice with a view of the Grossglockner glacier, for eight
hundred pounds in 1927; a flat in Budapest, overlooking the Danube, for nine
hundred pounds, in 1929; a copy of the Villa Medici in Rome, built by an
Irish millionaire at Southampton, Long Island, N.Y., for three thousand
pounds, in 1942; a medieval tower near Asolo, all fitted and furnished with
antiques, left by an American widow, and offered over dinner in a New York
apartment, for five thousand dollars, in 1944; I found later it included a car,
in a garage made out of the dungeon. And the bargains less than a century ago!
The ancient castle at Cagnes, inhabited by Henri Grimaldi II, with its Carlone
ceiling, was sold in 1875 for 8,000 francs (£320). The town of Cagnes bought it
as late as 1939 for £1,400.

a vine pergola, hens walking about, an innkeeper with a three days' growth of beard, in a sleeveless vest, old pants, and slippers, and four customers having lunch, one a local drunk, an old toothless peasant of seventy, roaring out songs in a cracked voice. I ordered a *fiasco* of wine, one of those large-bottomed bottles enswathed in plaited straw, common all over Italy. But here a *fiasco* of wine meant something different, and my order ended in a fiasco in the English sense of the word. I had thought the innkeeper looked surprised by my order. He returned with a bottle holding almost a gallon. He must have thought we were there for an all-night carouse. The error rectified, we became the best of friends. The whole inn took an interest in us. Half-naked, barefooted youths came in out of the hot noon for their midday drink. A group by the wall debated our nationality. We satisfied their curiosity, and declined joining a sextette from 'Lucia di Lammermoor' led by the old Bacchus, noisier as he grew more inarticulate. The innkeeper went out and brought in a bowl of apricots and peaches for us, gathered from his trees. My guest declared that he would like to live in Italy for ever, a considerable confession for a Californian. After an hour we left to a loud chorus of *Buon' giorno*, and went through the bead curtains into the blazing day. We walked up the road to Lusignano, amid orchards of pears, peaches, apricots, persimmons, and vineyards blue with a wash of copper sulphate. We came to Lusignano and failed to find the villa of Madame de Genlis. But we found an enchanting old village. It had gone to sleep for three centuries. We came to a little square, 'Piazza di Lengueglia', it said. So this had been a territory of the vanished Counts of Lengueglia. It had a delightful arched baroque screen at one end. Once upon a time this had framed a vista of vine-covered fields and hills; now it framed the ghastly chimney of a brickyard.

We mounted the silent high street. The black eyes of old crònes peered at us from behind barred windows. We turned left up a leafy alley and came into the grassy courtyard of a deserted palazzo. It was superbly placed on a plateau commanding the valley, the towers of Albenga, and the blue sea. An archway led to a derelict orchard of peach trees. The wine we had consumed and the heat of the day overcoming us, we stretched ourselves on the green grass in the shade of the peach trees and consumed the fruit fallen about us. Then we dozed a while. But we were here for a purpose, to find the villa of Madame de Genlis, so after an hour we rose, to discover that we had been under observation by an old crone in black who emerged out of the ruined house. She was white-haired and was busily knitting. She said she lived there. I wondered then, as often in these places, how and on what. There she was, waiting for death, an old grandmother, withered, no longer capable of work, existing on a little *polenta* and fruit. Well enough in the summer so glorious here, but in the winter, when the icy winds screamed down from the mountains, when the dark came early, and there was no fuel in the leaking house except some gathered sticks?

I apologized for eating the peaches. She smiled. They belonged to no one. And the great house, in which she lived with a married son and his six children? The old castle belonged to no one. No, she did not know to whom it had belonged, or its history, or when it was deserted, or why.

Down in the piazza a woman told us the villa we sought was up the road towards Villanova, only a few hundred yards on the left. Count Cipollini lived there. We started off for the villa. We found the gate and began to mount a long drive of chestnut trees. The villa spread itself high on a terrace above us, the valley fell away below. Long before we arrived, the barking of dogs filled the afternoon with alarm. Finally we came to a fortress-like wall with a great gate. We rang the bell and stirred up the dogs in the courtyard afresh. We waited. No one came. We rang again and waited awhile. I composed an apologetic explanatory speech for a drowsy domestic who would awake an annoyed count from his siesta. Mad dogs and Englishmen walk in the noonday sun and disturb the peace that follows a plenitude of spaghetti and wine.

We rang a third time. More echoes and canine uproar. Nothing. I was now quite sure Madame de Genlis had not lived here. We walked back down the drive and returned towards San Fedele.

In the village we came to the old church of San Giovanni,

with its fading fresco, its door with a black marble lintel carved with a primitive Annunciation, and a twelfth-century bell-tower. There was a large villa opposite, built into the hillside, abutting on the Via Costa down which we had come. Was it the Genlis villa? It was palatial and had a long façade, ochre-yellow, with green shutters, above flights of steps that mounted under a leafy pergola to a wide balustraded terrace. Below, behind a high wall fronting the road, was a large vineyard and garden. There was a long arcaded avenue of roses leading to a Madonna in an alcove by the first flight of steps. I hesitated to walk in. Over the gate it said 'Institute for Teachers (Registered) of the Ursuline Order of Jesus'. It was a convent school!

I ventured in. A young nun with a mouth filled with silver teeth answered my query. She did not know if this had been the villa of Madame de Genlis. She bade me mount. I mounted in the golden afternoon under the rose pergola. It was like going to call on Cardinal d'Este. One was steadily diminished by the progressive grandeur of the approach. At last I came to the long terrace with its silent fountain, its magnificent vista of the Albenga valley and the sea. It was all very true to form. Anywhere in Italy if you come to a villa of a grandeur no one can afford to live in, you will find it is inhabited by nuns, or priests, who pay no rates and trust in God. They have become the owners of all these villas that would otherwise fall into decay.

I timidly rang a bell. Nuns in coifs are creatures of another world for me. A pleasant young sister came to the door and half opened it, as became caution with a foreign male, and probably a heretic at that. Madame de Genlis? Never heard of her. I carefully refrained from saying she had been the *amie* of the Duc d'Orléans, and emphasized her fame as a governess in the French Royal Family. The Ursuline Order is a French one, it might establish a link. No, she had never heard of Madame de Genlis, but she would go and ask the Mother Superior. She shut the door. I waited and tried not to run. Did Mother Superiors have siestas? I speculated on how many sister-housemaids it took to run a vast villa like this, how much income it required. After a

long wait the door opened, a little wider. The Mother
Superior stood there. She looked neither a mother nor in any
way superior. I had imagined an old lady in billowing black
skirts with spectacles, large feet, and a rosary dangling from
a robust middle. Instead, she was scarcely middle-aged, slim,
erect, alert, and precise. She resembled a schoolmistress, and
that is exactly what she was, for I learnt presently that she
was the headmistress of a high-class girls' boarding school
with a French curriculum. We talked in French, Italian
being less facile, as I thought. Madame de Genlis had left
no ghost there. In vain I explained who she was. Not one of
her hundred works, poor woman, had ever been heard of.
Nothing was known of her presence in this villa one hundred
and fifty years ago. I tried to work backwards. Nothing was
known of anyone who had lived in the villa fifty or a hundred
years ago. This was a French Ursuline Convent School.

I was prepared to go back to the patron saint of the
Order, St Ursula, daughter of a King of Britain who, to
avoid marriage to a heathen prince, went on a pilgrimage to
Rome with eleven thousand virgins. On the way they were
all massacred at Cologne by the Huns.[1] But I refrained. I
did not wish to become tiresome. I could evoke no desire to
make any link with history. I retreated down the splendid
steps. Nevertheless, I thought that this was the villa. It had
a splendour such as Madame de Genlis had always contrived to have about her, the friend of kings, dukes, and
princes.

I pursued my quest. It involved letters to four foreign
countries. I went to Nice and spent two days in the French
library. I read eighteen volumes of Madame de Genlis's
works. Not a mention in her *Mémoires* or elsewhere of the
villa at San Fedele—Lusignano! Not a single letter headed
with that address! It was significant, I thought, that the villa

[1] The Order, a famous teaching one, was actually founded in Italy in 1537
by St Angela of Brescia. Its mission was the tending of the sick and poor and the
teaching of children. The French branch was founded in Paris in 1610. Its
high scholastic qualifications have dominated the Order. It was to the Ursuline
Convent in Rome that the wives of the Old Pretender and the Young Pretender retreated from their bullying husbands; and there, during the French
Revolution, the royal princesses, Madame Victoire and Madame Adelaide,
took refuge.

belonged to a French Order. Possibly some devout French-woman had bequeathed it to the Order. Possibly it was in the possession of a French owner when Madame de Genlis had rented it or had been lent it.

In the afternoon we waited for the bus into Albenga. The innkeeper informed us that it was very late. He led us along to a fruit-packing shed on the roadside. They were loading an open lorry with crates of pears, peaches, apricots, and tomatoes. In a few minutes the innkeeper arranged our transport. And so it was, among crates of fruit, that we were carried into Albenga. Strange to know that this very produce of the Albengan valley among which I sat, conveyed to England by plane, might be gracing a London dinner-table twenty-four hours later.

I persisted in my quest. Three days later two Italian friends motored me back to Lusignano. "The local *parroco* will know, if anyone does," said my friends. We called on the priest. Like Don Raffaele, Don Lanteri lived upstairs in a room with a window overlooking his church. He did not know. I told him of our inability to reach Count Cipollini in his fortress-villa. He took us by a back path through an olive grove right up to the door of the villa. We were most hospitably received by the Countess in a large salon with an altar at one end, a rare privilege accorded by the Church to a few villas. No, Madame de Genlis had never lived there. She did not know where she had lived. "Perhaps I know where it is," said Don Lanteri, and leaving the villa he led us up the main street of Lusignano. At the top he turned left. I knew at once where he was taking us—back to the ruined castle where we had rested in the peach orchard! It seemed it had once been the castle of the Cipollini family, which had been ruined by a tutor who had embezzled the fortunes of two orphans, one the heir, left to his charge. Don Lanteri pushed open a door on the ground floor. It was the ancient salon of the castle, with a domed ceiling, now used as a barn and utterly ruined. The old crone I had seen there on my previous visit emerged and joyously greeted me. I had to confess to Don Lanteri that I had already seen the place. "It is where she should have lived," I said.

I departed from Lusignano baffled. By this time I had half a dozen scouts questing for clues. Don Lanteri said he would write to an antiquarian friend who might know. In Diano Marina lived a professor who was the learned archivist of a library of topography and history covering Liguria. Alas, the professor dashed all my hopes even in the matter of the derivation of the name Lusignano. The village had nothing to do with the Kings of Cyprus. They had not been exiled there, although it was true that the Knights Templars, long associated with Cyprus, had held land in the vicinity. The name of the village had been derived from an ancient Roman family called Lucinia, and just as the village of Antagnano had taken its name from the family of Antonia, so Lusignano had been derived from Lucinia. Moreover, referring to my vain attempts, following the lead of the Berrys in their book, to discover the actual villa wherein Madame de Genlis was stated to have dwelt, the professor dismissed my authorities. "My researches in regard to the villa that interests you have also been negative. There are no documents to be found telling about the stay of Madame de Genlis in Lusignano except for a few lines which mention it in the Berrys' book, and I have not been able to find the source of their information. It is possible that they collected this during one of their peregrinations through the Riviera, but I have not found any mention of the fact among their manuscripts and notations in our library."

I made further inquiries through the following months, reluctant to admit defeat in my quest. I wrote to the publishers of *At the Western Gate*, a book written twenty-four years earlier, and out of print. To my delight, I received a reply from its author—"I am sorry to say that all my notes for the book were destroyed, so unfortunately I cannot give you the information you ask for. I am afraid that my age and infirmities would probably make it unreliable! I can only say that I was very careful to verify my statements when writing the book, so I feel pretty sure I had good reason for making this one."

That told me nothing new about Madame de Genlis at Lusignano, but it spurred on my quest. A friend, Contessa

Brizio, who had taken me to the Cipollinis, and the parish priest, Don Lanteri, at Lusignano, now enlisted the aid of Signor Luigi Costa, an Albengan lawyer whose family had resided in the Albenga valley for several centuries. He could tell me nothing about Madame de Genlis' villa at Lusignano, but he informed me that the village had once been called Roxinetum. Its name was changed in the fourteenth century to Lusignano. Since Jacques I had been made a hostage of Genoa in 1372, the presence of the Lusignans in the village seemed confirmed by this change of name. So far so good, but of Madame de Genlis and her villa, nothing.

Defeated after two years of inquiries and a large correspondence, I sent the proofs of this chapter to press, with the mystery unsolved. A week later I chanced upon a book that gave me the key to the whole story. The ruined castle of Lusignano that I had visited with my young American friend, and later with Don Lanteri, was, after all, the home of Madame de Genlis, as I had thought it should be! It was set forth in *The Heroines of Genoa*, by Edgecumbe Staley, an Englishman who, around 1912, had investigated the Genoese and Ligurian archives.

The Lusignan kings of Cyprus had long been involved with the Genoese and the Venetians, for both Republics had coveted the island. The Dowager-Queen Elizabeth, mother of Pierre II, took for a lover a Genoese admiral, Pietro Gontado. After the victories in Cyprus, in 1373, of Pietro Fregoso, the Republic rewarded "the great ornament and glory of his native city" with the gift of the Palazzo Fregoso, the forerunner of the magnificent Palazzo Doria-Pamfili in Genoa. Here, a few years later, Otto Lusignan, the brother of the hostage, Jacques I of Cyprus, was sumptuously entertained by Doge Fregoso. Part of the entertainment was a masque in which eight hundred beautiful young Genoese ladies performed, clad in little more than gold gauze sewn over with pearls. This so bewitched the dashing Otto that he planned a castle in a remote part of Liguria where he might indulge in similar revels. So while his nephew Janus returned to Cyprus to ascend the throne, and to fall a prisoner of the Sultan of Egypt, he built, in 1416, the castle of Lusignano.

It had a romantic history until the eighteenth century, when, deserted, Madame de Genlis took up residence there. She wrote a romance around it, called *Adèle et Théodore*, giving French names to the Italian characters, and named her abode 'Arcadia'. She also wrote there, around 1780, *Les Veillées du Château*, 'Late Evenings at the Castle', probably suggested by her surroundings. Madame de Genlis, given to flights of imagination, probably embroidered the facts of her tale, but there seems to have been an historical basis concerning events at the castle or villa.

In the suite of the King of Sardinia, Amadeo II, was the elderly Duke of Cerifalco, a man of great wealth. At an entertainment given by Genoa to the sovereign, the Duke fell in love with a girl of sixteen, Angela. His wealth stirred the venality of her parents, who betrothed her to the Duke, despite the fact that she had a fiancé, young Ambrogio, Count Belvedere, handsome but penniless. As soon as the wedding festivities ended the Duke took away his bride to his castle at Lusignano, anxious to shut her away from envious eyes. The Duke's suspicions were quieted by the birth of a daughter. But young Ambrogio had secretly followed and had trysts with the young Duchess. One day they were surprised in a wood by the Duke, who was wounded in an affray. Ambrogio, unrecognized, fled and the husband carried off his swooning wife. In vain he demanded her lover's name. He then locked her in her chamber, drugged her, and gave out that she was dead. On the third day, as she would not divulge the name, he conveyed her to a dungeon in the castle. He then had a waxen image of the Duchess made and held a false funeral. Meanwhile he fed his prisoner with his own hands through a secret opening, always demanding her lover's name and always meeting with a refusal.

The months passed into years. The Duke fell ill and, dying, revealed that his wife was still alive. The news came to young Ambrogio, who suddenly appeared before the imprisoned Duchess and released her. But, after nine years, it was too late. Though only twenty-seven, her beauty had fled and she was a physical wreck. She refused the pleading of the gallant Ambrogio, and, in the singular manner of high romance, handed to him her ten-year-old daughter. And thereupon she disappeared from the castle of Lusignano.

In her *Mémoires* Madame de Genlis declares that when visiting Rome with the Duchess de Chartres, she met the Duchess of Cerifalco, who was the daughter of Prince Palestrina. It seems that actually the Duke confessed to his valet that he had imprisoned a woman who had been guilty of a misdemeanour. The valet hurried to the dungeon, where he found the Duchess, who had been without food for three days. She sent a note to her father, who appealed to the King, who sent a posse of soldiers and had her released. Madame de Genlis said that the Duchess's father showed her the slip of paper with the message and she was greatly moved by it. The poor Duchess at forty looked sixty and only appeared for a few minutes at the Roman garden party given by her father in honour of the Duchess de Chartres.

So ended my two years' quest regarding Madame de Genlis at Lusignano. I had been misled by the ambiguity of the description of the castle's location—"a large villa with a walled garden on the left side of the road as one goes up the valley". I had thought this alluded to the valley of Albenga, but at the top of the climbing main street of Lusignano a small valley opens on the left, with a long walled garden leading to the ruinous castle, where the old crone had seen my friend and me eating the fallen peaches. It is a site of such beauty, looking down the valley to Albenga and the blue Mediterranean sea, that, had I chanced upon it before the Palazzo Vairo, I might have sought to buy it and restore it—with a dungeon in reserve!

CHAPTER TWELVE

ADDIO!

WITH the closing of the year Alassio began to grow festive again after the pleasant stupor into which it had fallen when all the summer and autumn holiday-makers had departed and not a sun umbrella or deck-chair remained on the beach. Christmas decorations began to appear in the shop windows; there were coloured lights for Christmas-trees, and the ever-popular model of the manger, showing the Virgin and Child with Joseph, the three kings, the shepherds, the ox and the donkey. I found it a little difficult to address Christmas-cards to my friends in England and America. It seemed out of season to be doing this on an open terrace where the sun was so strong that I had to lower the awning at midday, while in the sea some confirmed bathers continued their daily dip.

Inside the dim parish church the air of Christmas was not so incongruous. Parents with their children flocked to gaze in delight at the large and realistic manger built in one of the corners of the church. All over Italy, Bethlehem mangers come forth with an almost competitive zeal. They compensate, in their elaborate construction, for much that is missing from the Italian child's concept of Christmas. There are no stockings to hang up. Italian children wear short socks.

The journeys of Santa Klaus with his reindeer and sleigh would be difficult around the Mediterranean shore where snow is unknown. It is otherwise in snow-covered Germany, where Santa Klaus became a popular legend. The very name puzzles the Italian child. *Santa* is the feminine name for saint, *santo* is the masculine form. He should therefore be San Klaus or Santo Klaus. Indeed, for the Italian child his name is not Santa Klaus at all. He is San Niccolo. He got his other name Klaus in a curious, roundabout way from Germany, whence he was carried by Dutch emigrants to New York, who held a San Klaus holiday.

St Nicholas, the real Father Christmas, had his origin in Asia Minor, at the seaport town of Parara. Created Bishop of Myra in Lycia, he was the patron saint of sailors, merchants, and pawnbrokers. The legend runs that, hearing of an impoverished nobleman with three daughters for whom he could not provide, St Nicholas threw a bag of gold into each maiden's window in order to provide her with a dowry. He did this unseen by night. The three bags of gold became transformed into three balls of gold, and were put up as their patron saint's sign by all pawnbrokers. Nicholas was also the saint and protector of little children. After his death the parents of Myra used to make presents on his birthday, December 6th, to their children to remind them of his goodness. Because of the stealth by which he helped the poor nobleman's daughters, the gifts used to be left where the children, finding them, could think that they came from the saint himself. Somehow Nicholas was transported to Russia, where he was made a patron saint, and in that snowy country he got his long beard, warm red gown, top-boots, reindeer, and sleigh.

In Italy there are no Father Christmases, with red coats mantled with snow, standing in stores, shop windows, or depicted on Christmas-cards. The Madonna and Bambino supplant him in the Italian Christmas, which is called *Natale*—the Birthday of the Holy Child. The children are compensated, however, on the eve of Epiphany, January 5th, when the Befana, a fairy, brings presents down the chimney for the children, and waits sing in the streets. In Italy you do not mind your p's and q's but your a's and o's, for while a *befana* is a fairy, a *befano* is an ugly man.

There is a great celebration in the parish church of Alassio on Christmas Eve. The manger is illuminated, the altar sparkles with candles. Everyone seems to be present in Sant' Ambrogio for the midnight Mass. Not a corner is empty, from the great doors to the choir. The priests are all in their embroidered vestments and copes, the acolytes are in spotless collars. The service begins. At the *Gloria in Excelsis* of the Mass an old shepherd from the hills appears in the great west door. He slowly walks down the nave and up to the altar, carrying in his arms a newborn lamb. The dark eyes of the lovely creature shine in its woolly white head. While the shepherd holds it, kneeling, the priest blesses it. Then, rising with the blessed lamb in his arms, the shepherd without a word or gesture turns and walks down the nave, through the west door, and out into the night. He will carry the lamb up into the hills, returning it to the flock, which shares the blessing it has received. In the church they sing a special carol originally set to shepherds' pipes.

I came home after midnight through the illuminated streets echoing with voices exchanging greetings of *Buon Natale*. Going on to my terrace I looked down upon Alassio with its lights. A crescent moon hung low over the mountains, the clear sky was spangled with stars. A light breeze came in from the calm bay. The loveliness of it all enfolded the valley, the hills, the sea. The bells rang their Christmas tidings from the campanile. Then I heard other bells out of the past, the bells of Westminster Abbey that by radio had rung in my old Chiltern cottage while the fire burned cheerily and the candles in the silver candelabra cast a soft light on the Christmas fare spread beneath the old oak beams; and outside, the poplars in my garden swayed, netting a misty moon. The heartache for old lost things of beauty seized me momentarily. But it is useless to repine, and I had much cause for gratitude, listening to the ghostly bells of the past and the joyous bells of the present. I had a sense of the kindness of Providence that had fulfilled a boy's dream and brought me here in content to enjoy the lapsing years at what might seem to many the Portal to Paradise.